THE RISE OF RONALD REAGAN

 THE RISE OF

RONALD REAGAN

by BILL BOYARSKY

 RANDOM HOUSE · NEW YORK

SECOND PRINTING

Library of Congress Catalog Card Number: 68-18261

To the ladies of the house,

Nancy, Robin and Jennie

Acknowledgments

THE WAY to write a book is to marry a girl who can edit, research, organize material, suggest ideas and type. I was fortunate enough to find such a girl—my wife, Nancy—who, by her work on this book, more than repaid me for putting her through the last two years of the University of California at Berkeley early in our marriage. She suggested I write it. She did much of the important research. Among her discoveries were three boxes of the California Democratic party's files from the 1966 election, which State Chairman Charles Warren was kind enough to let me borrow. By poking through the California State Library she found Ronald Reagan's testimony before congressional committees in the 1940s and valuable information about his movie career. She also edited my copy and made revisions, helping put the book into shape for speedy delivery to the publisher. And she typed the manuscript.

Many others were most helpful. Some have provided information in private conversation and asked that I not use their names. Others can be thanked publicly. Among them are Lyn Nofziger, Nancy Reynolds and Edwin Meese III of

Governor Reagan's staff. Assembly Speaker Jesse Unruh, former Governor Edmund G. Brown and Brown's old finance director, Hale Champion, provided valuable information. So did Bill Roberts of the firm of Spencer-Roberts and Hafner, practitioners in the art of political public relations. Reagan's brother Neil is a storehouse of information about the Reagan family's early days. Clark Kerr, the former president of the University of California, shared his story with me. The Los Angeles *Times* and the Sacramento *Bee* allowed me the use of their libraries.

Finally, thanks to my friends who report political and government news in California. Many have supplied me with information and advice. Three were particularly helpful in looking over the manuscript and sharing their recollections of the past few years, James Wrightson of the McClatchy Newspapers and Jerry Rankin and Bill Stall of the Associated Press.

Sacramento, California
January, 1968

CONTENTS

THE RISE OF RONALD REAGAN

☒ **CHAPTER ONE**

THE STATE

FOR ALMOST ONE HUNDRED YEARS, the governors of California have stepped up to the oak rostrum of the assembly chambers in Sacramento and announced their plans for governing the state. On January 31, 1967, it was Ronald Reagan's turn. He walked from his wood-paneled office in a corner of the capitol and down the hallways crowded with visiting schoolchildren, took an elevator to the second floor and entered the green room where legislators have watched over California since it was a rural state grown rich on gold. In his hand was his first budget message for the people who had elected him by almost a million votes three months before. The message, fresh from the state printing plant, would tell in seven and a half pages how the new governor intended to make good on his campaign promise to cut down government and put California on the conservative path. It was a memorable day for the conservatives of the Republican party who had pleaded for power for years and watched in bitter disappointment as it was denied them. Now Reagan, an unabashed conservative, was the governor of the nation's most populous state. Now he would have a chance to change the course of one of the union's most liberal state governments, which had not only welcomed the largest domestic immigration in American history, but readily supplied the newcomers with free schools, parks and highways—and with generous welfare aid if they lost their jobs.

Accompanying Reagan upstairs was a committee of three senators and five assemblymen, whose job was to escort the governor into the legislative sanctuary. In the ritual of government, they were the symbols of a strong-minded legislative branch, still controlled by Democrats despite Reagan's victory and filled with Republicans who had voted for the expensive programs Reagan had pledged to cut.

The party went up in the elevator and into the chamber where eighty assemblymen and forty senators were waiting. There was a stirring, and heads turned when Reagan entered the room. He looked like a governor, just as another Republican, Warren G. Harding, had looked like a President. Reagan's face was even-featured, heavily tanned and deeply wrinkled, with a dozen deep lines reaching out from each eye when he smiled. Four more lines stretched across his forehead. But his hair, remarkably, was brown and thick despite his fifty-six years. His jaw was firm, with no sagging double chin. His body was well tended, without a middle-age paunch breaking the cut of his carefully tailored dark-blue suit. He walked briskly, with the controlled grace learned in twenty-nine years as a motion picture and television star. From his first film to his last, he had a touch of magnetism that helped him stand out from long-forgotten co-stars, and later from the politicians who ran against him. He was in some big movies—*King's Row* and *Brother Rat*—and some small ones—*International Squadron* and *Cattle Queen of Montana*. He was never, by his own admission, a "whole actor." But on the screen and later on television, Reagan projected something of a star quality, a warm, sympathetic and friendly manner. There is a chatty, next-door-neighbor quality to his conversation. Football, children and the tribulations of commuting to work on the Los Angeles freeways are subjects that interest him.

Seldom has a more inexperienced person stepped into a more difficult job—but it worried neither him nor a majority of the voters. "Once in a while," he said, "when you come to a tough problem, you choose someone who doesn't know anything about it because he doesn't know what you can't do."

Reagan left the welcoming committee, stepped onto the rostrum and shook hands with the Democratic leaders of the legislature. First there was Jesse M. Unruh, the speaker of the state assembly and the surviving star of the state Democratic party. Reagan shook hands with Unruh and then greeted the senate's Democratic leader, the president pro tem Hugh M. Burns. Burns had his own sort of power. An old, wise and tired man, his loyalties were to his own farm-city constituency and to the business-oriented lobbyists who influenced the senate. Once, Reagan's predecessor, Edmund G. Brown, had asked Burns for support on an issue. Burns granted it, but Brown later confided to a friend, "I'll be paying for that for years."

Up in the balcony was the governor's wife, Nancy—wide-eyed, attractive, a Chicago debutante who had graduated from Smith College, gone to work as a movie actress and ended up as the wife of a governor. Like her husband, Nancy Reagan was deeply conservative. In public she smiled often and said little. But in private she was keenly interested in what happened to the state, and to Reagan's career. A reporter was in the governor's private office on a confusing day early in his administration. Reagan had made a statement in Sacramento, and his finance director had contradicted it in Los Angeles. The phone rang. Reagan picked it up and apologized to the reporter, explaining, "It's my wife."

"Yes, dear," he said several times. Finally he said of the finance director, "No, dear, I don't think he was being insubordinate. It's just when I say something in Sacramento, and he says something in Los Angeles, we'll have to get together." The reporter carried away the impression that Mrs. Reagan had considerable influence in running the state government.

The assembly room was ringed with television cameras and bright lights. At one time left to the care of a few news service reporters and resident newspaper correspondents, the capitol was now big news. Editors and television news directors, bored with Reagan's predecessor, were curious about the new governor.

Reagan prepared to speak. The applause was polite and unenthusiastic. The night before, Reagan had unnecessarily antagonized the legislature by a speech on a fifteen-minute television show paid for by his political backers. He had said that Brown had "looted and drained" California's economic resources, an unfortunate choice of words which offended the legislators who had supported Brown's programs. "I have tried to maintain a 'wait and see' attitude on the governor's program, and I intend to do so, but it is difficult to maintain your composure in the face of criticism of this type," said Senator Burns.

The clapping stopped when the governor began to speak. Never adept at unpracticed reading of a script, Reagan stumbled often. A Democratic senator shifted his pipe to the other side of his mouth and shook his head in disagreement and disbelief. The audience was silent and unresponsive. But finally the governor roused the legislators with a quip. "You know, one of the economies we won't effect is in regard to the state printing plant. I propose they use darker ink." Then he put on his reading glasses and said, "I was hoping I wouldn't have to do that. The next time they make the Rockne movie, I'll play Rockne." He had played the young football hero, George Gipp, when the movie was made in the late 1930s.

What Reagan read was the financial blueprint for the biggest retrenchment of California government since the Depression. Every department of the state government was to share the burden of the unaccustomed economies, even the University of California and the colleges, the traditional recipients of special consideration by previous governors. "We have fallen heir," he said, "to the most serious fiscal dilemma that has faced the state of California for more than a decade."

It was a new message for Californians. For the past quarter of a century, the government had lived up to a standard set by another Republican, Earl Warren, a moderate who believed the state should step in and assist social progress. In 1953 President Eisenhower appointed him Chief Justice of the United States, but his policies still influenced the two administrations that followed him. For years Warren had stood on the assembly rostrum, telling of his plans in a high-pitched, slow-moving delivery, a typical pretelevision politician. He talked of a state moving forward, always expanding services to help a growing population. The administrations of Warren and the men who followed him, Goodwin J. Knight and Brown, tended to melt into one long, moderate reign.

California is a warm and friendly land, growing in a way that is beyond control. If you considered California a nation, its economy would be fifth among the nations of the Western world. Only the gross national products of the United States, Great Britain, West Germany and France are greater. Newcomers create the state's main problem—or blessing. Even some of the pre-World War II migrants, notably the dusty Okies of the 1930s, brought problems with them, but they eventually won their share of California's prosperity and were absorbed into the community. But in World War II shipyards and aircraft factories lured thousands of the unskilled to southern California and the San Francisco Bay area. The migration continued after the war. Servicemen who had liked the place, Negroes searching for long-denied opportunity, easterners just tired of the cold and damp weather were among the newcomers; they moved into the rural outskirts of metropolitan areas, filling out the cities of the Central Valley and now even building homes on the barren foothills of the Sierra Nevada.

The state government had surpassed the visions of the New Deal in many ways. While eastern states suffered from drought, California, with little federal help, built a storage dam that dwarfed the pyramids and a water aqueduct that stretched almost the length of the state. Easterners paid tolls on their highways. Californians did not; their gasoline taxes were set aside to pay for freeways. The range of state services was dazzling—parks, generous welfare, liberal medical aid to the poor—and governors Warren, Knight and Brown believed California was rich enough to pay for it all, and more. "In Washington," Brown once boasted, "they call it the Great Society. We just call it California."

Reagan took a different view. He came from a Republican party that had changed since the days of Earl Warren. The party came under the control of residents of the growing suburbs, young managers and professional men and their families, often newcomers, who had built islands of prosperity and security in a changing world and were deeply interested in conserving what they had. In 1958 the Republican party had been shattered when United States Senator William F. Knowland pushed Knight aside, took the governorship nomination for himself and lost to Brown in a futile campaign on a "right to work" platform. The elements of labor which had supported the Republicans in the past went over to the Democrats. Six years later, conservatives took over the party, forced out the heirs of Earl Warren and helped Barry Goldwater win the Presidential primary.

The Democratic party had also become more conservative as its adherents moved into the suburbs. Reagan was speaking to these suburbanites, Democrats and Republicans, as he delivered his budget message. He was counting on these people, rather than the legislators and lobbyists listening in the assembly chamber, to provide the main support for his economy crusade.

"There is no doubt," he said, "that tremendous pressure will be applied by many special-interest groups in an attempt to force a relaxation of economy measures. The legislature, of course, must consider these concerns, but pressure should not overrule sound judgment."

His message of unrelenting economy was more warmly received outside of the capitol. Public-opinion polls showed wide approval. But to those in the assembly chamber that day, the most memorable recollection was the cold silence. As the governor concluded, a Democratic legislator turned to reporters and said: "The budget will still go up, as it has every year." The economies were unpopular with the politicians—but they were made even more unpalatable by the governor's asking the legislature and the judiciary to cut their own budgets.

There was silence when he finished his speech and then

only scattered applause. The legislators had heard their guest's message, and most of them didn't like it. Now, with nothing left to say, Reagan left the rostrum, this time without the legislative escort. The ritual of the occasion provides the governor with guides into the chamber but requires that he find his own way out. Back down the halls he went, exchanging small talk with Philip Battaglia, his executive secretary, and Paul Beck, an assistant press secretary. Striding quickly—Reagan at his usual fast pace—the party reached the elevator, went down to the main floor and into the side door of the governor's office. Nancy was waiting for him in his small inner office, which she had redecorated with the sturdy furniture of Colonial America as an inauguration present. It was almost lunchtime and there was a long afternoon ahead. The governor had given his orders. Now he put the machinery of state government into action to carry them out.

⊠ **CHAPTER TWO**

THE MAN

DURING HIS FIRST YEAR AS GOVERNOR, Ronald
Reagan worked at an uncluttered desk in an attractively
furnished office tucked away in a quiet, well-protected corner
of the California capitol's executive suite. The office provided little evidence of the inner man, for Reagan divides
his life into compartments—public and private—and they do
not overlap. At work he is friendly but impersonal, reluctant
to draw those around him into his life. Reagan does not need
people. Self-contained, he prefers spending a day on his
ranch working with a hired hand to being in a room filled
with friends. So distant is he that even his closest professional
associates feel they don't know him very well, and strangers
are baffled by his personality.

He is intelligent but not brilliant; quick-witted but without deep intellectual curiosity. He talks in long, rambling
sentences, and once he has found an answer to a question, he
will use it over and over again, clinging to familiar words as
if they are part of a movie script. The same phrases, and
even the same paragraphs, appear in speech after speech. A

visitor once mentioned that three of Reagan's old movies had been on television the day before. One of them was the life story of Grover Cleveland Alexander, the baseball pitcher, and the film was one of Reagan's favorites. Reagan was immediately reminded of an anecdote. He told how the studio bosses tried to disguise Alexander's epileptic seizures by portraying them as fainting spells; but that had only served to anger the public and the critics, who thought the studio had another motive in mind—using the fainting spells to cover up a more famous Alexander affliction, alcoholism.

The story was interesting, but it had been told before, and in the same words, in Reagan's autobiography. The visitor felt he had pushed a button marked "Grover Cleveland Alexander," and the story had come out, just as questions about the Vietnam war, the University of California and state mental hospitals drew identical answers day after day.

The same fondness for the familiar was apparent in his campaign for governor. An audience had once liked the way Reagan ended a speech: "You and I can start a prairie fire that will sweep across the country and restore to government a full measure of confidence." Pleased, he used "prairie fire" from then on, and it became his standard ending, coming with such predictable monotony that reporters closed their notebooks when they heard it, knowing it was time to leave.

In his speeches he grasps for the familiar, and at work he looks for simple answers. Details bore him and the internal workings of government leave him puzzled. When he was asked about the progress of his Creative Society program halfway through his first legislative session, Reagan said: "Well, I haven't talked to my legislative task force on this, so I don't know the state of their preparations." But he sometimes would take a boyish delight in trivia. He broke a logjam in his office mail room by applying some of the methods he used in handling his Hollywood mail. Under his direction, all of the envelopes, which had previously been saved and clipped to the incoming letters, were thrown away. Return addresses were written on those few letters that lacked them. This simple procedure, he found, saved time and valuable filing space.

Instead of ponderous reports, Reagan's staff gives him "mini-memos," one-page summaries of state problems, divided into the issue, facts, reasoning, conclusions and recommendations. An assistant, William P. Clark, Jr., said: "It has been found that almost any issue can be reduced to a single page. At times, if the governor wants to go into the thing in more depth, he will request more detailed reports. He is a late-night reader. But in contrast to the last administration, we do not give him the full reports unless he specifically requests them."

His lack of sophistication also adds to the impression that he is a simple man. He reads the comic strip "Peanuts" every morning, and when cartoonist Charles Schulz came to the capitol, Reagan proclaimed it "Peanuts Day" in California and happily brought Schulz home to lunch with the family. *Newsweek* magazine took a look at this side of Reagan's personality, his tastes and his manner of speaking, and summed it up this way: "Holy Toledo! Macaroni and cheese! Vanilla ice cream! Peanut butter!"

In one of his less sophisticated moments, Reagan readily confided to a reporter that he did not discount the possibility of flying saucers. That happened early in his political career, weeks before he became a candidate for governor. It was during a tour through the Central Valley farm country of California, and with him were a campaign aide, a friend and a reporter. It was late at night; everyone in the car was tired from a long evening and the drowsy conversation turned to

THE RISE OF RONALD REAGAN

the surrounding countryside and finally to the stars shining clearly above. Someone mentioned flying saucers. Reagan said he thought unidentified flying objects existed; so did the friend. Reagan said he had an acquaintance, a Navy reserve pilot, who had seen UFOs while on a flight through the Midwest.

Reagan reads the astrology columns of newspapers, an interest that resulted in one of the more farcical disputes of his administration. He had decided to be sworn in as governor at 12:10 A.M. on January 2. His reason: "The law prescribes that at midnight it is the end of the present administration. I hate to be a pessimist, but accidents may happen. I don't want anything to interfere." He also noted there were several football bowl games on television on January 2 and didn't want to interfere with those.

Former governor Brown thought the hour peculiar. "My only guess is that it's because he believes in astrology. I understand he does," said Brown. Two astrologers agreed with Brown's guess. In San Francisco, Gavin Chester Arthur, a newsboy astrologer who was the grandson of Chester A. Arthur, twenty-first President of the United States, noted that Jupiter, the sign of kings and the symbol of prosperity and fame, would be high in the sky the moment of the inauguration. "I truly suspect that Reagan was advised by an astrologer because no better time could be picked," said Arthur. "It's not just a coincidence," said Louise Huebner, an astrologist in Los Angeles.

This made Reagan angry. "He does not believe in astrology," said Battaglia, his executive secretary. "He is not guided by the stars nor do we intend to have stargazers in the administration." Reagan finally moved up the inauguration to 12:01 A.M.

Even though he is outwardly unsophisticated, there is

a more complex personality under Reagan's glossy, well-tailored Hollywood exterior. But it is not readily apparent, for he carefully keeps the world away from his inner self and his private life. So great is his interest in shutting out the world that he appears preoccupied with security. Bulletproof glass was placed in the windows of his office. The outer doors of the executive suite are always locked; under Reagan's predecessor they were not. But security was increased even more when Negro militants carrying loaded rifles stalked through the capitol and entered the assembly chamber to protest new gun control laws. Since this incident, only those with appointments were admitted to the executive suite. Once inside, visitors walked down a long corridor, turned right and passed by the open door of the security section, a department Reagan added to the governor's office. In charge was Arthur Van Court, a husky former Los Angeles police officer who, although given the official title of travel secretary, always carried a gun and was considered Reagan's bodyguard. Usually seated in the office was Reagan's armed California Highway Patrol driver. Thus two guns were generally available when Reagan was in the office. Van Court even accompanied the Reagans on their vacations.

"It's not the governor's idea," claimed Reagan's close advisor, Lyn Nofziger. Nofziger said he had insisted on the security, sometimes over Reagan's objections. No matter whose idea it was, Reagan was given tight protection from the beginning. Early in his campaign for governor, Reagan hired his first bodyguard, another former Los Angeles policeman, William Friedman. Completely devoted to the governor, Friedman's zeal sometimes surprised even Reagan's aides. Nofziger, then the newly hired press secretary, and Battaglia, then the campaign chairman, were returning to a hotel room after the bar closed early one morning. Battaglia made considerable noise as he tried to put the key in the lock. Across the hall a door swung open, and Friedman, dressed in undershorts, appeared, holding a pistol. "Don't worry," said Nofziger. "It's just us assassins."

One newspaper veteran of Hollywood thought the concern with security was inherited from Reagan's days in films. Celebrities, he said, are beset with more fears than the average man—fears that their children may be kidnapped or that they might be blackmailed or that they will be pummeled by an overenthusiastic crowd.

The night Reagan was inaugurated, the capitol was sealed off to the public. Thirty armed state policemen carrying walkie-talkies patrolled the building while the governor took his oath of office in the rotunda. Two days later, as he paraded through the streets of Sacramento in a triumphant inaugural procession, state police and highway patrolmen, some with shotguns, accompanied him. When he gave his speech from the capitol steps, eighty uniformed officers and plainclothesmen were on hand. State policemen were on the roofs of nearby buildings. And at the inaugural ball that night, there were 125 highway patrolmen, fifty national guard troopers and a number of state police.

Only the precautions taken for a visit by President Johnson in 1964 exceeded the security preparations for the inaugural, a source of amusement to members of the Sacramento police department who remembered how Governor Brown used to stroll through the downtown area without a bodyguard. During Brown's inaugural, the state went about the pageantry with a trace of embarrassment, more worried about disturbing the residents of Sacramento than protecting the governor. The state adjutant general, for example, warned the public that three 105-millimeter howitzers would be firing blanks during the ceremony, and "although harmless, [would] make a lot of noise."

Van Court worked hard to shield Reagan from the public. In September, 1967, Reagan drove to San Francisco for a conference on medical aid to the poor—a program he had just trimmed. Angry recipients were waiting outside the hall to confront him. But at the end of Reagan's speech, Van Court tricked the crowd by making a false start toward one exit and then taking the governor out the other. Earlier in the year, on a hot summer day, a young girl approached Reagan on the steps of the capitol. A former mental patient, she had been fasting for two days on the steps, holding a sign protesting reductions in aid to the state mental hospitals. As she talked to Reagan, Van Court nervously stepped between the governor and the girl, seemingly afraid that she would hit the governor with her cardboard sign.

Along with the security goes an almost total blackout on news of Mrs. Reagan and their children—Patricia, fourteen, and Skipper, nine. Governor Brown enjoyed confiding tidbits of his private life: "I've been watching television and my wife has been trying to straighten out the checkbook." But Reagan is silent about his family. Did he have friends in Sacramento? "I don't know," said one of his closest associates. "He has always kept his private life separate from his career." One legislator who went to a meeting at Reagan's home at night recalled being ushered out at 10 P.M. because it was the governor's bedtime. Another remembered spending time in the downstairs den, where Reagan showed off an electric train. "I think he leaves work at five P.M., goes home to Nancy and doesn't worry about a thing until he comes back at nine in the morning," said a Republican legislator who often quarreled with Reagan.

Nancy, his wife, is as important an influence as any in Reagan's life. To the public she is a pretty woman who stands at the side of her husband on television and in newspaper pictures, looking at him wide-eyed, almost too adoring to be true. Mrs. Reagan has grace, style and her husband's determination. She was determined, for example, that the family move out of the eighty-nine-year-old executive mansion, a wooden house in a run-down area that had been labeled for years as a firetrap. And she wanted the reason to be made clear—that it was concern for the safety of their children, not any dislike for the poor families living around the old house. In announcing the decision, however, Reagan said he was moving because Skipper had no playmates. (Both children attend private schools.) Mrs. Reagan called press secretary Nofziger aside and told him to emphasize that the main reason was safety.

Mrs. Reagan was also determined to improve the executive suite. Old furniture was discarded and a spacious outer office was redecorated with bright-red rugs, burlap wall covering and the heavy oak furniture of Spanish California. "Hearst Colonial," a visitor remarked, comparing it to the garish furniture in William Randolph Hearst's castle in San Simeon, California. She found pictures, engravings and documents from the early gold-rush days of California and meticulously supervised while state workers hung them on the walls.

Most important, she built a happy home, and Reagan loves it deeply. She is in charge of the family's private life, which she calls "preciously limited," and she does not like to share it with the public. "When you have a small child at home, you are limited as to what you can get involved in," she said. "I don't mean to imply I will stay aloof, but as anyone with children knows, they come first." As a result, home is where Reagan is natural and relaxed. Only rarely do outsiders glimpse the inner man. But when he is tired, the shell will sometimes crack.

A month before the gubernatorial election of November, 1966, he stopped in the small northern California city of Chico in the middle of a long day of speechmaking; tired, he submitted to a news conference. Reporters asked him about a speech in which he had appeared to shift his stand on the state open-housing law. Reagan wanted to take a nap, but the questions continued, and finally he said: "Well, at this time of the day, I'm not sure what I'm talking about, I'm so pooped." Reporters continued the questions. "You're boring in, aren't you?" said Reagan. "You're boring in because you caught me so pooped." Press aides finally broke it up. Reagan napped and came out cheerful and refreshed.

Usually his private world remains carefully hidden, as it was in Hollywood, where he was able to keep his personal life separate from his career. As an actor he had built his image on the screen and that was how the public knew him. Most often, it is different with a politician. When a politician runs for office, he is forced to parade his private self before the public, who like to judge a candidate on the basis of his style and temperament as well as on his stand on issues. Before he had made a single political speech, the public knew Reagan as a friendly, sincere, hard-working sort of fellow, one who had no major vices. The producers had picked Reagan as Shirley Temple's first grown-up boy friend in *That Hagen Girl,* confident that his forthright honesty wouldn't damage her virginal charm. In *Voice of the Turtle* he was the puritan-minded soldier who insisted that Eleanor Parker sleep in another room when a rainstorm forced him to spend a night in her apartment. In *Bedtime for Bonzo* he played a well-meaning and good-natured scientist who was raising a chim-

[19]

panzee to prove to his prospective father-in-law that environment is more important than heredity—and that his own father's criminal background was not important. Even when Reagan portrayed a playboy, the character was sanitized by the script and by Reagan's own clean-cut manner. In his films, whiskey bottles and pool cues were taken from the hands of baseball pitcher Grover Cleveland Alexander and George Gipp, the old Notre Dame football hero.

California Democrats never understood the danger they faced from his ready-made appeal. Instead they poked fun at his acting background. "This time I am running against an actor," said Governor Brown. "I just can't act, and he can't govern, believe me." Reagan knew better and emphasized his film career. "I've got a warm spot in my heart for Huntington Park; my first picture for Warners had its sneak preview in Huntington Park in 1937," he told the appreciative Huntington Park Republican Women's Club.

The overwhelming impact of that appeal became apparent on his first political trips. The combination of the celebrity's fame, the wisecracking humor and healthy, suntanned good looks made him an instant hit. There was excitement when he walked up to the platform with that quick stride and smiled a greeting. The speeches themselves were a cut above the standard conservative dogma. He added sparks to tired *Reader's Digest* stories of government waste. He reminded some listeners of evangelist Billy Graham. Graham had a way of taking familiar fundamentalist sermons against sin, and with his zeal, making them sound unique. Reagan did that with his appeals for old-fashioned individualism.

He is popular with women, an appeal that campaign assistant Dick Woodward liked to call "the hormone vote." The phrase was born late one night at the end of a political tour, when an oversized blonde grabbed Reagan and enthusiastically hugged him. "We call that the hormone vote," said Woodward. "We got her but lost her husband."

Reagan did not lose her husband's vote, or the votes of many husbands in the campaign, for he has a forthright masculine manner that smacks of horses, riding boots and football. The first stop of a tour one night was the home of a wealthy businessman who had invited some of the leaders of the agricultural aristocracy of his county to meet the potential governor. Almost two hundred people crowded into the flat, ranch-style home, decorated in front and in the hallways with Arizona flagstone that looked out of place in the flat fields of the farming valley. The people stood patiently on the receiving line that had become part of every Reagan appearance. Youngsters not yet born when he made his first movie asked for his autograph. "I think you're wonderful," said a woman. "Keep it up," said a man. Reagan —still at a loss in the give-and-take of political small talk —just flashed his boyish grin, occasionally bit his lip in apparent embarrassment and repeated softly, "Well, thank you." But even though he had little to say, the people reacted warmly. They were meeting someone they already knew—the Ronald Reagan whom they had seen the other night on the late show.

Back in the car, Reagan relaxed. The wife of the businessman had loaded down Reagan with a sack of tiny canapés, gooey combinations of mayonnaise, fish, olives and meat, and a jar filled with hot coffee. Freed from the obligation of impressing strangers, Reagan became a different, more likable man. That was another facet of his personality— even some of his most severe critics liked him and enjoyed being with him. The verdict of friend and foe: "He's a damn nice guy." Seated in the back seat, he handed out canapés and napkins, joked about the food and shook his head at the impossibility of pouring coffee from the wide-rimmed jar. The car sped over the narrow road and Reagan looked over the notes for his speech. He was reminded of a newspaper column that had angered him. The columnist had said he gave the same speech each time. It wasn't true, said Reagan: he had three basic speeches. Sometimes he would use the beginning of one, the middle of another and the climax of a third. By alternating them, like decks of a triple-decker sandwich, he actually could give many different speeches.

A celebrity's built-in appeal, however, was only part of the reason for Reagan's instant success. The public, who came to look at him, stayed because they were fascinated by what he had to say. He spoke about what they felt were the problems of the day, carefully pointing his message to specific audiences. Not a wit, but a wisecracker, he relieved the gloom of his conservative message with such remarks as: "I think the reason Bobby Kennedy is so excited about poverty is that he never had any."

He could sense an audience's worries—and exploit them in a dramatic speech. That was apparent in a talk to a group of middle-aged women in one of Los Angeles' older suburbs in April, 1966. "Once we've come to the retirement age," he said, "we can't live in our homes. We can't keep pace with the spiraling property tax. The people of California are being squeezed." As taxes went up, Reagan said, morality declined. He told of a dance at the University of California at Berkeley, a dance that showed Berkeley had "finally reached a point where the morality gap is so great that we can no longer ignore it." He told how the dance, sponsored by a committee protesting the Vietnam war and held in the men's gymnasium, had drawn the attention of the district attorney, whose report told "a story of what can best be described as an orgy." The catch words in the speech—Berkeley, morality and, finally, orgy—had assured Reagan the attention of every woman in the room. Pictures, he said, had been displayed on a giant screen in the gymnasium, "pictures of men and women, nude, in sensuous poses, provocative, fondling." It was heady material for the women's club, a dramatic portrayal of the morality message.

Built-in appeal and a popular message were not the only reasons Reagan was a political hit. Just as important—and maybe more important—was his skill on television, his ability to handle himself in front of the cameras. "He's a great performer," said a television newsman. "He plays to the camera all the time." Reagan approached political appearances on television as he approached the movies, as a business that required dedication and hard work. Just before a television appearance with United States Senator Robert F. Kennedy, Reagan sat tense and silent, not hearing the chatter of his assistants. But once the show began, Reagan was calm and quick-witted as he answered questions from hostile college students, handling himself more impressively than Kennedy.

As an actor he learned to control his voice and body movements to create a desired impression. "It has taken me many years to get used to seeing myself as others see me," wrote Reagan in his autobiography. "Very few of us ever see ourselves except as we look directly at ourselves in a mirror. Thus we don't know how we look from behind, from the side, walking, standing, moving normally through a room. It is quite a jolt."

Professional training gives him an advantage over politicians whose knowledge is limited to government. When most politicians are reading a speech on television, their eyes dart back and forth as they read the teleprompter. But

Reagan follows it with ease and even audaciously looks away without losing his place. That is important. For it means he is able to look directly at the audience, establishing direct communication; or he can look downward in a characteristic gesture that also brings him closer to the folks at home—grimacing in disgust with his opponents.

He has ease, superb timing and "empathy with an audience," said Nancy Reynolds, a former television newswoman Reagan hired to take charge of his television activities. "He started in a profession where he memorized scripts. He had a retentive memory, and I'm sure that comes from reading a script."

Reagan was not the first to use television so effectively. Dwight D. Eisenhower was aware of the possibilities of the medium and hired television producer Robert Montgomery to advise him. And John F. Kennedy, with his youth, good looks and vigorous manner, dominated the small screen as effectively as does Reagan. But Reagan was the first politician to neglect the traditional pageantry of the political campaign—long rallies, handshaking tours, dawn-to-midnight schedules—and rely so heavily on television. He emerged as television finally came to dominate American politics and was quick to realize that old methods were obsolete. No one before him had been more qualified, by looks or by training, to take advantage of the new era.

Every element of Reagan's appeal—the prepacked image, the performer's speaking ability and the conservative message —came together on the television screen. His shortcomings were not apparent and his star shone brightly. Television permitted him to demolish the charge that he was too inexperienced for office—just as the first television debate with Richard M. Nixon permitted John F. Kennedy to puncture the charge that he was too young for the Presidency. As governor, Reagan used television as Franklin D. Roosevelt used the radio two and three decades before. Roosevelt talked directly to the people in his fireside chats, appealing over the heads of recalcitrant congressmen. The warm rich voice evoked confidence and friendship, and when he died, millions felt the sharp pain that accompanies the death of a friend or relative. Radio took Roosevelt out of the impersonality of the printed page and into the home. Reagan modernized the fireside chat, and in his first few months in office filmed fifteen minute- and two-minute films, handing them out to television stations around the state. The aim was to present Reagan without the editorial comment of newspapers who were critical of his reductions in state programs. By all the standards of Reagan's show business background, the reports were a success. The ratings were high and public-opinion polls showed a majority of Californians approved of the way Reagan was doing his job, even after he saddled the state with a record tax increase and budget.

On the surface, California, and possibly the nation, had reached the long-prophesied era of the manufactured candidate—the product carefully picked and nurtured by public-relations specialists and then sold to the voters on television. But Reagan was more than a manufactured candidate. No doubt the techniques he used changed American politics, made them more visual and made strategists think of simple issues that could be discussed in short telecasts. His success, however, is due as much to his message as to the medium he uses to spread it. He deeply believes in what he is saying and says it with a sincerity that reaches out of the screen and into the living room.

Reagan arrived at his conservative philosophy late in life. The change came when he was in his thirties and forties, and it had come slowly. Even when he was forty-five, he apparently had not arrived at a clearly defined political philosophy. At that age he began making speeches for General Electric, and the company president, Ralph Cordiner, became concerned over his difficulties in answering audiences' questions. "I told him," Cordiner recalled, " 'You'd better get yourself a philosophy, something you can stand for and something you think this country stands for.' I think this is when he really started to change."

Those who find a philosophy in middle age, after years of wandering, often develop a stubborn faith, and that is what happened to Reagan. Once he arrived at his philosophy, Reagan clung to it with a determination that is sometimes found among late converts to a religious faith. There is a fervor in him when he talks about the philosophy, and he conveys it to the audience whether he is on television or in a hall. Reagan is a true believer, and when Californians became more conservative, he was the best-qualified spokesman for their new cause.

Without this deep commitment to conservatism, Reagan would have been just another celebrity in the parade of actors and actresses who appear each election year to help their favorite candidates and then return to private life. He was committed, however, and ready to accept when his party summoned him.

CHAPTER THREE

A HUMBLE BEGINNING

THERE IS IN AMERICAN LITERATURE a portrait of the Midwest of the 1920s—conservative, materialistic, admiring of the businessman, intolerant of social service, foreigners and dissenters. It is the Midwest described by Sinclair Lewis, and its typical community was Zenith, "the Zip City, Zeal, Zest and Zowie—1 million in 1935." Zenith's typical citizen was George F. Babbitt, who said of politics: "I'll tell you—and my stand on this is just the same as it was four years ago and eight years ago and it'll be my stand four years from now. What I tell everybody, and it can't be too generally understood, is that what we need first, last and all the time is a good, sound business administration." It was, in the words of Lewis' biographer, Mark Schorer, "the world of the little businessman. . . . He boasts and boosts with all his fellows, sings and cheers and prays with the throng, derides all difference, denounces all dissent— and all to climb with the crowd. With the supremacy of public relations, he abolishes human relations."

Ronald Reagan grew up in this era and in one of these communities. He was a boy of nine in 1920. But unlike Lewis, he loves the small towns, admires the conservative men who run them and looks back on his youth with fond memories. Reagan was shaped by the small towns of the Midwest, and that explains in large part the simple moral and conservative approach he brought to public life. Where Lewis satirized the Midwest communities, Reagan glorifies them. He enthusiastically accepts the values that Lewis criticized. As a result, he is deeply respectful of business; determinedly conservative; mistrusting of change; unintellectual and slightly suspicious of higher education; firmly wedded to the Protestant religion of his boyhood; convinced that, as his father said, "All men were created equal and [that] man's own ambition determines what happens to him the rest of his life." As he has done with all the values of his boyhood, Reagan applies this to public life and opposes state intervention in the problems of minorities. He likes neither open-housing laws nor big welfare programs. He has clung to these values all his life. In 1947, when he was a Democrat, his ideas didn't sound much different from his pronouncements as a conservative Republican twenty years later.

He has remained, through his life, a small-town boy from the Midwest, boosting its values, doubting the worth of other backgrounds, certain that the simple answers of his youth were still valid in his adulthood. He believes strongly that any individual, if determined enough, can succeed without the help of big government. "For two hundred years," he once said, "American business and industry have fought the greatest war on poverty the world has ever known. At the height of the great Depression, it was employing ninety percent of the nation's workers." Yet Reagan's own father was unemployed by the Depression and didn't find work until he got a government job administering relief, a reward for campaigning for Franklin D. Roosevelt in 1932. Later, his father was in charge of the local Works Progress Administration.

Reagan was born in Tampico, Illinois, on February 11, 1911, in a five-room flat above the H. C. Pitney General Store, where his father sold shoes. His father, John Edward Reagan, once commented that his son looked "like a fat Dutchman." The name stuck and Reagan was "Dutch" to his friends ever since. His brother Neil, then two years old, was brought into the bedroom to see the new baby, but he wouldn't look at him. His parents had promised him a sister, and he was disappointed.

There was only one block of paved street in Tampico, and the main communication with the outside world was through the two passenger trains that stopped each day at the small station near the grain elevator; they were local trains connecting the villages of the area. Reagan loved this village of twelve hundred people and wrote of it in his autobiography: "There were woods, and mysteries, life and death among the small creatures, hunting and fishing; these were the days when I learned the real riches of rags." It was a vigorous dissent against the view of the Midwest taken by Sinclair Lewis, who fled the area and became a socialist. In *Main Street* Lewis described a similar town, picturing it through the eyes of his heroine, Carol Kennicott. She wanted to run away from the village because "oozing out of every drab wall she felt a forbidding spirit she could not conquer." Even the drab town jewelry store depressed her. But in Reagan's memories, the Tampico jewelry store was a wonderful place, owned by a kindly childless couple, Aunt Emma and Uncle Jim, who gave him an allowance of ten cents a week, hot chocolate and permission to spend hours "hidden in a corner downstairs in Uncle Jim's jewelry store, with its curious relics, faint lights from the gold and silver and bronze, lulled by the erratic ticking of a dozen clocks and the drone of customers who came in."

Soon after Dutch was born, the family moved out of the flat to a house. The general store was across the railroad tracks from the house, and a park with a Civil War cannon was nearby. On the porch, Reagan's father hung a swing, and children would swing on it sideways instead of back and forth, shattering the midwestern evening quiet with the squeaking and thumping. Downstairs was a living room, a kitchen, a parlor and a service porch. Upstairs was the luxury of three bedrooms.

They were a close family. The father distressed his religious wife (she was Protestant of Scottish-English descent, and he was an Irish Catholic) by periodic drinking binges, but even in their most distressing moments together, she would say: "The Lord will provide." Most of the time he was sober and hard-working, always watching for better-paying jobs. There were many light moments in their lives. He and his wife were in the Parent-Teachers Association, and one night he put on a crepe-paper hula skirt, smeared make-up on his face, put on a wig and appeared with his wife in the P.T.A. talent show. Other nights the Reagans—devoted to amateur theatricals—would bring the drama group over to their home to rehearse for a play at the Tampico Opera House, located in an upstairs room in the town with space for about one hundred folding chairs. The boys would sneak behind a corner and watch the rehearsals. Afterward there was a big pot of oyster stew for everybody.

Within the close-knit family there was a strong bond between the brothers that continued through their lives. Later, when they were young men, Neil passed up college to work in a cement plant. Reagan went to college equipped with his proudest possession, a new, shiny black steamer trunk. When he came home at the end of his junior year, he told Neil he had made arrangements for him to also go to college, having lined up an athletic scholarship and a part-time job. Neil refused. When the new semester began, Neil came home from the cement plant one night and found his brother gone, but the steamer trunk remained in the middle of his bedroom.

"Nelle," he said to his mother, "I thought Dutch was leaving." The boys always called their parents by their first names.

"He has," replied his mother, "but your brother left that in case you changed your mind about going to college. He packed up all his things in cardboard boxes and shipped them down to school."

Neil considered the generous gift and his mother's unspoken rebuke for a moment and then said: "If that's the case, I'll go to college. I'll pack and go tomorrow."

During Reagan's early childhood, his father searched constantly for advancement, a quest that kept the family moving throughout Illinois. A job at Marshall Field's Department Store brought the Reagans to the South Side of Chicago when Dutch was two. But instead of improving the family fortunes, the move turned out to be a disaster. Jack Reagan's salary was so low that the family had to live in a flat lighted by a gas jet that provided light only if someone put a quarter in the meter down the hall—"If we had a quarter," Neil Reagan recalled later. On Saturdays, Neil was sent to the butcher shop with a dime for a soupbone. He'd also beg some liver for a nonexistent cat—and then bring it home for the main course for Sunday dinner. The mother would make a big pot of soup with the bone and keep it on the stove the rest of the week, adding carrots and potatoes. "That was the entrée," said Neil. For breakfast she would buy a carton of rolled Quaker Oats and serve it each day with condensed milk. When there were football games at the nearby University of Chicago stadium, Mrs. Reagan would make popcorn, put it in bags and send the boys out to try, without much success, to sell it. She made all the clothes for the boys.

The family lived in the flat on Cottage Way for almost two years, and finally Jack Reagan found a job that returned them to rural Illinois, this time Galesburg. He bought a bike to ride to work at the O. T. Johnson Department Store, and the family rose to new economic heights by moving into a rented two-story frame house, their first with hardwood floors. Big lawns were in front and back, just right for the football games the boys enjoyed. In three years his father found a better job in Monmouth, a city of between 35,000 and 40,000 people with three colleges nearby. In another two years, his old employer from Tampico, H. C. Pitney, asked him back for a year. Wearing the bibbed overalls of the era, eight-year-old Reagan would trudge off to the two-story country school each day. In the summer, Ronald and Neil sometimes spent a week on the farm of their parents' friends, the Lutyens, where they hauled water to the men thrashing grain in the fields and stuffed themselves with fried chicken, pie and cold watermelon when the women brought the heavy noonday meals out to the fields. Of that period of his childhood, Reagan wrote: "Those were the happiest times of my life."

It was a picture-book boyhood, something out of an old Norman Rockwell cover for the *Saturday Evening Post* or a Booth Tarkington novel. It was *Tom Sawyer* and *Huckleberry Finn* without the tragedy of Nigger Jim's slavery. There were, of course, some bleak times. Sometimes children would drown in the deep canal outside of town where everyone swam. And once, when Reagan and his friend Monkey Winchell were playing with a gun, Monkey fired it and blew a hole in the ceiling. Another time Jack Reagan bought a carload of potatoes for speculation and made his two sons sit in the car for days, sorting them. But mostly there were good times. Football and other sports occupied most of Reagan's time. Undersized and near-sighted, he was introduced to football in games in the park, with a lopsided ball. He would enthusiastically charge down the field with the other boys and jump into the battling pile of youngsters scrambling for the ball.

When Reagan was nine the family moved again. H. C. Pitney, the general store owner, agreed to become a partner with Reagan's father in a high-quality shoe store in Dixon, Illinois. The father would do the work while Pitney put up the capital. Reagan lived there from the age of nine until he was twenty-one. Here, in the schools, on the playing field and at home, Reagan's character was shaped. "All of us have to have a place to go back to," he said. "Dixon is that place for me."

In 1920 Dixon was a town of 10,000 located on the Rock River about one hundred miles west of Chicago. Driving into town on the Lincoln Highway from the rolling hills surrounding Dixon, you headed into the business district. The streets were lined with trees, many of which were later felled by disease and road projects. Now there are petunias instead of trees on the streets, and every July the city, grown to 20,000, has a petunia festival. The main street—then, as now—was Galena Avenue. Over it was the rustic memorial arch, built of wood, to honor the dead of World War I. Near the arch was the post office and the leading hotel, the Nachusa House, where Abraham Lincoln once slept, and the Nachusa Tavern, where, according to local legend, he

had debated Stephen A. Douglas. Boynton-Richards and the
Daile Clothing Company were the big retail stores downtown. On the other side of town was Lowell Park, a 320-acre,
city-owned area rich in historic tradition. The land was given
to Dixon by the family of James Russell Lowell, who liked
to spend time watching the Rock River. Today the river
is too polluted for swimming.

The town's schools were also along the river. The elemen-
tary school was built during the Civil War. Next to it was
Northside High, a sturdy red-brick building with big bay
windows of the post-Civil War period. Here Reagan came
in 1927, five feet three inches tall, weighing one hundred
eight pounds. He was near-sighted and wore thick, black-
rimmed glasses. With his friends, he walked through the
main door and up the big stairway. At the top of the stairs
was a study hall. To the right was the principal's office.
Classrooms were on the left and upstairs on the third floor.
The building was dark, solid, dignified and almost pretty,
with trees in front and a yard of grass and pavement. About
one hundred fifty students, equally divided between boys and
girls, attended the school.

Reagan's greatest challenge was not in the classroom but
on the nearby football field. He couldn't see the ball well
enough to catch it, and he was too small at first to play in
the line. But the game, he remembered as an adult, "was a
matter of life and death. Every year at the beginning of the
football season you were kind of ready for summer to end.
You'd begin to think about the smell of burning leaves. The
new high school uniforms would be put on display in a
store downtown. Your heroes were the high school stars.
They seemed like grown men." To make the high school
team was "your goal and aim in life. Everything is a game
except football," he said. "It is the last thing in our civilized

life where a man can physically throw himself, his full body, into combat with another man."

It took Reagan two years to make the high school varsity, but in his junior year, when he weighed one hundred twenty pounds and was "still a stringbean," he made the team. His bad eyes prevented him from playing where he wanted, at end or in the backfield. Instead he was a guard. But that didn't reduce the satisfaction the game gave him, and he retained his love for football as an adult. No role was more enjoyable to him than that of George Gipp in the Knute Rockne movie. In public life he liked to put his problems in the context of a football game. Handed a defeat in the legislature, he assured Republicans that it was only half time and that "there are still two quarters left to play." As governor he gave a staff job to Jack Kemp, the quarterback of the Buffalo Bills. Kemp, an articulate and intelligent man, used to complain that in their private conversations he wanted to talk politics while Reagan insisted on talking football. When a photographer took pictures of Reagan and Kemp, they tossed a ball back and forth for him in the governor's office. After the photographer finished, the two engaged in a forty-five-minute game of catch.

Football was the main interest in his life, but he had others. For a time young Reagan and his brother had a museum and zoo in the loft of the carriage house in back of their home. Their father gave them an old display case and they filled it with a collection of birds' eggs and butterflies. In the summer they had to pick tomato worms and potato bugs from their father's vegetable gardens. One year he gave them each a set of prize pigeons, which multiplied quickly. They also raised rabbits and persuaded a friend who had goats to join them in putting on circuses in a tent along the side of the house. But when the friend and Neil Reagan decided to go out of the circus business and into the meat and poultry business with the pigeons and rabbits, Dutch withdrew. "He couldn't go for killing," said Neil.

There were also overnight hikes with the Y.M.C.A. youth group—Reagan was too poor for a boy scout uniform—and swimming lessons at the Y.M.C.A. pool. And he shared the interest of his parents and brother in acting. The man who first taught Reagan about acting was B. J. Fraser, a slender, tweedy drama and English teacher. When Reagan was governor, Fraser was still living in Dixon, retired from the school, but alert, busy with an insurance business and willing to talk at length about his former student. Fraser thought the young Reagan "had possibilities" as an actor, but it was almost unheard of in the Midwest of those days for anyone to choose the theater as a career.

Reagan remembered himself as an indifferent student, concerned only with making the grades needed to remain eligible for football and other activities. But Fraser said: "He was quite interested in literature and English. He was an above-average student. He was curious. He was original and creative, and he had a quality that not too many high school kids had. He did what he started." Brother Neil recalled Reagan was "never one to crack a book"; instead he had "a truly photographic mind," an ability to read a large amount of material and absorb it. Throughout his life, those around him would comment on his memory. As an actor he learned scripts easily and remembered them. Later on, he could read summaries of complex government documents quickly and absorb them well enough to discuss them in public.

Reagan also wrote for the high school yearbook, enthusiastically took part in student government and clubs and was one of the few youngsters in town who planned to go to college. But he did not know what he wanted to do after that.

The happy boyhood produced the optimistic adult. Except for the two years on the South Side of Chicago, his growing up was a catalog of pleasant memories. When he reminisces about his childhood, it becomes clear that it was then that he learned the lessons that govern his life. He was asked once if he had a happy childhood. "Oh, yes," said Reagan. "Not a blissful, idyllic thing, but as you look back through the rosy glow of time, yes. I realize now, looking back on it, that we were poor, but I didn't know it at the time." Growing philosophical, he went on: "I think this is one thing that might be wrong today. The government seems intent on telling people they are poor. One of the reasons we didn't know it was that my mother was always finding someone who needed help."

The life of rural Illinois provided him with the material with which he justified the conservative opinions of his adulthood. There were, for example, the part-time and summer jobs that furnished him with spending money and helped him through college. For seven summers he was the lifeguard at Lowell Park, and during that time he pulled seventy-seven people from the water. In the mornings he would pick up hamburgers and other supplies for the park and then go on duty at the beach until swimming ended at night. "It was great," he said. "There was no place to spend money. I could save twenty dollars a week and, of course, they fed me, and if it was too crowded, they brought food down to me." The hours were so long that he didn't have time for girls, although they remembered him years later as the handsome lifeguard at the beach.

Many young men have such jobs and are enriched only with a little spending money. Reagan carried away something more; he left his lifeguard's post on the Rock River with a philosophy about independence and working. Looking back, he liked to say he had advantages the government now denies children. "This whole thing about teen-agers and summer jobs" annoyed him. "We have taken jobs away from them. We have taken them away in some instances by way of unions, but more by way of our own social legislation, and I think we've got to make some exceptions." As a teenager, he once worked for a company that remodeled old houses. At the end of every week, Reagan recalled, "The boss paid you out of his pocket in cash. He didn't have to sit down and do a lot of paper work for social security and all those things. Now don't get me wrong. I'm not criticizing it for the legitimate work force, but for the kids who have to go through school, it seems to me, we could make some exceptions; the employer today is resisting hiring the teenager part time because of these fringes and these excessive things and the paper work, and I would think social security could wait until a fellow becomes a legitimate member of the working force instead of being a kid in school with a summer job."

The values of the Midwest were also a great influence on his views about the problems of poverty and bigotry. As governor, he opposed laws to stop bigotry in housing, although he was raised to respect minorities and personally was not a bigot. But such laws represented collective action through the state, something alien to the lessons of his youth. He much preferred individual action, such as that his father took when he refused to permit his sons to see *Birth of a Nation* because "it deals with the Ku Klux Klan against the colored folks and I'm damned if anyone in this family will go see it." During the Depression Reagan's father was traveling, and a hotel clerk assured him, "We don't permit a Jew in the place." The father walked out after telling the clerk: "I'm a Catholic, and if it's come to a point where you won't take Jews, you won't take Catholics." The father spent the night in his car and became so ill that he later suffered a heart attack.

Government efforts to help the poor, such as the War on Poverty, were considered unnecessary by Reagan, and he was irritated by the way the Kennedy brother-in-law, Sargent Shriver, led the federal antipoverty program. "I was born in a small town back in the Midwest, and I was in poverty before the rich folks got hold of it," he said. Reagan believed that the poor should work hard and pull themselves up by their bootstraps, as he and his brother did. Welfare rolls, in his view, were full of the lazy. "Because most people believe in reward for productive labor, they voted against giving that reward to those who are able but unwilling to work," he said of his election as governor. His thoughts on assisting the poor and distressed came from his mother, who taught him that 10 percent of what he earned was the Lord's share. After receiving permission from a minister, Reagan sent ten dollars a month from his first job to his brother in college. Then, "just to gild the lily," he gave ten cents each day to the first man on the street who asked him for coffee.

That sort of generosity was part of Reagan's family's life. Years later in southern California, his brother found a poor family, gave them food and clothing and a Christmas tree and then wrote a poem to Reagan saying the good deed was Neil's Christmas present to him.

As a political candidate and later as governor, Reagan tried vainly to translate that sort of private generosity to public life. As a candidate he proposed a unique, neighbor-to-neighbor solution to one of California's greatest problems, floods. In one of the worst flood years, 1964, it took a Navy aircraft carrier, helicopters, planes, and one thousand two hundred airmen, marines and soldiers—all at federal expense —for the rescue operation. Afterward, millions of dollars in low-interest government loans helped rebuild the area. Reagan questioned the federal help. He said he had a better way, taking advantage of the good will of concerned citizens who wanted to help their neighbors. "Suppose," he asked, "it happened next year? What do you think would happen if a governor of California, instead of calling Washington, would get on the radio and television and say to the people of California: 'These are our neighbors, our fellow Californians, this is what they need. I am appointing a citizens committee and shortly you will be told what it is that you can do to help your neighbors.' " In this way, Reagan said, "we could solve the problem and we wouldn't have to set foot across the borders of California and I think everyone in the state would like it better that way." This simple philosophy was also at the hearts of Reagan's solutions to the complicated urban problems of the 1960s.

His opponents mocked such ideas. They said government was so big, complex and expensive that it had to be left to experts. "This is your citizen pilot," said Governor Brown, in a campaign speech parodying Reagan's "citizen politician" slogan. "I've never flown a plane before, but don't worry. I've always had a deep interest in aviation." But once again Reagan's opponents were wrong. Nobody, of course, would entrust his life to an untrained pilot. But Californians did not feel that way about their government. They agreed with Reagan that the professionals had been in charge too long. He came along at a time when people were looking for simpler answers, when they were tired of big government. He assured them that easy answers were available. "We have been told," he said, "that the problems are too complex for simple answers, until gradually we have accepted government by mystery; there seems to have evolved a special kind of government language, incomprehensible to simple citizens like ourselves." Reagan's complaints of rule "by an intellectual elite in a distant capital"—what he called "the puzzle palaces on the Potomac"—rang true to people who were as suspicious as he was of the intellectuals and progressives who promised peace and prosperity that never seemed to come. Hoping for simpler answers from an earlier time, they turned to Reagan. He looked and acted like—in fact he was—the homespun, small-town American boy whom politicians always pretended to be. Although he had lived in Hollywood since 1937, he still talked like the boy from Dixon, Illinois. Told of the complexities of the state's big water project, he said: "It's a little more complicated than laying down by a crick bank and getting a bellyful." He often shook his head in sorrow that his own son wasn't being raised in the country.

God, Home and Country—that's what Reagan believes in, and that is what he sells so well on television and before live audiences. To critics, Reagan's philosophy is midcentury Babbittry, thoughtless boasting and dangerous oversimplification of problems that can be solved only by cooperation of every talented and expert element of society, including government. But this is an era when the experts seemingly have failed. Negroes burst out of their slums in violence, undeterred by the inefficient War on Poverty. College students defy the courts in their protests against the Vietnam war. Parents worry that their children will be swept away by the troubled hippie and drug elements of society.

When Reagan came along with his message of the virtues of the old values, the voters began to think that maybe folks had the right idea back then in Dixon, Illinois.

CHAPTER FOUR

COLLEGE HERO

EUREKA, ILLINOIS, is even smaller than Dixon. Today, as in Reagan's youth, it is a town of less than three thousand people built around Eureka College, a Disciples of Christ school. Its slogan is "City on the Go—with Young Men on the Go." Old homes, some of them built more than a century ago, are shaded by maple trees. Only five men are on the police force, and there hasn't been a robbery in town for almost a decade. No bars are allowed and no liquor is sold within city limits. It was in this small college community where Dutch Reagan, fulfilling an ambition he had had since he was a teen-ager, enrolled as a freshman in September, 1928. Puritan rules governed Eureka, giving a highly moral tone to the school. The young man who grew up to run for public office on a morality platform could not have found a more suitable alma mater.

But in 1928 there was an undercurrent of unrest and rebelliousness against authority at Eureka, and surprisingly Reagan found himself in the middle of it. At seventeen, Reagan did not look like a candidate for student rebel. By now he was approaching one hundred seventy-five pounds, a handsome, smiling, self-assured young man with horn-rimmed glasses and thick auburn hair parted in the middle. He was neatly dressed and obedient to authority the day he arrived at Eureka, his clothes packed in his new steamer trunk, four hundred dollars in lifeguard wages in his savings. There was a scholarship for half of his tuition awaiting him, awarded because of athletic ability, not good grades. His main goal was to make the football team. He had already been pledged to a fraternity, Tau Kappa Epsilon. Well-liked, popular and conventional in high school, he was awaiting the same sort of experience in college. But he arrived to find morale low on the campus. Signs of unhappiness against the strict rules were evident. Backsliders ignored the no-smoking rule and went across the street between classes for cigarettes, sending up a thick blue haze of smoke into the air. The administration said that girls must be in Lyda's Wood, the women's dormitory, at 9:30 P.M. on weekdays and at midnight on Saturdays, but some girls slipped out for after-hours dates, sticking a pin in the front-door lock so they could get back in, a staggering offense on that disciplined campus.

Elsewhere, it was the Jazz Age, the Roaring Twenties, the time of flaming youth. Movies, novels and lurid newspaper stories told of college students drinking home-made gin, of immorality, of rejection of traditional American standards. But at Eureka, in the ivy-covered brick buildings and at chapel, where attendance was required each day, President Bert Wilson fought the tide. Eureka students who were caught drinking were dismissed. The year before Reagan enrolled, there had been an ugly scene when students defied the ban on dancing at the annual get-acquainted party. One of the rebels was the daughter of the chairman of the board of trustees; another was the chairman's nephew. They were among a group of about eight students who persuaded the orchestra leader to put aside his regular chamber music and play dance music. When the orchestra started, the rebels began to dance. Furious, President Wilson ordered the band to stop playing, led the violators up to the platform, made them sit down as a sign of disgrace and publicly chastised them. Even respectable places off campus were not free from the rules. The president penalized students caught attending the twice-a-week family night dances at the American Legion Hall, even those who were there with their parents. He took away grade points needed for graduation from some of the students and required others to remain on campus.

Now, a spirit of rebellion was on the campus, even though the ban on dancing had been relaxed. An underground movement to force out President Wilson had been started, and it had been joined by some of the faculty, for the declining economy of the Midwest had forced the already unpopular administration to propose some budget cuts that affected staff as well as students. As Reagan remembered it, the economies were the reason for the strike. Others, however, recalled it differently and said that the real motive was a rebelliousness against the unreasonably strict administration. In a 1967 article for *West* magazine about Reagan's college days, Thomas Driscoll concluded: "No doubt the students seized upon the cutback as the issue they could use to get rid of Wilson and his puritan restrictions. Faculty members were upset by it because it called for combining several departments and eliminating a few others, with the eventual dismissal of six or seven professors and the downgrading of several more. Later, it became clear that a number of professors were actively stirring up the students, working with equal fervor for Wilson's removal."

The tradition at Eureka was that freshmen were supposed

to remain silent, and the leadership of the dissenting students was in the hands of the upperclassmen. But as a boy, and as a young man, Dutch Reagan was never one to remain silent. He was audacious, a quality that was not softened by the passing of the years. As a legacy from his Irish shoe salesman father, he inherited brashness and the love of making a speech for a cause. Sometimes the speech was more important than the cause—as in the months following World War II, when Reagan spoke enthusiastically before veterans and labor groups and later found to his amazement that their views were far to the left of his. In Eureka's student rebellion Reagan found his first cause, and he joined with an eagerness that surprised some of his fellow students.

Quick of tongue and eager to help, Reagan was made a freshman representative on the student committee, and when the trustees accepted Wilson's economies, he was one of one hundred forty-three students who signed a petition asking for the President's resignation. When the trustees refused to act on the petition, the students disobeyed the campus rules and prepared to strike. A strike was contrary to all of the traditions of the little school, but powerful forces were at work. The night the trustees turned down the students, the college bell announced a meeting in the chapel. Faculty and students, some of them roused from beds and wearing coats over their pajamas, crowded into the chapel, which was big enough for only two hundred fifty people. Eureka graduates from around the town were also there, unhappy with Wilson because of a statement in which he indicated he thought the town was too small to support the college. They also wanted the trustees to demand his resignation.

Speeches were made by student leaders criticizing the administration. Then it was time for Reagan, the freshman representative, to speak. He did not call for a return to law and order or ask the students to protest to the trustees through established channels. Nor did he—as he did as governor—criticize the faculty for supporting the students. Instead he offered a resolution calling for a student strike. He had been asked to introduce the strike motion because the upperclassmen did not want to be accused of having a vested interest in preventing cutbacks they felt might affect their chance to graduate. His motion was adopted unanimously, and when classes resumed, all but a few students stayed away. Professors joined the protest, taking roll and reporting none of the missing students absent. It was complete defiance of the rules. As an adult Reagan liked to give the strike more respectability by recalling how students meticulously continued to study. But as others remembered, the strikers sat on the steps of homes across from the school, smoked cigarettes and engaged in a week-long bull session. "If any studying was done, it was a pretext," said one graduate. Pressure on Wilson grew. Even some of the trustees privately were sympathetic to the students. Finally Wilson submitted his resignation on December 7. "Other avenues of service are open to me, and a burden will be lifted from my shoulders if tonight I know that I am freed from any further connection with this unfortunate situation," he said. The students met again and accepted their complete victory. With Wilson gone, they graciously said that in view of the "fine spirited statement made last evening by President Wilson . . . we instruct our leaders to withdraw our petition." Now, the students said, they recognized they were dealing with matters that concerned the trustees and did not "presume to dictate what their action shall be in any matters affecting the policy and the program of the school. . . . We love Eureka College." That abruptly put an end to the student unrest.

So out of tune was the revolt with the traditions and think-

ing at Eureka College that it took two or three years for it
to dwindle as a topic of conversation. But life did settle back
into a routine, and the strike assumed its place as just another
memory of college—a momentary display of youthful spirit.
Surprisingly, neither Reagan nor the other participants were
to find any resemblance between it and a student rebellion
of another day, the 1964 free-speech revolt at the University
of California at Berkeley. Reagan drew a distinction between
the two student movements. He said that the Eureka strike
had the backing of nearly all the faculty, and that made it
different from the protest at Berkeley. But when University
of California faculty members and students protested his own
budget cuts, Reagan said: "It is disturbing to see supposedly
mature members of the academic community inciting students to intemperate acts with inflammatory charges." For
despite his three-week fling as a student rebel, Reagan learned
no lessons from Eureka that would prepare him for his later
confrontation with the big and complex system of university
and college campuses, a system which drew students from
every level of society—some of them questioning, searching
rebels and others just as conventional as Reagan was in college. Eureka's puritanical atmosphere did not prepare him
for the intellectual ferment, the hippies, the coffee houses,
the interracial couples, the long-haired beardies, the undisciplined demonstrations of the University of California at
Berkeley.

Except for those few weeks, the rest of his college life was
so typical of a student of that time and place that it could
have been used as a plot for a Hollywood college movie of
the thirties and forties. The happy college of his youth, in
fact, didn't seem too different from the fictitious college
Reagan taught at in the fanciful movie of the forties, *Working Her Way Through College*.

Home was the Tau Kappa Epsilon fraternity house. His friends from the fraternity were among his friends later in life. As governor he still corresponds with some of them. When Reagan moved into the Teke house, the kitchen, dining room and living room were crowded into a very small area on the first floor. But once again his eagerness came to the surface, and he and two friends, Enos (Bud) Cole and Elmer Fisher, decided that the house needed a new dining area. They ripped out the old basement so it could be re-modeled into a dining room and kitchen. "We mainly tore things down and someone who had the skill put things back," said Cole.

Reagan was an average student, and there are no intel-lectual triumphs among his memories of college. By his own account, there was not the fierce commitment to scholarly excellence at Eureka that was found at Harvard, Columbia, the University of California, the University of Chicago or others. "The student who was going into pre-law was going to have to work harder for a good grade than I was because the professor knew that all I wanted was a diploma, that there wasn't a chance in the world that the actual subject matter was going to be vital to me, that I would have to re-member it, so he wouldn't be as strict with me." He majored in economics, and as in high school, his photographic memory got him through examinations. His extracurricular activities were so extensive that they left little time for studying. Reagan was on the football team. He was also cheerleader during basketball season, president of the student council, active on the yearbook and the student newspaper, the school's best swimmer, and a member of the debate team and the dramatic club. He was elected president of the boosters club three years in a row. As he said later: "I was so busy with these other things that I apportioned only a certain amount of time to study. A C average was required for eligibility for outside activities. I set my goals at maintaining eligibility. I know that wasn't right, but it also made room and time for other things that I think were valuable."

Most important was the football field, flanked by wooden stands where Eureka's team ran out every Saturday for its weekly battles in the "Little 19," a conference of small colleges. "I remember him best as the freshman who stuck with the football squad all fall, although he never even got a first-class jersey. . . . It was difficult not to get one at Eureka," said Howard Short, the manager of the football team. Reagan sulked on the bench through his first year, believing that coach Ralph McKenzie didn't appreciate him. But in the second year, friends commented on his "pay day pepper," as he attracted McKenzie's attention in some bruising practices. Early in the year he was elevated to first string guard next to Pebe Leitch, the right tackle, the team captain and his roommate in the fraternity house. "Dutch was not an outstanding football player, but he was a good plugger, dedicated, put out a lot, had a lot of spirit and desire," said Coach McKenzie.

On fall evenings, Reagan, Pebe Leitch, Bud Cole, and later Neil Reagan would walk back to the Teke house from football practice, college heroes in an era when life from September through November revolved around the football team. There was the homecoming show each year when each of the fraternities and sororities put on "stunts" or skits. Reagan was forever ready to give a speech, act in a play, somersault through the air in the acrobatics of a basketball cheerleader or do an imitation of a radio sportscaster in a fraternity skit.

In the winter, now that the restrictions against dancing were lifted, students had a Christmas dance. By Reagan's second year, the Depression had hit the parents of most of the Eureka students, and that simplified the campus social life. Reagan would often visit his girl friend, Margaret Cleaver, daughter of a Eureka minister. At nights, young men and women without any money would go on dates to the drugstore for a ten-cent cherry phosphate. Sometimes they would dance in the living rooms of fraternity houses or walk through the walnut orchard in back of the campus. Few had cars, so the lover's lane was a graveyard within walking distance of the campus. At the fraternity house the boys would play pinochle, with the loser required to walk eight or ten blocks downtown to bring back hamburgers and malted milks.

In this idyllic setting Reagan used his activities to develop what was later to become his profession. He became seriously interested in acting. Drama was taught by Miss Ellen Marie Johnston, and under her guidance he became as convincing on the stage as he was when giving a strike speech in the chapel. With others in the small college's drama group, he traveled to Northwestern University for an annual one-act play contest. The Eureka players made the finals in the competition with their performance of *Aria da Campo*, Edna St. Vincent Millay's play about the foolishness of war. They didn't win first prize, but there was a bit of unexpected glory for Reagan, something he would remember when he wondered what to do with his life. He received an individual acting award and bounded out of his seat with a big smile as he hurried toward the stage to receive it. "The fact was, I suppose, that I just liked showing off," he said.

At home, Jack Reagan's Fashion Boot Shop staggered under the Depression and finally went out of business. Reagan had to provide for himself, and in addition to washing dishes at the fraternity, he was the school's swimming coach and teacher and worked in the kitchen of the girls' dormitory. Every Saturday, when there wasn't a football game, he and the other hashers would scour the cupboard doors, working their way around the kitchen, giving each door a quick wipe. The housemother followed them, holding a pencil and writing "brush here" on each of the doors. Inevitably, the boys would do them over again.

This was his life at Eureka—content, centered on the campus, for the most part unaware of the powerful political currents sweeping the nation. Here there was none of the tumult of the big-city campuses. No radicals on soapboxes called for the overthrow of the government. At Eureka the Depression was an economic inconvenience and not a sign of a sick social system. In 1932 Reagan graduated, taking part in the symbolic cutting of the ivy vines—a tradition for Eureka graduates. He left college without prospects of a job, but he was not bitter. Forever the optimist, he was confident that something would turn up.

He was, by the standards of the great universities of today, undereducated. By his own admission he had not taken advantage of even the limited opportunities at Eureka. But even with his minimum college education, Reagan left college with no regrets. He believed then—as he believes as an adult—that he had chosen the correct course in dedicating his energies to activities outside the classroom. There is more to college, he believes, than books. He makes a distinction between knowledge and wisdom. Knowledge is acquaintance with facts. It means expensive and often obscure research conducted in equally expensive facilities. But more than knowledge is needed. He said: "What good is it to teach someone all the facts if they don't know how to live and if they don't know the use of them for the solutions of the problems they are going to meet as life goes on?" Young people need wisdom, a virtue which in his view is something else altogether. It is an ability to deal with the world; it is based on experience, good judgment and discretion rather than knowledge of facts. Wisdom comes with growing up. He believes that Eureka gave him wisdom—an ability to continue to learn and grow—even though his academic record was spotty.

Perhaps of everything he learned at Eureka, his ideas on education would most significantly affect his political philosophy. He values folk wisdom, an awareness of the hard-headed practical ways of the world. And the small college of his youth gave better individual care than does the well-equipped big state university. He drew from his own college years a concept of education that made him hostile to big universities, especially to the University of California—committed as it is to intellectual perfection and academic freedom. He is uniquely unsuited to sit on the Board of Regents of the University, a job he holds as governor. His complete conviction of the superiority of his own education prejudices him against the extremes of freedom of expression on college and university campuses.

In later life he became more of a reader, grasping for the books that he was told to read in college but never did. On his adult list of reading priorities is *The Decline and Fall of the Roman Empire* and other books "of the type of thing they tried to force me to read then, outside reading and those sort of things." But his do-it-yourself education did not make him more sympathetic to the scholars of the state university and colleges. He was ill at ease among them and their students. He liked to lecture college students rather than participate in the give-and-take of ideas. When he addressed them, it was often in the nature of a dramatic confrontation from which someone had to emerge a winner and someone had to leave a loser.

He made visits to his alma mater and received honors from it. He returned in 1947 and was the grand marshal of the annual Pumpkin Parade. A decade later he visited the campus again, stood among the buildings, talked with old friends. On that day he put on an academic gown and walked over the green grass that covered the campus. He now was one of Eureka's most famous sons, a future member of the board of trustees, and he had come back to receive an honorary degree of Doctor of Humane Letters. As usual, his wife Nancy watched proudly as he accepted the degree and made a speech in reply. Like his scholarships, the degree was awarded more for outside activities than for intellectual attainment. It was given for "understanding and exposing Communists and their influence" while he was president of the Screen Actors Guild.

In 1967 he came back to Eureka once more on a cold September evening—this time as the conquering hero, Eureka's most prominent graduate. He was governor of California and, more important, a potential candidate for President. He had been invited to dedicate the college's new library, and the student body, the faculty and the townspeople were seated on chairs outside the new building to hear him. On the platform Illinois' most famous Republican politicians were with Reagan, senators Everett Dirksen and Charles Percy. The band played and the student chorus sang as the audience pulled their coats around themselves to keep out the cold.

For Reagan it was an important occasion. He was beginning a tour of three states, and this was to be a showpiece speech, one that would set the tone for a tour that his ad-

visers hoped would start a serious Reagan-for-President movement. In it he would address himself to one of his critics'
favorite points—that he was out of tune with youth and
hostile to education. He began with a joke, a reference to
his own undistinguished grades in college. "Ten years ago,
in cap and gown, I stood in this place to receive an honorary
degree—a happening which only compounded an already
heavy burden of guilt. I had always figured the first degree
you gave me was honorary." The audience laughed. He went
on to say: "As the day nears when classroom and playing
field must give way to the larger arena, with its problems
of inequality and human misunderstanding, it is easy to look
at those in that area [adult life] and demand to know why
problems haven't been solved." There was no recognition in
this speech that the college students of today had already
entered into adult life, that college was no longer a peaceful
interlude between high school and a job. Students were man-
ning the antiwar protest lines and serving in the civil rights
movement. Some would soon leave school to fight in Vietnam
or join the Peace Corps. These young people had accepted
their responsibilities already, without waiting for the formality of a college diploma. They were participating in the
"larger arena" of life.

The silence continued as Reagan rambled through a tor-
tured explanation of why the older generation and the
younger generation could not communicate. It was because
of "horizontal stratification"—generations talked only to
themselves. "This horizontal stratification has led to lateral
communication, and it is highly essential that we restore
vertical dialogue if not an outright recognition of the naturalness and rightness of a vertical structuring of society." Then
he defended the older generation in a tone that was con-
descending to the students and as hackneyed as anything

written in Hollywood by a script writer for a B movie. "That fellow with the thickening waist and the thinning hair who is sometimes unreasonable about your allowance or letting you have the car, his life seems a little dull to you now as he reports for his daily nine-to-five chores or looks forward to lowering a golf handicap or catching a fish no one wants to eat. I wish you could have known him a few years back on a landing craft at Normandy or Tarawa or on a weekend pass in Peoria. He was quite a guy." Reagan spoke in clichés that night, lecturing to an audience he seemed to think was composed of children. At the end there was an automatic bow to the books in the library as he urged the students to read Aristotle, Plato and Socrates, Maimonides and the "man from Galilee."

They listened while he lectured. Parents, he said, have given too much to their children. "We are the classic example of giving to you what we never had . . . from TV to wheels and dental care to Little League. But I am afraid we shortchanged you on responsibilities or the right to earn for yourselves. All too often, because we had to earn, we wanted to give. Our motives have been laudable, but our judgment has been bad. 'No' was either a dirty word or dropped from our vocabulary."

The students stood up and applauded politely when he finished. He might be, after all, the first Eureka graduate to become President. But Dutch Reagan, class of '32, had lost contact with the students of the sixties. His speech had shown the size of the gap between him and his college days and the college generation of the present. He had talked to them as if they were students of the Eureka of his day, when the drama club and football team were more important than studies and the world outside of the campus.

⊠ CHAPTER FIVE

HOLLYWOOD

ALMOST EVERY AFTERNOON between April and September in the mid-thirties, Reagan sat behind a desk in a six-by-eight studio on the first floor of radio station WHO, the National Broadcasting Company's affiliate in Des Moines, Iowa. In front of him was a big square microphone with the call letters—the *H* flanked by flashes of lightning—printed on the sides. Reagan, his hair parted in the middle and combed back in the pompadour style of the times, waited impatiently for a Western Union operator in the next room, visible through a big window, to hand him a piece of paper through a slot. On the paper was written a brief description of the action in a Chicago Cubs or White Sox baseball game that was being played more than one hundred miles away. "Hartnett singles to right," might be typed on the paper, the bare outline of an exciting moment at Wrigley Field, and it was up to Reagan to reconstruct from this a vivid word picture of what was happening at the ball park. He had already described the pitcher, looking toward first, winding up and throwing the ball. All he had to work with was one brief sentence. From his imagination he filled in the rest.

The engineer, who also read the message, cracked a small bat on a piece of wood, imitating the sharp sound of Gabby Hartnett's bat hitting the baseball, and then turned up the volume of a phonograph record of crowd noises so it sounded like the thousands who were yelling at Wrigley Field. At the crack of the bat, Reagan would tell how Hartnett scrambled down the first-base line, describing the chagrin of the opposing pitcher. His voice would rise in excitement as he told —still from his imagination—how the right fielder threw the ball back into the infield and Hartnett wisely held up at first base. Then Reagan would picture how the opposing manager walked out to the mound, held a worried conversation with the pitcher and returned to the dugout. Finally the Western Union operator would begin typing out another message he was receiving from Chicago, and Reagan would have the pitcher go into his stretch again, faking the action until he was handed news of the latest play. Some of those who heard Reagan "recreate" these games still recall his performances. "You would think from hearing those ball games you were sitting in Wrigley Field," said Republican congressman H.R. Gross of Iowa, then WHO's top newscaster.

In this WHO studio, on the edge of downtown Des Moines, Reagan began the training that would eventually take him to Hollywood. Before television, major-league baseball was brought to most of the nation by talkative men who read Western Union's fragmented accounts of a game being played many miles away and recreated the action. This is how Reagan perfected his speaking ability and learned how to sell soap, cars and major-league baseball by the power of his voice.

Reagan was one of the best play-by-play men in the Mid-west, a nonstop talker who was so garrulous that he wasn't even flustered when the wire occasionally broke down and he had to improvise until service was restored. Once, when the wire failed in the middle of a game and Reagan was ad-libbing until it was repaired, the station manager ran downstairs from his office, looked into the studio and yelled, "When the hell are you going to get the game on?" Reagan signaled that the profanity was going over the airwaves and continued talking.

His success in the college play contest at Northwestern had stirred his ambitions to become an actor, and that led him into radio. Without prospects of a job following graduation, he returned to Dixon in the middle of the Depression for a final summer as lifeguard at Lowell Park. "After college, he didn't know what he wanted to do, not really," said his wife, Nancy, who has heard the story of his youth many times. "Becoming a sports announcer was not the career that he set out to follow. That just kind of happened." Radio was part of show business, an important part in small towns such as Dixon, and when the summer ended Reagan tried for a job in it. The big stations in Chicago, WBBM, WGN and the rest, turned him down, but he was advised to visit the smaller outlying stations. Most of his classmates, hoping for careers in more conventional fields, were unemployed, but Reagan, who has always been able to find work, was hired on his first stop. Peter MacArthur, the program man-ager of WOC of Davenport, Iowa, put him to work part-time to broadcast the remaining four University of Iowa football games. He was paid only five dollars for the first game, between Iowa and the University of Minnesota, and ten dollars each for the remaining three.

By the beginning of 1933 he became a full-time staff announcer at one hundred dollars a month. In April he was shifted to WHO in Des Moines. This was the golden age of radio, and Dutch Reagan was a leading announcer at WHO, NBC's 50,000-watt prize in the area, a clear channel station that could be heard in Iowa, Missouri, Minnesota and the western Illinois country where Reagan grew up. Besides recreating baseball games, he covered track meets and football games. He also interviewed people outside the sports world, among them Aimee Semple McPherson, the evangelist, and Leslie Howard, the actor. On occasional Saturday nights he announced the station's big three-hour barn dance program in Shrine Auditorium, a country music show that was as popular as the WLS *Barn Dance* in Chicago, one of the most famous midwestern country music shows of the era. Reagan's brother Neil, who was also with WHO, remembered that at one time "we had ninety-five hillbillies on the staff." Dutch also wrote a sports column for a newspaper that was published briefly, and during football season when Iowa was playing away from home, he handled the public-address system for the Drake University football games.

Gross, the newscaster, remembers that even in those days Reagan loved to give speeches. So popular was he in WHO's big listening area that the station often sent him to talk to high school father-and-son banquets or before clubs. Gross, who also liked to make speeches and often accompanied him, recalls that Reagan, as he did in his later political talks, ended his speeches with a strong morality plea. "He would tell sports stories," said Gross, "plus some solid morality—urging his audiences to stay away from drink, cigarettes and cheating."

Reagan lived in an apartment near the nurses' quarters for Broadlawn General Hospital. One night he broke up a robbery. "I heard a girl on the walk outside my window say,

'That's all the money I have.' I looked down and saw a guy poking a gun at her." Reagan had three guns in his room, but all were empty. But he pointed an empty gun out the window and yelled: "I have a forty-five in my hand, and I'm going to let you have it. Get going." The bandit ran away and Reagan put on his robe and escorted the girl back to the nurses' quarters. "I was shaking all over, and she wasn't even scared," Reagan said. "Just kept saying, 'To think, a little squirt like that trying to hold me up.' "

Neil Reagan said his brother was "probably the best on the staff" of the station. Neil is now in advertising, the vice-president of McCann-Erickson agency in Los Angeles. One day he was asked to assess, as an advertising man and not as a brother, the single quality that Reagan showed in those days that was to make him successful in radio, films and later politics. "I would say it in one word. It is what you strive for in directing any dramatic show—credibility as far as the audience is concerned. If you have that, you don't have to worry about anything."

"I was doing pretty well in the sports announcing thing," recalled Reagan. "All the dreams down deep of being an actor had died." But in 1937 one of the hillbilly bands at the station stirred up the dreams again by signing a contract to appear in a Gene Autry movie. It was Autry's custom to hire for each film a country music band from a major section such as WHO, and when the movie played in the area, the local musicians would guarantee a large audience. The same year, Reagan accompanied the Chicago Cubs to Southern California for spring training at Catalina Island, which was owned by the same Wrigley family that operated the baseball team. "Suddenly the whole thing awoke," said Reagan. "It seemed more possible. I visited WHO's western band on the set." Their agent, also a friend from Des Moines, arranged for Reagan to read for a casting director in Hollywood who offered him no hope. He had lunch with another friend from Des Moines, Joy Hodges, a singer, who was more helpful. First she suggested that he remove his glasses in front of the camera, and then she introduced him to an agent, Bill Meiklejohn. Reagan and Meiklejohn talked for a while, and then the agent called Warner Brothers and asked for Max Arnow, the casting director. "I have another Robert Taylor in my office," said Meiklejohn. Warners gave Reagan a screen test and was impressed enough to offer him a contract. Reagan had already left for the East with the Cubs, and when he arrived home, the news was awaiting him. "I thought I'd probably hear from the test by Thursday," he said. "When no word came I thought, Aren't they ever going to tell me I didn't make it? I was nervous as could be, but I couldn't explain why to those who asked me because I hadn't said anything about the test." Friday, he received the telegram saying: "SCREEN TEST OKAY. MAILING $200 A WEEK CONTRACT." Reagan leaped into the air and whooped with joy. "I didn't read the rest of the telegram until that night."

Joy Hodges jubilantly wired back to the Des Moines *Register* and *Tribune:* "MAYBE SCOOP YOU DO HAVE POTENTIAL STAR IN YOUR MIDST DUTCH REAGAN LOCAL SPORTS ANNOUNCER SIGNED LONG TERM WARNER BROS CONTRACT FRIDAY THEY CONSIDER HIM GREATEST BET SINCE TAYLOR WITHOUT GLASSES I DON'T MIND TAKING SOME CREDIT MY OWN IDEA AND EFFORTS HIS TALENT CINCHED IT HOWEVER." The contract was important news in Des Moines, and the *Register* and *Tribune* recorded the event in a long story. Reagan told the paper: "I'd rather act than anything else. But I didn't think anyone would go home and give their husband arsenic after seeing me, so I turned to radio as a second choice." His contract guaranteed him six months' work at Warners, with options to extend it running over a seven-year period. "I may be out there for only six months," he said. "Of course I hope it doesn't turn out that way—but you never can tell." He said: "I've never had a thrill like this before. I'll admit it's got my head spinning like a top."

Despite Meiklejohn's enthusiasm, Reagan was no Robert Taylor. In his show business career, which lasted until January, 1966, when he formally announced he was running for governor, Reagan would never be a great movie star, a first-ranking personality like Robert Taylor, Gary Cooper, Clark Gable or Errol Flynn. But given a good role, he was a believable actor, one who worked hard at his craft. He improved slowly over the years and did not fritter away his limited talents by dissipating, as so many of his colleagues did. Untemperamental and easygoing, he followed the advice of those more experienced, and as a result developed strong friendships with producers and with influential columnists such as Hedda Hopper. In many of his roles Reagan was a victim of the poorly written movies ground out by Hollywood's film factories in the thirties, forties and fifties by inept writers, directors and producers. The major studios owned their own theaters in those days and produced more than six hundred pictures a year for a receptive market, which did not face the competition of television. Most of the films were mediocre at best, and too often a success that should have boosted Reagan to stardom was followed by a disaster over which he had no control. In 1939 he was thoroughly convincing in his role in *Knute Rockne—All American*, an early success. But soon after he was cast in a film appropriately called *The Bad Man* and found himself caught between two of Hollywood's most famous hams, Wallace Beery and Lionel Barrymore. "Sheer nickelodeon," said the reviewer for *Scribners*

Magazine. "It is as crude and primitive as anything I saw in the old five-cent silent days in Bloomfield, Illinois, when I was a child in curls and pinafores." The reviewer for *Time* pinpointed Reagan's dilemma: "Both dialogue and action . . . are resolved into a prolonged contest between the stallion snorts of actor Beery and the crosspatch snuffles of actor Barrymore." As for the others, including Reagan, they "seem to walk through their parts in a mechanical daze."

Reagan treated his screen career with unusual objectivity. "He was never fooled by his publicity," said Taft Schreiber, who, as head of Music Corporation of America's Revue Productions, later brought Reagan into television. "The motion picture business was just a part of his evolution, as was radio before." Movies were never an art form to Reagan. Like Schreiber, he referred to movies as "the picture business" and there was always a heavy emphasis on the business end of it. When television came in, many of his more famous colleagues, out of work in the declining motion picture industry, were too proud to go on the new medium. But Reagan willingly switched as public tastes changed.

Personally he was, as he liked to confess when he was older, "a square." "He wasn't a night club kid," said Robert Taylor. "When I first met him, he was vitally interested in athletics and keeping himself in great condition." He lived simply in an apartment, drove the convertible he brought out with him from Iowa and owned only four suits. Even today he dislikes buying new clothes, and as a result, some of his suits have the padded shoulders and wide pants cuffs popular several years ago. Flynn, Bogart and other Warner players caroused at night, and Reagan occasionally joined the social life of Hollywood. But he also found time to make a speech to the San Fernando Y.M.C.A. in those early days on "clean sportsmanship, health rules and the importance of team play." His home life was important to him. After his first movie, he brought his parents to California, and Neil followed a year or so later. By 1939 he was ready for marriage, and that year he became engaged to Jane Wyman, twenty-four, an actress who had been divorced the year before from Myron Futterman, a manufacturer. They met while working on a picture, and she said at the time, "It was love at first sight." They were married on January 26, 1940, at the Wee Kirk O'Heather, a popular Hollywood wedding chapel, and then went on a short honeymoon to Palm Springs.

Hollywood, recalled Schreiber, was filled with all kinds of stars, but "talk to any actor," said Schreiber, "and all he can talk about is his box office." Reagan was a man apart with many other interests—horses, politics, sports. Schreiber recalled: "He was knowledgeable. He could carry on a conversation beyond acting—football, FDR; he was a totally interested man." He had another quality that endeared him to Schreiber and others at MCA: "He only had this one agency. This was it. It wasn't the agent's fault if things didn't go well. Most actors blamed their agents. He understood. He had a very sound grasp of the situation."

On the screen there was a certain sameness to his performances. As Schreiber saw it, there were two types of actors in Hollywood. Some had "screen magic that somehow on celluloid jumped out at the audience." Reagan was not that type. "He was not a Clark Gable," said Schreiber. Reagan developed slowly; as Schreiber said: "By the time he was doing great roles, he was doing a good job." His career, said his wife, Nancy, "wasn't a sudden skyrocketing that is followed as often by a sudden decline. It was a nice steady line." While not spectacular, he had staying power. Jeffrey Lynn, John

Hodiak, Jon Hall and other young men who were more promising than Reagan in those days dropped out, but Reagan continued working.

His first movie at Warners in 1937 was a quickie that was noted briefly in a story in the Los Angeles *Times:* "A departure in the exploitation of talent is to be accomplished by Warner Brothers when that studio films a new subject called *Inside Story.* It seems this organization is to experiment with a radio sports announcer and news writer, one Ronald Reagan from Des Moines, Iowa, who will have the lead opposite June Travis." The movie was eventually called *Love Is on the Air,* and like some of his other early movies, it has disappeared into the vaults of Hollywood, so poorly done it has never been shown on television.

His parents were proud when they saw the movie in a special screening in Des Moines which was covered by the *Register* and the *Tribune.* The paper's reporter noted that his mother wiped away her tears with a lace-trimmed handkerchief as she watched him on the screen. "That's my boy," she said. "That's my Dutch." She added: "That's the way he is at home. He's just as natural as can be. He's no Robert Taylor. He's just himself." His father commented: "He doesn't change. He'll always be the same."

He made more than twenty B pictures during the early years of his career under his producer, Byrnie Foy, who was the eldest of the little Foys in the vaudeville act. In 1940 his break came when he persuaded Warners to give him his first good role, that of Gipp in the Rockne movie. He had wanted to do a film about the football hero since first going to work at Warners and had even considered writing it himself. He asked his colleagues how to write a screenplay. Some of Warners' writers liked his idea, handed in the story themselves and sold the studio on it. Reagan soon heard that the film was not only written, but was being cast. When he asked the producer for the Gipp part, he was rejected on the grounds that he didn't look like a football player. Reagan protested that he had played the game and, as a matter of fact, looked more like a football player than the slouching Gipp. The producer still refused. Realizing that the man didn't believe anything until he saw it on film, Reagan went home and dug out a picture of himself in a Eureka football uniform. He got the part. The film was really about Rockne, the Notre Dame football coach, who was played by Pat O'Brien. Gipp died of pneumonia early in the picture, but his memory lived on because of a deathbed request he made of Rockne—that when Notre Dame was behind one day, he would ask the boys "to win one for the Gipper." Reagan played the Gipper as if he were Dutch Reagan at Eureka. Although George Gipp in real life was an undisciplined athlete who ignored the lessons of Reagan's Y.M.C.A. lecture, Reagan portrayed him as a courteous, soft-spoken young man. In the film Gipper visited Rockne's home and talked over his troubles with the coach and his wife, just as Dutch Reagan used to visit faculty members' homes on cold Eureka evenings. As a result, Reagan gave one of his better performances.

The critics were not enthusiastic about the film, but they praised Reagan. He remarked that the role "was the springboard which bounced me into a wider variety of parts in pictures. Before that I always played a jet-propelled newspaperman who solved more crimes than a lie detector." So convincing was he that he was chosen in the 1940–41 exhibitor's poll as one of the five "Stars of Tomorrow," the young players most likely to emerge from the season as successes.

In 1941 Reagan gave the best performance of his career

in the movie that made him a star, *King's Row*. In it he played Drake McCugh, the town sport. McCugh was injured in an accident and came under the care of Dr. Gordon, who disapproved of McCugh because he was dating his daughter. To punish McCugh, Gordon amputated his legs, and when the young man awoke, he looked down at his body and cried: "Where's the rest of me?" the line that provided Reagan with the title for his autobiography. Reviewers praised the whole cast, as well as Reagan. *Commonweal* called it a "splendid performance." *The New Yorker* said that the film will "give you that rare glow which comes from seeing a job crisply done, competently and with confidence." The picture was a success, Reagan's salary at Warners was tripled and a columnist for the Los Angeles *Times* reported that only Errol Flynn received more fan mail than Reagan at the studio. "It will behoove Warners to set about getting good roles for Mr. Reagan from this point on," the columnist said. "Incidentally, it should be remarked that his is an instance that should be of benefit to the psychology of younger players who figure they ought to soar right to the top. It took Reagan plenty of time to hit the pace that counted."

When he entered politics, his opponents would mock his ability as an actor, but critics throughout his career were often kinder. When he played a wartime serviceman in *Voice of the Turtle* in 1947, *Newsweek,* sharing the opinion of other reviewers, called his portrayal "sensitive." Bosley Crowther of the *New York Times* was generally unimpressed with the 1949 comedy *John Loves Mary,* but he said Reagan's performance in it had "dignity." *The Girl from Jones Beach* was a 1949 piece of fluff, but Richard L. Coe of the Washington *Post* said Reagan made his role "as painless as he can." Crowther admired him in it as "a fellow who has a cheerful way of looking at dames," and said he was "thoroughly capable of getting the most that is to be had out of the major comedy encounters that develop in the film." Some reviewers, such as Howard Barnes of the *Herald Tribune,* panned him: "Reagan's acting is so casual that it seems like mere improvisation for much of the time." But generally, when he was given good material, he would turn in a professional performance. He was working steadily, and in 1946 and 1948 he earned over $150,000 a year. While never a great actor, he was far from a failure.

In 1941, with *King's Row* a popular success, his career once again slowed down—this time because of World War II. Lew Wasserman, his MCA agent and today one of the Democratic party's major financial contributors, negotiated another raise from Warners just before Reagan, a reserve second lieutenant in the cavalry, was ordered to active duty. On April 19, 1942, Reagan said good-by to his wife and their infant daughter Maureen, boarded a train at the Glendale station for San Francisco, where he reported for a month's duty at Fort Mason, and then was shifted back to Hollywood, where he spent the rest of the war. Reagan was one of the stars ordered into the "Culver City Commandoes," the First Motion Picture Unit of the Army Air Force, which harnessed the technology that produced *Hell's Angels, Dawn Patrol* and other airplane films to make training and combat movies for the Air Force and produce morale-boosting pictures for the home front. Reagan, George Montgomery, Arthur Kennedy, Clark Gable, Alan Ladd, Craig Stevens and Van Heflin were some of the actors who served among the one thousand men in the unit. Most were skilled film technicians, brought together by the Air Force after the phenomenal success of two animated recruiting pictures, *Win Your Wings* and *Beyond the Line of Duty.* A half million Air Force volunteers had written on their questionnaires that they had been persuaded to enlist by one or both of the films. So impressed was the Air Force that the unit was established. Like most of the unit, Reagan had two jobs—he was personnel officer and narrator for training films. For a while he was detached to play in the film *This Is the Army*.

The unit's first headquarters was the old Vitagraph studio, but in the fall of 1942 the men shifted to the nine-acre Hal Roach Studio in Culver City. Barracks and a mess hall were built, but it still was a most unmilitary post, called Fort Roach or Fort Wacky by the rest of Hollywood because of the way the stars chafed under military discipline. Reagan, on duty all night, filed a report to the commanding officer, stunt pilot Paul Mantz, which said of the post: "Very poor place to make pictures. Recommend entire post be transferred as near to 42nd Street and Broadway as possible. Also suggest several Westerns be made to round out the program." Under irregularities and disturbances Reagan wrote: "3 A.M.—post attacked by three regiments of Japanese infantry. Led cavalry charge and repulsed enemy. Quiet resumed." One afternoon after a military-minded officer had marched the Hollywood soldiers four abreast to the flagpole, Reagan, who was watching, shouted: "Splendid body of men. With half this many, I could conquer M-G-M." General H. H. Arnold, the Air Force chief of staff, saw a studio gag film put together from all the mistakes made during the year and asked the unit to make him one for a party in the Pentagon. Reagan played a general, with a cigar in his mouth, briefing a bomber squadron. As he pointed to the target, the map rolled up, uncovering a pretty girl.

The unit, however, did work the Air Force considered vital. Reagan was the narrator for one of its most difficult projects, *Target Tokyo*. It was a training film to prepare the pilots of B-29 superfortresses for the fire-bombing raids on Japan. Special-effects men went to Washington and studied the landmarks the pilots would follow from Saipan to the target of Ota, the site of a plant producing new fighter planes. The files in Washington, along with newspaper photographs, travel brochures and books, provided the details for a ninety-by-ninety scale model of the route to Ota, built of cheesecloth, plaster, matchsticks and piano wire. Above the model was a camera crane, and the camera moved over the set as if it were a B-29 on a bomb run. Reagan, playing the briefing officer, described the route, and to the pilots watching it on Saipan months later, it gave an invaluable glimpse of what faced them.

The unit made the classic film about a flying fortress, William Wyler's *The Memphis Belle*. That was one of the best-known Fort Roach productions, but just as valuable were briefer films about B-17s. Midway through the war, absenteeism hit the Boeing plant at Seattle, Washington, where the B-17s were made. The First made two ten-minute films which were shown with the newsreels at civilian theaters, telling how the planes from Seattle were helping win the war, and soon absenteeism decreased. Secretary of War Henry Stimson, concerned over the failure of women to volunteer for work in Connecticut Valley ball-bearing plants, asked the unit to make a civilian recruiting film for the area. Other home front films urged women to become bus drivers and asked Americans to open their homes to war workers who couldn't find housing.

The First was often called in for emergency situations at the war front. Pilots were afraid the extra gas tank on the speedy new P-38 lightning fighter plane would explode in flames if hit by enemy bullets. The unit's film convinced the pilots that the plane was safe. Flying and ground crews discovered that the American P-40 fighter and the Japanese Zero looked practically alike at one thousand-yard distances, and American crews were shooting down their own planes by mistake. When a Zero was captured, it was brought to San Diego and flown side by side with a P-40. Film unit crews filmed the planes from all angles, showing how to tell them apart, and the prints were rushed to the South Pacific to clear up the confusion.

As part of the unit, Reagan performed a useful job, but later on he magnified it into one of his qualifications for the governorship. When his experience was questioned, he would reply that he had served in World War II as adjutant of an Air Force base. Never did he explain that the base was located in the film community, within driving distance of his home.

By 1945 the war was nearing an end. The final months of the war brought two developments that would have a profound effect on Reagan's thinking. One was the personnel situation at Fort Roach, where Reagan was growing restive under the Government's command. Civilian workers had been ordered to serve at the post, which was chronically understaffed with servicemen, and Reagan was unhappy with federal regulations that prevented him, as personnel officer and adjutant, from firing the incompetent or unneeded ones. Another development was the troubled Hollywood labor conditions of the postwar period. Two powerful union groups—the Conference of Studio Unions and the International Alliance of Theatrical Stage Employees—were fighting for control of the studio workers, and Reagan's union, the Screen Actors Guild, was trying to help settle the dispute. Reagan would rejoin the board of the Screen Actors Guild after his discharge on September 12, 1945, and become one of the union's most vocal leaders.

He was thirty-four years old and ready to move on to another stage in his life. The movie career, which had seemed important when he was twenty-six, now did not satisfy him. The union would soon occupy much of his life. His career would suffer and his marriage fail. But in the end he would find a new career, more promising than the one he began at Warner Brothers less than a decade before.

CHAPTER SIX

THE LIBERAL YEARS

IN HIS FIFTIES, as the conservative governor of California, Reagan—like a man sheepishly confessing a boyhood indiscretion—liked to recall his youthful days as a "bleeding-heart liberal." He often told a story of how he joined left-wing organizations after World War II and learned, almost too late, that he had been duped. It was a convincing confessional to his conservative audiences of later years. They loved him even more for his frank admission of early mistakes. The story, however, was an exaggeration. Reagan was a Democrat; he was a union leader. But never, by the standards of postwar Hollywood, was he a militant participant in the liberal causes of the time.

In 1947 five hundred members of Hollywood's liberal community rose to protest against the House Un-American Activities Committee investigation into communism in Hollywood. Reagan was not among them. Reflecting a liberal view, the "Talk of the Town" section of *The New Yorker* said: "If the producers in Hollywood are sincere in their belief in America, they need not worry about Communists. All they need to do is make a good picture. A movie man who has made a good picture, a newspaper publisher who has put out a good issue, can walk through aisles of Communists on his way to work in the morning and when he sits down the chair will feel solid under him and the room will not go round and round." Reagan, however, was worried about communism. He supported the committee investigation and appeared as a friendly witness. He also favored the blacklist imposed by the producers on writers who refused to testify. As a union leader, Reagan led the Screen Actors Guild across picket lines to keep the studios running in the face of a strike by a union that he considered Communist-dominated.

It is a fact that Reagan flirted briefly with an organization that was later accused of being a communist front. But he scurried out of it as soon as he was informed of its leftist orientation and his joining seems born more of naïveté than true belief. This was just months after the long war in which the Soviet Union had been the United States' ally. For years everyone had loved the Russians. Children sent their dimes to help Russian refugees. Public schools taught Russian history. Even the conservative boss of Reagan's studio, Jack Warner, had made a movie friendly to Russia during the war —*Mission to Moscow*. When criticized for the film afterward, Warner replied: "This picture was made when our country was fighting for its existence, with Russia one of our allies. It was made to fulfill the same wartime purposes for which we made such pictures as *Air Force, This Is the Army, Objective Burma, Destination Tokyo, Action in the North Atlantic* and many more."

Politically unsophisticated, Reagan returned to a civilian life full of the idealism generated by the war. He eagerly joined organizations that advertised the humanitarian goals of preserving world peace, ending poverty and opposing such postwar exponents of racism as Gerald L. K. Smith. Like many veterans, Reagan worried about the danger of Nazism in postwar America.

There is no doubt that he was more liberal in his younger years than he is now. As a young man he had been committed to Franklin D. Roosevelt, whose New Deal had given his father a job and who was the nation's Commander-in-chief during the war. But it was a personal and emotional loyalty, and Reagan said he thought little about the social programs Roosevelt advocated. When Roosevelt died in 1945, Reagan recalls he was left without political roots. He supported Democrat Harry S. Truman for President in 1948, choosing Truman's Fair Deal domestic program over the Republican alternative offered by Thomas E. Dewey. He campaigned for Helen Gahagan Douglas, a liberal Democrat who lost to Richard M. Nixon in California's United States Senate race in 1950.

But beneath the surface there was a strong conservative streak, the legacy of Reagan's Midwest boyhood. His support of Truman, for example, was not the act of extreme liberalism. That was the year the most ardent liberals bolted the Democratic party and worked for the Progressive party candidate, Henry A. Wallace, a critic of President Truman's strong stand against communist aggression in Europe. "Progressives want a genuine two-party country and not a country operated by a fake one-party system under the guise of a bipartisan bloc," said Wallace, the former Vice-President of the United States. Praising Truman for his anticommunist stand, Reagan remained with the Democratic party. Two months before the election of 1948, Reagan sounded like a sedate businessman when he told the Rotary Club in Los Angeles how his union fought the Communists. "We are for the free-enterprise system," he said. Then, in words that would not be out of place in a Reagan campaign speech almost two decades later, he added: "We are against statism. We have fought our little Red brothers all along the line."

His later opponents would have done well to study his record in those postwar years, for it shows him to have been a knowledgeable and articulate spokesman for his point of view. He was in the middle of day-to-day battles and testified at length before congressional committees. His basic political instincts were sharpened during this period, and he emerged from it a battle-hardened and polished advocate of the conservative cause.

Reagan's first taste of Hollywood politics had come in 1938 when he was a reluctant recruit for the Screen Actors Guild. The young man from the Midwest had seen no need for unions when he came to Hollywood, but an actress, Helen Broderick, persuaded him that the guild was needed to improve the salaries and working conditions of the screen players. The union was unique. It was organized and later run by rich men and women, the actors and actresses who sometimes made more than $100,000 a year. These wealthy people set the tone for the union, and as a result it has always been conservative. Unlike the auto workers, the miners, the steel workers or other unions, the guild did not campaign for Democratic candidates. It couldn't. Too many of its leaders and members were conservative Republicans. Among its past presidents are United States Senator George Murphy, who has been active for years in Republican politics, and Robert Montgomery, who was the television adviser to Republican President Eisenhower.

The guild's main interest was bread-and-butter issues. It was formed in March of 1933 when producers forced contract players to take a 50-percent pay cut from their fifteen-dollar-a-day pay and freelancers to accept a 20 percent reduction.

There was no overtime or premium pay for holidays, and an actor who was promised pay for nine days of work often found that those days were stretched over many weeks. The guild was incorporated on June 30, 1933, and by the time the first meeting was held on July 12, such well-established stars as Alan Mowbray, James and Lucille Gleason, Leon Ames and Boris Karloff had joined. Other prominent actors soon followed. Among them were Robert Montgomery, Groucho Marx, Ralph Bellamy, George Raft, Chester Morris, Fredric March, Gary Cooper, Spencer Tracy, Miriam Hopkins, Paul Muni, James Cagney and Eddie Cantor. "I am not here because of what I can do for myself, but to see what I can do for the little fellow who has never been protected and who can't do anything for himself," said Cantor at one of the first meetings.

Reagan became active quickly. He was appointed to the board of directors to fill a vacancy in the young contract player category, and when he attended his first board meeting, any doubts he had about joining a union were dispelled. Seated there were the stars with the greatest prestige—the men and women Reagan looked up to, whose example he wanted to follow. Being in the same room with them was an impressive experience for the young man. At first he sat and watched the senior leaders of the union who were in the middle of the fight to rid Hollywood unions of hoodlum influence.

At the center of the controversy were two union leaders, George Browne and Willie Bioff. Browne was president of the International Alliance of Theatrical Stage Employees, which represented everyone from movie projectionists to stagehands. Bioff was his personal representative. These two men, who controlled most of the studio workers, were accused of extortion by the Federal Government in 1941. They were charged with taking more than $550,000 from five major studios under a threat of "you pay us or we'll break your business." They were convicted and sent to prison. The fight against Bioff and Browne began long before the trial, and in 1939 the guild withdrew from the AFL's Central Labor Council in Los Angeles because, according to *Daily Variety,* the actors objected to the support that council leaders gave to Bioff. Bioff was resisting extradition to Illinois, where he still had time to serve on an old six-months' jail sentence for pandering in Chicago. "For some time, it has been apparent to the Screen Actors Guild that the officers and controlling faction of the Los Angeles Central Labor Council have not conducted affairs along the lines of democratic, honest unionism," said Kenneth Thomson, the guild's executive secretary. The action was supported unanimously by the board of directors.

In 1941 the long fight over hoodlum control of the unions resulted in a development that was to cause even more bitter labor troubles after the war. A union leader who had opposed Browne and Bioff, Herbert Sorrell of the painters union, formed the Conference of Studio Unions. This was the beginning of the fight between the conference and the alliance. It would have been easy for the movie labor force to take sides if it were a simple choice between a gangster-dominated union and an honest one. But by the end of World War II the picture was hopelessly confused. Sorrell himself provided much of the controversy. He was, remembered an acquaintance, about five feet eleven inches tall, with "a busted nose and cauliflowered ears. . . . I think he told me he used to be a heavyweight boxer at one time." Even before he formed the conference, Sorrell had been praised for his opposition to the extortionists, Bioff and Browne. It took courage to oppose those two in the late 1930s when their power was almost unchallenged. "Sorrell let Bioff know that this town would not be big enough for both of them if Willie tried any monkeyshines," the trade newspaper *Variety* said in an editorial on December 18, 1939. But years later, the California legislature's Joint Fact-Finding Committee on Un-American Activities was to say in an official report filed with the legislature: "Herbert K. Sorrell is a secret member of the Communist Party. The Conference of Studio Unions, headed by Sorrell, on strike for over a year, is Communist dominated, inspired and directed for the purpose of capturing the American Federation of Labor unions in the motion picture industry." Sorrell denied the charge and told the United States House Education and Labor Subcommittee in 1948: "I am not now nor ever have been a member of the Communist Party."

By the end of World War II the International Alliance, now rid of Brown and Bioff, and Sorrell's Conference of Studio Unions were locked in a struggle for control of the studio work force. The alliance's new Hollywood boss was Roy Brewer. He and Sorrell were implacable foes and this complicated the situation. In March, 1945, the conference, a coalition of painters, janitors, machinists, guards, office workers and others, called a strike when it was denied jurisdiction over seventy-seven set decorators' jobs. It was a violent strike. The International Alliance, which also controlled many studio jobs, claimed jurisdiction over the set decorators, too. The alliance sent its workers through the conference's picket lines, supplying the manpower to keep the studios operating. Pickets fought with other employees at the Warner lot. Bricks were thrown, cars overturned and men injured. The conference charged that the alliance was corrupt and too friendly with the producers. The alliance replied that the conference was dominated by Communists.

In October, 1945, less than a month after Reagan was discharged, the guild pulled its members off work because it feared they would be injured by crossing the Conference of Studio Union picket lines. Twenty days later, the strike was temporarily settled. But in July, 1946, the dispute over control of the set designers resumed again. This time Reagan took an active role in the Screen Actors Guild's efforts to end the strike, which lasted only two days. As he later told the House Education and Labor Subcommittee:

"We again found ourselves with the prospect of actors that were going to be unemployed by reason of the slowdown in production. . . . I suggested that it was about time we forget all the rules and regulations and red tape and go back to the town hall meeting idea, that the guild take the lead and try to get all the leading parties to sit down at a table in one room and hammer this out . . . instead of talking through the newspapers. If we couldn't succeed, we would at least know which side or what individuals had failed to cooperate, which was more than we had been able to learn up to then. We formed this committee, and as testified here, it was largely as a result of this committee the meeting in Beverly Hills was called and the strike was settled."

Despite Reagan's optimism, this settlement was only temporary. Under the Treaty of Beverly Hills, neither union was given final control of the decorators. Negotiations were merely postponed. Differences became deeper. In August, 1946, an American Federation of Labor arbitration board issued a new ruling. Sorrell interpreted it to mean that the Conference of Studio Unions was given jurisdiction over the set decorators. In September he pulled his men out again—maintaining that they were striking over more than the control of the set decorators. Wages and hours were involved, Sorrell said. Brewer of the International Alliance called it a jurisdictional strike and supplied men to take over the jobs vacated by the conference strikers. The guild tried once again to arrange a settlement but failed. Finally, as Reagan recalled later, "We decided we had done everything we could do, and on that basis we decided that it was a jurisdictional strike, and we so reported to the membership." On October 2, the guild voted 2,748 to 509 to cross Sorrell's picket lines and join the International Alliance in keeping the studios going.

Reagan later said that he was threatened with disfigurement if he gave to the guild a report that was favorable to the International Alliance. Testifying in a 1954 lawsuit that grew out of the old labor troubles, Reagan said: "I was out on location in the country when I was called to the telephone at an oil station. I was told that if I made the report a squad was ready to take care of me and fix my face so I would never be in pictures again." For a time, police guarded his home and he carried a gun. During this period he was one of several actors preparing to board a bus that would take them across the picket lines. Just before they climbed aboard, the bus was bombed and burned.

The Screen Actors Guild leaders made another attempt to settle the strike by traveling to Chicago to the American Federation of Labor convention to ask for a resolution to set up permanent arbitration machinery in the motion picture industry to settle future labor disputes. Reagan, Jane Wyman, Walter Pidgeon, Dick Powell, Alexis Smith, Gene Kelly, Robert Taylor, George Murphy and Robert Montgomery arrived at the convention with plenty of fanfare, but as Reagan told the House Labor Committee, the stars found it a frustrating experience.

"We descended on Chicago by plane and train," testified Reagan. "I might add we realized, being a small union, at the AF of L convention, that our greatest weapon, which happens to be the one weapon which goes with our type of work, was publicity. We knew if we could drop ten or fifteen actors or actresses on any city in America they are bound to get their names in the papers and this we did."

There was something almost comic about the picture he drew before the investigating committee, as he told of the rebuffs given the stars by labor leaders obviously unimpressed by the Hollywood contingent. "We found, when we arrived there—speaking of confusion—that we had made a mistake and did not have our resolution before the resolutions committee in time, under the rules, for it to be considered." This blow was followed by a desperate search for help. "We saw several international presidents, trying to find out what we could," said Reagan. "We were told on several hands that we were helpless. The upshot was, however, they did accept our resolution. They put it before the convention . . . and it was unanimously passed by the convention." But the American Federation of Labor never put the resolution into effect, and when the House committee's counsel, Irving G. McCann, asked Reagan in 1948: "What is wrong with the AF of L?" Reagan replied: "Sir, that is calling for a conclusion of the witness." As the years passed, his loyalty to the Screen Actors Guild never wavered, but he became more and more hostile to organized labor's national leadership.

Reagan was becoming better known as a union leader than as an actor. At the studio he was working in a soon-to-be-forgotten film, *Night Unto Night*. But at union headquarters he was at the center of the industry. Watching Reagan, Harpo Marx, Gregory Peck, Robert Taylor and Franchot Tone participate in board deliberations during the strike, columnist Hedda Hopper admiringly wrote: "I thought never had so much glamour gone out on a limb for so many fellow players."

Years later Peck would be one of Hollywood's most enthusiastic campaigners against Reagan in the 1966 election. Governor Brown was so appreciative that he suggested Peck run for the United States Senate, but Peck declined.

In May, 1947, a glimpse of Reagan's philosophy was provided in an interview with Miss Hopper. "Our highest aim should be the cultivation of the freedom of the individual for therein lies the highest dignity of man," he said. "Tyranny is tyranny, and whether it comes from right, left or center, it is evil." The way to fight communism, he said, is to improve America. "The Reds know that if we can make America a decent living place for all of our people their cause is lost here. So they seek to infiltrate liberal organizations just to smear and discredit them. I've already pulled out of one organization that I joined in completely good faith. One day I woke up, looked about and found it was Commie-dominated. You can't blame a man for aligning himself with an institution he thinks is humanitarian, but you can blame him if he deliberately remains with it after he knows it has fallen into the hands of the Reds. I can name you one organization that is so obviously controlled by the Communists that all members must be aware of it. So I must believe that any who choose to support it must be, at least, Communist sympathizers. Otherwise, knowing what they must know, why don't they get out?"

The organization from which Reagan resigned was the Hollywood Independent Committee of the Arts, Sciences and Professions, one of the social action groups that abounded in Hollywood during and just after World War II. In addition to his membership in this organization, he joined the liberal American Veterans Committee and the United World Federalists, which advocated world government. But he quit the veterans committee quickly. And the United World Federalists was a dreamy sort of organization—far removed from the main currents of political thought.

In 1947 the California legislature's Joint Fact-Finding Committee on Un-American Activities said that the Hollywood Independent Committee of the Arts, Sciences and Professions was one of "two key Communist fronts in California." But by that time Reagan had left. His disillusionment began, in fact, at his first board meeting, when James Roosevelt, son of the late President, proposed a declaration repudiating communism. A fight followed and Reagan spoke on Roosevelt's behalf. John Howard Lawson and Dalton Trumbo, two screen writers, criticized Reagan. Later in the evening Reagan, Roosevelt and a few others met to plan strategy. Reagan recalls proposing that "we reaffirm our belief in free enterprise and the democratic system and repudiate communism as desirable for the United States." The proposal was rejected by the executive committee and Roosevelt and Reagan quit the organization.

Reagan and congressional and legislative investigators contended that communist influence prevented the organization from condemning the Communist party. But Mrs. Ellenore Abowitz, an official, gave another reason to the California legislative committee: "Our theory is that in these days, the immediate danger to our form of government is fascism."

Arguments over communism were becoming increasingly bitter by 1947. The House Un-American Activities Committee sent a subcommittee to begin a new investigation on communism in the film industry. Jack L. Warner told the subcommittee that he had fired six writers because "what they were doing was taking your money and supposedly writing your scripts and trying to get these doctrines into the films, working for the party or whatever the term is." Many Hollywood personalities bridled at the committee's methods. *Life* magazine reported that John Garfield, Paul Draper, Lauren Bacall, Humphrey Bogart, John Huston, June Havoc and Danny Kaye were among those who flew to Washington to protest the committee's next round of hearings. "The whole procedure is as if I came out before an audience of five thousand and before I'd said a word the audience shouted 'you stink,' " Kaye said. Bogart later recanted and said: "I went to Washington because I felt fellow Americans were being deprived of their constitutional rights. I see now that my trip was ill advised, foolish and impetuous, but at the time it seemed the thing to do."

As president of the Screen Actors Guild, Reagan joined two past presidents, Montgomery and Murphy, in telling the committee how Hollywood had resisted communism. The hearings were a circus, for the publicity-conscious chairman, J. Parnell Thomas, had called some of the biggest stars to testify. One of the committee members was a young congressman, Richard M. Nixon of California, who was building a reputation as a Communist-hunter. Every day, lines of women waited outside the committee room for a chance to see Robert Taylor, Gary Cooper, Robert Montgomery and others. While the stars brought the publicity, the committee's real targets were a group of screen writers and directors who had decided they would not answer any questions dealing with their political beliefs or memberships in organizations. They cited the First Amendment, guaranteeing the freedom of Americans to speak, write or assemble.

According to one witness, the Communists, like the committee, considered the actors as window dressing to help obtain publicity. Howard Rushmore, a journalist who said he belonged to the Communist party from 1938 to 1939, testified before the committee that the party didn't have much use for actors. "The general line would be that the stars were, 99 percent of them, political morons, and they added some other uncomplimentary things, which I wouldn't care to repeat, but the Communist party per se had great contempt for the stars of Hollywood," he testified.

When Reagan appeared before the committee he answered the questions in a clear, concise way even though he was angry with the committee counsel, Robert Stripling. Stripling had come to his hotel room the night before and demanded that Reagan tell him what he planned to say on the witness stand the next day. Reagan later claimed he was "conditioned as a liberal to think of the committee as a pretty venal bunch"—even though he cooperated fully with the investigators and did not join others in criticism of the committee. He was unhappy with Stripling's request, but he answered his questions anyway, telling how the guild had fought the Communists. Apparently that was not what Stripling wanted to hear, for Reagan said the counsel did not ask him the same questions on the witness stand.

Reagan was a contrast to some other friendly actor-witnesses, like Gary Cooper, who testified it would be a good idea to outlaw the Communist party "although I have never read Karl Marx and I don't know the basis of communism, beyond what I have picked up from hearsay. From what I hear, I don't like it because it isn't on the level."

Reagan testified: "There has been a small clique within the Screen Actors Guild which has consistently opposed the policies of the guild board and officers of the guild, as evidenced by votes on various issues. That small clique referred to has been suspected of more or less following the tactics that we associate with the Communist party."

Counsel Stripling asked: "Would you refer to them as a disruptive influence within the guild?"

Reagan: "I would say that at times they have attempted to be a disruptive influence."

Stripling: "Has it ever been reported to you that certain members of the guild were Communists?"

Reagan: "Yes, sir; I have heard different discussions and some of them tagged as Communists."

Stripling: "Have you heard that from any reliable source?"

Reagan: "Well, I considered the source as reliable at the time."

Stripling: "Would you say that this clique has attempted to dominate the guild?"

Reagan: "Well, sir, by attempting to put over their own particular views on various issues, I guess in regard to that you would have to say that our side was attempting to dominate, too, because we were fighting just as hard to put over our views. . . .

"I would say of these people, the best thing to do is make democracy work. In the Screen Actors Guild we make it work by insuring everyone a vote and by keeping everyone informed. I believe that, as Thomas Jefferson put it, if all the American people know all of the facts they will never make a mistake. Whether the party should be outlawed, I agree with the gentleman who preceded me that it is a matter for the government to decide. As a citizen, I would hesitate, or not like, to see any political party outlawed on the basis of its political ideology. However, if it is proven that an organization is an agent of a power, a foreign power, or in any way not a legitimate political party, and I think the government is capable of proving that, then that is another matter." Several years later, after his thinking had shifted more to the right, he would conclude that the Communist party was not a political party but part of a Soviet Union conspiracy.

Stripling questioned Reagan about another experience he had had with one of the groups of that era. Reagan told how he had been duped into sponsoring a recital that was under the auspices of the Joint Anti-Fascist Refugee Committee, a group that both the counsel and Reagan felt was too far to the left. Reagan said: "I was called several weeks ago. There happened at the time in Hollywood to be a financial drive on to raise money to build a badly needed hospital in a certain section of town, called the All Nations Hospital. I think the purpose of the building is so obvious by the title that it has the support of most of the people of Hollywood— or of Los Angeles, I should say. Certainly of most of the doctors, because it is very badly needed.

"Some time ago I was called to the telephone. A woman introduced herself by name. Knowing that I didn't know her, I didn't make any particular note of her name and I couldn't give it now. She told me that there would be a recital held at which Paul Robeson would sing and she said that all the money for the tickets would go to the hospital and asked if she could use my name as one of the sponsors. I hesitated for a moment because I don't think that Mr. Robeson's and my political views coincide at all, and then I thought I was being a little stupid because, I thought, here is an occasion where Mr. Robeson is perhaps appearing as an artist and certainly the object, raising money, is above any political consideration—it is a hospital supported by everyone. I have contributed money myself. So I felt a little bit as if I had been stuffy for a minute and I said, certainly you can use my name.

"I left town for a couple of weeks, and when I returned,

I was handed a newspaper story that said this recital was held at the Shrine Auditorium in Los Angeles under the auspices of the Joint Anti-Fascist Refugee Committee. The principal speaker was Emil Lustig. Robert Burman took up a collection and remnants of the Abraham Lincoln Brigade were paraded up to the platform. I did not in the newspaper story see one word about the hospital. I called the newspaper and said, 'I am not accustomed to writing to editors, but I would like to explain my position,' and he laughed and said, 'You needn't bother, you are about the fiftieth person who has called with the same idea, including most of the legitimate doctors who also had been listed as sponsors of that affair.' "

Mr. Stripling: "Would you say from your observation that this is typical of the tactics or strategy of the Communists, to solicit and use the names of prominent people either to raise money or gain support?"

Reagan: "I think it is in keeping with their tactics, yes, sir."

Stripling: "Do you think there is anything democratic about these tactics?"

Reagan: "I do not, sir."

Following the hearings, the ten witnesses who had refused to answer the committee's questions were cited for contempt of Congress and eventually convicted. On the following day the Motion Picture Association of America blacklisted the ten. It promised to fire any of the witnesses under contract, and said: "We will not employ any of the ten until such time as he is acquitted or has purged himself of contempt and declared under oath that he is not a Communist." Reagan agreed with the association.

Compared to some of his colleagues, he was a moderate on the communist issue. He did not storm into the committee hearing like Sam Wood, the producer of *King's Row,* who testified that Communists were making a constant effort to subvert pictures. "If you go back into the pictures, you will find frequently the banker or the man in public life, the doctor, any one of them would be the heavy in the picture. I think it is particularly bad if that is constantly shown, if every night you go into the pictures you see a dishonest banker or senator, you begin to think the whole system is wrong. That is the way they work on it." Nor did Reagan go after the Communists with the enthusiasm of Adolphe Menjou, who said: "I am a witch hunter if the witches are Communists. I am a red baiter. I make no bones about it whatsoever." Menjou obligingly described his clothes to reporters before he testified: "A brown chalk-stripe suit, a tie made for me by Mr. Sulka, a Clark Gable shirt that he kindly let me copy and my hat is Homburg." Then he described for the congressmen how communist propaganda could be injected into movies. "I believe that under certain circumstances, a communistic director, a communistic writer, or a communistic actor, even if he were under orders from the head of the studio not to inject communism or un-Americanism or subversion into pictures, could easily subvert that order, under proper circumstances, by a look, by an inflection, by a change in the voice. I think it could be easily done. I have never seen it done, but I think it could be done."

In today's ideological scale, Wood and Menjou would be to the far right, nervously looking for Communists under every rock—as do many of Reagan's present supporters. On the other side were the stars who attacked the committee. They formed the Committee for the First Amendment which condemned the investigation and defended the writers cited for contempt, the Hollywood Ten. Although many members of this committee in later years disavowed it, claiming they had been tricked into joining by Communists, its roster in 1947 contained some of Hollywood's biggest names—actors, actresses, writers, and directors who were active in liberal causes then and now. Another sixty personalities took part in hour-long broadcasts entitled *Hollywood Fights Back* that sought support for the blacklisted witnesses.

Reagan's replies to the committee were restrained. "I do not believe the Communists have ever at any time been able to use the motion picture screen as a sounding board for their philosophy or ideology," he said. *Life* magazine, impressed with his testimony, and that of Robert Montgomery and George Murphy, said they "made their points neatly, with a good deal of restraint and common sense, and left the stand without dragging their feet."

After the hearings Reagan returned home and faced the fact that his marriage was breaking up, and that his interest in politics was at least in part to blame. Today the marriage is a closed subject to Reagan and those around him, and Miss Wyman chooses not to speak of it either. But at the time, the breakup of what was considered one of Hollywood's happiest couples was big news. In December, 1947, Reagan told Hedda Hopper: "We had a tiff. That's right. But we've had tiffs before, as what couple married eight years hasn't. But I expect when Jane gets back from New York, we'll get back together all right."

He was wrong. In February, Miss Wyman's attorney, Lloyd Wright, Jr., said she was suing for divorce. There was a brief reconciliation in April, but the following month Miss Wyman filed a complaint in Los Angeles County Superior Court charging Reagan with extreme mental cruelty. In June the story of the divorce hearing was told in the Los Angeles *Times*. Miss Wyman, hatless, with her hair in a pageboy bob, explained to Judge Thurmond Clarke what had happened to the eight-year marriage. Reagan was not in the courtroom. She said the Screen Actors Guild was now occupying much of his time, and she did not share his interest. Reagan, she said, insisted that she attend meetings and be present during long discussions with his friends, but her ideas "were never considered important. Most of their discussions," she said, "were far above me."

It was not a matter of disagreeing with him, but simply that she could not match his interest. "Finally, there was nothing in common between us, nothing to sustain our marriage." She was awarded custody of the couple's two children, Maureen, seven, and Michael, three.

A bachelor again, Reagan moved into an apartment. He was kept busy with some good parts in undistinguished movies. He played in *John Loves Mary* with Patricia Neal and in a musical comedy that was a box-office success, and then went to England for a part in *The Hasty Heart*. Later he would remember it as a lonely period, a time of working and waiting for something better to come along.

CHAPTER SEVEN

A TIME FOR CHOOSING

In 1949 REAGAN completed work in London on *The Hasty Heart,* a touching story based on a popular play by John Patrick. Great Britain, trying to restore its economy, had forbidden American firms from removing their money from the country, and the only way the movie studios could use their big deposits in British banks was to make movies in England. Reagan had reluctantly accepted the part of Yank, an American soldier, for he had wanted to play in a Western. But *The Hasty Heart* turned out to be one of his better films. The stars were Patricia Neal and Richard Todd, who appeared in his first major role. He had to learn to play a bagpipe for the film, and Reagan suggested Todd wear earmuffs during the lessons. Todd politely turned down the suggestion. Much of the action took place in a hospital in Burma, and *Newsweek* commented that "Reagan and his fellow patients achieve an offhand naturalness that maintains them as distinct individuals." *The New Republic* disliked the plot—"one of the most barefaced tearjerkers ever concocted"—although it thought the film had "an admirably directed cast." *Christian Century* said the movie was "simple, effectively done."

But as before, this success was followed by a series of poor roles that robbed Reagan of whatever reputation he had as a proficient actor and box-office attraction. The next fifteen years would be a time of great change for Reagan. His movie career was failing and, what was more significant, his views on life and politics were changing. This period marked the transformation of the actor into the politician.

His career had a setback soon after his return to America. On a June night he was playing with some other stars in a benefit softball game for the City of Hope, a research hospital. "Bob Hope was pitching, and Bill Demarest, the umpire, had called two balls and one strike on me when I bunted," Reagan remembered. "The fellow on first stepped in front of the bag to block me off, and I hit him with all stops open. Anyway, my leg came apart like a wet cigar." His leg broken in four places, Reagan was hospitalized through most of the summer, lost a screen role and was limping for almost a year. "Funny thing about this accident," he told Al Wolf, sports columnist for the Los Angeles *Times*. "In three years of college football I played all but two minutes. And at guard, what's more. I had plenty of water wrestling matches while pulling out hysterical swimmers, but had no serious mishaps. And just a week before this softball game, I was taking a jumper over a hurdle only to have it smack the barrier good. Horse and I went head over heels into a lot of trees. But we were both lucky, just a couple of scratches."

At the studio, Reagan was arguing with Jack Warner over movie roles. Warners had promised him a part in a Western, *Ghost Mountain*, when he completed work on *The Hasty Heart*. But the box-office receipts for his film *That Hagen*

Girl were low, and the studio replaced him in the Western with the more popular Errol Flynn. Reagan was angry and Warners was in no hurry to make peace. Like other studios, the company was trying to trim overhead by reducing the number of players who were working on expensive long-term contracts. As a result, Lew Wasserman, one of Reagan's agents at MCA, negotiated a new deal. Warners would pay Reagan $75,000 a film for one picture a year over a three-year period. In addition, Reagan signed with Universal for one picture a year for five years at the same price. But there was no security in such contracts. If an actor turned down a bad role, he would not receive any money. When Reagan was a regular contract player, he was paid whether or not he worked.

In politics Reagan would often talk about personal freedom. But he was lost and unhappy when he was given his own freedom by Warners. "A star doesn't slip," he told Hedda Hopper. "He's ruined by bad stories and worse casting. I think if the producers would close up their private projection rooms and see pictures in regular theaters, they'd get some idea of what they're doing to our business." As good parts became harder to find, Reagan's unhappiness with the men who ran the studios intensified. At a meeting of the Screen Actors Guild, he complained that producers were reducing advertising budgets despite the drop in theater attendance. "No industry has ever been able to survive business reverses by cutting down advertising," he said.

Accustomed to accepting every role that came along at Warners, Reagan started out doing the same as a free-lancer. As a result he starred in a series of failures. *Storm Warning* with Ginger Rogers and Doris Day was a quickly forgotten film about the Ku Klux Klan. *The Last Outpost* at least gave him a chance to ride horses in a Western. He was aging and new faces were coming along. So, at the age of thirty-nine, he was cast as the father of a teen-ager in the movie *Louisa.* His daughter was Piper Laurie, eighteen, then a starlet on the Universal-International lot. "I thought they'd make me up to look old, maybe whiten my hair at the temples," said Reagan. "But they just washed my face and shoved me in."

Reagan remained active in the Screen Actors Guild, and if his interest in the union cost him one wife, it soon brought him another. Director Mervyn LeRoy telephoned, not to hire Reagan for a film but to ask his help as president of the guild. A young actress at Metro-Goldwyn-Mayer, Nancy Davis, had been receiving mail from left-wing organizations and had found her name in the *Hollywood Citizen News* among a list of people who, she recalls today, "had rather exotic political feelings." She brought her problem to LeRoy, and he suggested calling Reagan. As she tells the story, it looks as though Reagan was the victim of a plot—not communist but matrimonial. "Well, I knew Ronnie, but not personally, and Ronnie didn't know me from Adam, but I thought that was a dandy idea so I said: 'Yes, Mervyn, you do that, you call Ronald Reagan.'" After two days she hadn't heard from Reagan and she reminded LeRoy, an old friend of her family. As she stood next to him, he telephoned again. Reagan checked through files at the guild office, convinced himself of her loyalty and discovered that her name had been confused with that of another woman. He reported this to LeRoy, but LeRoy insisted that he take her out to dinner and tell her personally. Reagan began dating Nancy steadily, and on March 4, 1952, they were married. Reagan's friend William Holden was the best man and Mrs. Holden was matron of honor.

Associates in Hollywood said the marriage influenced Reagan's political thinking. Mrs. Reagan is a conservative. Her father is Dr. Loyal Davis, a wealthy and politically conservative surgeon in Chicago. Reagan deeply admires Nancy's parents, and he and his wife like to join them at their summer home in Phoenix, Arizona, every Easter.

Miss Davis' career—like Reagan's—was in the doldrums. She had never been a star like Miss Wyman, but merely a young actress in some unimportant films. To her, acting was something to do between college and marriage, and she all but retired after the wedding. Later, though, she would return to the studios for an occasional performance with Reagan. In 1956 they costarred in Reagan's last movie, *Hellcats of the Navy*, a low-budget film about the submarines in World War II. *The National Parent Teacher*—the only magazine to review it—said: "This black and white melodrama authentically, if routinely, portrays courage and initiative" in World War II. The magazine pointed out that the movie was technically well produced but complained that neither the director nor the cast made any effort at characterization. Reagan's movie career had come full circle. In the early days at Warners, making B movies for Byrnie Foy, Reagan had played in an undersea quickie, *Submarine D-1.*

A few months after the wedding, Mrs. Reagan became pregnant. The Reagans were living in a big new house in Pacific Palisades and were worried about making the mortgage payments. The Hollywood slump was at its worst, caused mainly by the competition of television, high labor costs and poor movies. Producers who couldn't have met his price in more prosperous days were calling him with free-lance offers for work in hastily made films. Actors and actresses more famous than Reagan found themselves out of work. "I grabbed everything," he said—accepting parts in movies he hated to see when they were shown in the theaters. His career was collapsing. "When I realized it, I feared it was too late," Reagan said. As a drastic solution he began refusing all bad parts in an attempt to salvage his star ranking. He refused a Universal picture and lost $75,000. Universal offered him two more films—$150,000 worth of work—and he turned them down. "I went fourteen months and turned down $500,000 worth of film, not counting percentages," he said. His wife remembers it as a difficult time. "You know, Ronnie didn't get into the so-called big money until after big taxes, so there was no residual, you had to keep on working. And it was hard. For any man it is demoralizing and for any wife watching him. Your heart breaks."

With Lew Wasserman now president of MCA, Art Park became Reagan's agent and tried hard to find him work. Park and others suggested he try a Las Vegas night club act. The Reagans felt out of place amid the bright lights of the gambling city, but he accepted anyway. Reagan was not, commented a columnist, "a typical night club entertainer." He was the master of ceremonies for a variety act that included the Continentals, a comedy dance team, and two other acts. He worked with the Continentals in a comedy routine and finished up with some semi-humorous comments.

His two weeks at the Last Frontier were a success. "He broke the record," said Mrs. Reagan. "They wanted him to extend and we could use the money." Offers came from night clubs in other parts of the country, but the Reagans declined. They didn't like the smoky rooms, the drinking and the late hours. "I'm sure that by most standards we're probably considered squares," said Mrs. Reagan, "and frankly I'm happy to be one. We're not night club people." At the Last Frontier they went back to their hotel room after Reagan's performances and relaxed with books they had brought from home. They only went into the gambling casino once, on their last night, cautiously bringing only five dollars with them.

Reagan also rejected offers to appear in plays in New York or in television series. Finally help came from an unexpected area, his union activities. As president of the guild, he had become an unofficial spokesman for the movie industry, often acting as the toastmaster at banquets, giving speeches pleading for a tax break for actors and promoting Hollywood. He would say: "I know the public has been fed a lot of drivel under the name of publicity, so we can understand their false ideas about us. But believe me, I have found this place to be pretty much a cross section of the U.S.A." He donated his time for much of this, but finally it paid off. In 1954 the General Electric Corporation was looking for a host for its new half-hour television series—a man who could act, sell General Electric products, help build the company's corporate image and visit G.E. plants to improve employee morale. "I could think of only one man, Reagan," recalled Taft Schreiber, who was in charge of Music Corporation of America's Revue Productions at the time. General Electric agreed, and Reagan's drought was over. Schreiber negotiated a $125,000-a-year contract for him, and later it was boosted to $150,000. G.E. was delighted, for Reagan was a superb television salesman. There was a joke in Hollywood about someone who watched him delivering an institutional advertisement for General Electric's nuclear submarine and remarked: "I really didn't need a submarine, but I've got one now."

Reagan's eight years with General Electric were important to his political development. He visited one hundred twenty-five plants, met 250,000 General Electric employees and spent hours in serious conversation with the conservative businessmen who ran the company. It was like a political campaign. He would shake hands with the workers in the plants. At lunch and dinner he spoke to clubs or other groups. At first his speeches were simple Hollywood boosting, but in his conversations with executives and workers he began to find, for the first time in his life, a coherent political philosophy. The people he met, he felt, were dissatisfied with the bigness of their union, their company and their government. General Electric's management complained of government harassment and expansion. Reagan began thinking about the huge federal projects that had been started under Roosevelt and realized that he did not approve of them. To General Electric's embarrassment, Reagan singled out one such project for special attention, the Tennessee Valley Authority, to which the company sold millions of dollars' worth of electrical equipment. Company officials came to Schreiber and said: "Doesn't he know what he's saying?" But Schreiber said that G.E. did not try to censor Reagan. He voluntarily deleted the reference to the TVA and substituted an attack on another aspect of big government.

In 1952 Reagan—still a Democrat—supported the Republican candidate for President, Dwight Eisenhower, and backed him again in 1956. By this time his philosophy was much like it is today. Typical of Reagan's speeches during his association with G.E. was a talk in May, 1958, to the Executives Club of Chicago. He began with a discussion of the troubles of the movie industry and concluded with a rousing attack on the government. Censorship, high taxes and government harassment had been wrecking the movies because studio chiefs had let "the planners and regulators get a foot in the door. This superstructure of government imposed on our original form is composed of bureaus and departments and is unchanged by any election," he said. "This hierarchy threatens to reverse the relationship of citizen and civil servant."

In Amarillo, Texas, a few years later, he said: "Medical care for the aged is a foot in the door of a government take-over of all medicine." When the American Medical Association was fighting Medicare, Reagan eagerly helped the doctors. He made a phonograph record which the physicians used to whip up enthusiasm for their battle against the health care plan. He criticized the income tax, "this progressive system spawned by Karl Marx and declared by him to be the prime essential of a socialist state." He became a campaigner against farm price supports and opposed urban renewal. He favored voluntary social security "so those who can make better provision for themselves are allowed to do so." He wanted the government out of the power business, opposing the needed rural electrification program of the New Deal.

He questioned every social program enacted since 1932, programs that had come into being under Roosevelt and Truman and had been continued by Republican President Eisenhower. Except among the die-hard right wing, debate had ceased in American life over such accepted plans as social security and the progressive income tax. Reagan was now intent on reviving that debate.

Often after these talks, someone from the audience would approach him and suggest that he run for public office. In California, when he spoke before Republican groups, listeners asked him to run for governor or United States senator. He always replied that he was an actor and could do more good for the nation speaking as a private citizen. "I think he sharpened his wits and saw what it might be like to be a politician—to be confronted with issues he had no total involvement in," Schreiber said of these days. "He began to speak out, and I think this is what made him a politician."

His association with General Electric did more than

sharpen his political philosophy. *The G.E. Theater* was an extremely successful show. It relied on the veteran big names of Hollywood as guest stars. Charles Laughton made his television debut on *The G.E. Theater*. Fred Astaire was in a non-dancing role. Tony Curtis played a bullfighter, and James Stewart starred in a Western version of Charles Dickens' *A Christmas Carol*. The show introduced more famous movie stars to television than any other series. But ratings dropped when *Bonanza* moved against it at 9 P.M. on Sunday nights. Reagan's show, in black and white, was no match for the appeal of the hour-long color Western. In 1962 General Electric dropped the show.

The long years with General Electric and the acquisition of valuable ranch land in the Malibu Hills north of Los Angeles had made Reagan wealthy. He had stepped down as Screen Actors Guild president, although he remained on the board of directors. In 1959 he was brought back as president during a time of crisis for the union. The guild was trying to win for its membership a share of the profits that studios were making from selling post-1948 movies to television. These films were bringing in large amounts of money, and the guild was prepared to strike for a percentage. Howard Keel, the president, was leaving Hollywood for a part in a New York play, and the guild needed a dynamic leader to keep the membership enthusiastic in case they walked off work. "We needed somebody who could speak, excite the membership, stir them up," said one guild worker. In the opinion of the nominating committee, Reagan was the best qualified, and so John Dales, the executive secretary, called him. Afraid that more controversy would hurt his career, Reagan consulted MCA. But Lew Wasserman, the president, advised him to go ahead and Reagan took over as president. There was no conflict in his mind between his conservative speeches on the road and his position on a union negotiating team. The guild, with its fourteen thousand members, remained a mixture of liberals and conservatives interested only in economic goals.

The producers rejected the guild's demands, and on March 7 the actors and actresses struck. Millionaires joined bit players in walking off the job. Alan Ladd, who was acting and producing, left the set of *One Foot in Hell,* from which he would receive 10 percent of the profits. Marilyn Monroe, Yves Montand and Tony Randall quit *Let's Make Love.* Clifton Webb looked around a quiet movie lot and said: "It's so awful, everything has stopped. In the barbershop, no one even talked." Most guildsmen supported the strike. Frank Sinatra summed up what many felt: "For the good of the entire motion picture industry, the Screen Actors Guild has compromised greatly from its original contract demands. I personally believe it is now time for all motion picture producers to do a little compromising."

But not everyone backed the strike—the first in the guild's history. John Wayne, who had originally joined Kirk Douglas, Lauren Bacall, Bing Crosby and some others in signing a pro-strike newspaper advertisement, later said: "I don't know what the hell they're striking about." The strike lasted six weeks and Reagan frequently was called upon to boost morale. In the end, the studios granted the actors payments for the television sales of their old films, and part of the money was used for a pension fund.

There was a two-year lapse between jobs after *The G.E. Theater,* but in 1964 the United States Borax Company needed a new host for its weekly dramatic show, *Death Valley Days.* Neil Reagan, now vice-president of the McCann-

Erickson advertising agency which handled the Borax account, suggested his brother, and Reagan was hired at about the same salary he received from G.E.

At the same time he plunged actively into Republican politics. In past years he had made speeches to help candidates raise money and draw crowds, but had not held an important position in any of the campaigns. In 1962 he changed his registration from Democratic to Republican, and in 1964 he was appointed state co-chairman of Citizens for Goldwater-Miller. Few of Goldwater's supporters were angrier than Reagan at the refusal of the moderate Republicans to support Goldwater in the general election. In a bitter speech to Los Angeles County Young Republicans after the election, Reagan said: "We don't intend to turn the Republican party over to the traitors in the battle just ended. The conservative philosophy was not repudiated" in the election. "We will have no more of those candidates who are pledged to the same socialist philosophy of our opposition."

These were impressive words to a few wealthy Goldwater Republicans who were beginning to recover from the disaster of 1964 and were looking toward the gubernatorial election of 1966. There were several reasons Reagan appealed to them. His philosophy was the same as theirs, and therefore the state would be in safe hands for business if he were in charge. He was the California Republican party's best orator. In the closing days of the Goldwater campaign, when even the die-hard supporters of the senator were conceding defeat, Reagan had made a televised fund-raising appeal that attracted wide attention. The speech, "A Time for Choosing," was along the same lines as the one he had been giving for years on the G.E. banquet circuit. This time he borrowed a line from Franklin Roosevelt and used it to emphasize his conservative message of desperation and despair. "You and I have a rendezvous with destiny. We will preserve for our children this, the last best hope for man on earth, or we will sentence them to take the last step into a thousand years of darkness." The speech was to party conservatives what William Jennings Bryan's "Cross of Gold" speech had been to the farmers and workers of the Democratic party in 1896, a rallying point, a promise of hope for the future. Bryan left the national convention a Presidential candidate. When conservatives flicked off their television sets that night in 1964, Reagan was as good as a candidate for governor.

His entrance in the race was assured by the victory in 1964 of his old friend George Murphy, who defeated Pierre Salinger, the former press secretary to Presidents Kennedy and Johnson. Murphy had proved that an acting career was more a help than a handicap. His old movies, still on television, made him seem like an old friend to the crowd and quickly established a rapport that made it easy for him to deliver his speeches. His performing skill permitted him to defeat Salinger, who was overweight and a poor speaker, in a television debate.

Thinking about all this were two wealthy men, Holmes Tuttle, an auto dealer who had known Reagan since 1947, and Henry Salvatori, an oil developer who had met Reagan socially in the late 1950s. "In 1965, after the Goldwater debacle," Tuttle said, "I called Henry Salvatori and some others, and we went to Ron and discussed the idea of his running for governor." Others also asked him to run. One supporter called Reagan while he was on location with *Death Valley Days.* Reagan declined, but several months after the 1964 election Tuttle came to Reagan's house and made another approach. "Holmes came up to the house specifically to see me," Reagan remembered later. "I gave him the usual thing about running for office." Finally Tuttle asked just one thing—"Would you agree not to give us a flat no? Just kick it around in your mind." Reagan agreed, and thus was born the Friends of Ronald Reagan, a group of supporters who mailed out thousands of letters signed by A. C. (Cy) Rubel, the former president of Union Oil Company. "Ronald Reagan, out of a deep sense of duty and dedication, is willing to serve as Republican candidate for governor, providing a substantial cross section of our party will unite behind his candidacy," the letter said. "To this end, Mr. Reagan has agreed to exhaustively explore the depth of feeling and the possible commitment to such an endeavor."

This was not, however, the humble effort of a few admirers. The address on the letterhead was 1300 West Olympic Boulevard, Los Angeles, the office of Bill Roberts and Stu Spencer, the founders of the political public-relations firm of Spencer-Roberts and Hafner. Roberts is tall and chubby. Spencer is short. Both are nervous, the proper emotional state for men whose livelihood depends on something as uncertain as winning a political campaign. Spencer and Roberts got their start in the business by managing a Republican congressional candidate's campaign after the Korean War and are late arrivals among California's political public-relations men. These professional campaign managers are now found in other states, but the idea for these firms first was conceived in California in the 1930s because of a feature of the California election law, the section that permits people to repeal or enact laws by popular vote. This is not a unique feature, but California, even in those days, had more wealthy special interests than most states—men who were willing to spend millions for a campaign that would change the law to protect their industries. Companies were soon organized to run these campaigns and they used imaginative methods to win for their clients. "Keep California Green" was the slogan of one campaign. Thinking it was a conservationist measure, Californians approved it. All the initiative did, however, was give a tax break to private golf clubs. The public-relations firms also managed the campaigns of individual candidates, taking charge of everything—fund raising, image building and organization. Spencer and Roberts had first made a name in the state by handling U.S. Senator Thomas H. Kuchel's successful reelection campaign in 1962. In 1964 the firm was in charge of New York Governor Nelson Rockefeller's unsuccessful primary campaign against Goldwater. When Reagan's friends began looking for professional advice, Goldwater told them he would never run a campaign in California again without Spencer and Roberts.

In April, 1965, Ralph Townsend, a Los Angeles-area businessman who was friendly with both Reagan and Stu Spencer, asked Spencer and Roberts if they would handle the Reagan campaign. They did not immediately agree. First they lunched with Townsend, Reagan and Neil Reagan at a private club in Los Angeles, the Cave de Roy, and then had two more meetings with Reagan at his house. But before Spencer and Roberts would take the account, they had to be assured of one thing. On record—made in scores of speeches —Reagan was as conservative as Goldwater. And his fighting words to the Young Republicans after the 1964 election made it clear that he did not approve of taking the moderates back into the Republican party. Roberts did not believe an ultra-conservative would win the governorship in California. He told Reagan that neither he nor Spencer wanted to be associated with another futile Goldwater crusade. Reagan replied that neither did he. Without specifically saying so, he implied he would agree to moderate his conservative statements—and work with more liberal Republicans—in the interests of winning an election. From then on he began moving toward a more moderate position in his speeches. He was, said Roberts, "a reasonable guy with a sense of humor who didn't take himself too seriously."

"By September," said Roberts, "his feet were in concrete on running for governor. He had made a mental commitment," even though the formal announcement would not be made until early the following year.

Since Reagan, Roberts and Spencer had decided against selling Reagan's conservative ideas, something else had to be offered to the voters, a framework that would allow him to appeal to Californians of varying political beliefs. It was the Creative Society, a vague hodgepodge of ideas put together under a title obviously inspired by Lyndon Johnson's Great Society. It was concocted by an ultraconservative minister friend of Reagan's, the Reverend W. S. McBirnie, who is a radio commentator in addition to being the spiritual leader of a church. His fifteen-minute radio program, *Voice of Americanism,* sponsored by his Center for American Research and Education, is heard throughout California, often on small radio stations that feature fundamentalist radio ministers who mix religion with right-wing politics. He describes himself as a "hard-line conservative," and on his broadcasts he warns each day of the "international communist conspiracy." He preaches an uncompromising message against any accommodation with the Soviet Union. He denounces as leftist such established institutions and people as the National Council of Churches and George Kennan, former ambassador to the Soviet Union and Yugoslavia.

During the campaign, one of McBirnie's letters of political advice to Reagan came into Governor Brown's possession.

Reagan charged that the governor's aides had stolen it. Brown seized upon the letter as evidence to back up his claim that Reagan was an extremist. Brown said of McBirnie: "He appears on the same platform with Robert Welch [founder of the John Birch Society]. He has said our newspapers are infiltrated by Communists, and he has called Senator Tom Kuchel a California disgrace. Mr. McBirnie has also accepted an award from Billy James Hargis' anti-Catholic, anti-Semitic Christian Crusade, an organization that described the National Council of Churches as 'guilty of treason to God and Country.'" McBirnie replied that Brown was lying. He acknowledged, however, that Hargis once offered him an award, but he did not accept it, although he considers Hargis' group a patriotic organization. As for the newspapers, McBirnie said that testimony before the House Un-American Activities Committee had convinced him that Communists had infiltrated them.

McBirnie, in short, is a spokesman for ultraconservatives in California. Yet when the Friends of Ronald Reagan began meeting in Reagan's house with Bill Roberts to begin planning the campaign, McBirnie was there. "Late in the spring of 1965," said McBirnie, "I wrote Ronnie and I talked to him about having worked on the inside of the Nixon campaign, and we talked about Nixon's speeches." Finally, McBirnie said, Reagan "asked me to be a member of the initial circle of counselors."

It was after one of the meetings that McBirnie thought up the phrase Creative Society. There was some grumbling among the advisers that the Reagan campaign needed a slogan. While McBirnie was driving back to Glendale on the freeway, the idea of the Creative Society was born. In essence it was this: Politicians should be catalysts to harness all the resources of the private sector of the nation to solve America's problems. "How do you get that creative energy loaned to government? You get businessmen to volunteer as one-dollar-a-year men as during the war. . . . I sat up all night," recalled McBirnie. "I wrote him a long letter, formulated the whole thing as a structure." Reagan liked the idea and began using the phrase in his speeches. Brown strongly criticized Reagan for accepting advice from McBirnie, but Reagan replied: "I'm very proud to have had the help of Dr. McBirnie, and he has been of inestimable help in expressing the philosophy of the Creative Society. But it is the same philosophy which I have held and expressed for the last fifteen years many times in speeches." McBirnie, too, said: "I did not create the Creative Society; I gave it formulation. The Creative Society is Ronnie's."

Once elected governor, Reagan would no longer rely on McBirnie's advice. McBirnie, however, still kept in touch with the Reagans and even arranged for them to be presented with a baby elephant from the son of the deposed King of Albania, an admirer of the governor. The Reagans donated the elephant—named G.O.P.—to the Sacramento Zoo.

In the fall Reagan talked to the Tulare County Industrial Management Association in Visalia, in the farm country, and a volunteer worker reported to Democratic headquarters: "Polite applause greeted his introduction, and he was more warmly applauded after he concluded. Spontaneous applause greeted his responses to several questions." More important, the Democrat said, "I talked with a member of the Republican Central Committee . . . who was in attendance at a small meeting of the Central Committee addressed by Reagan prior to the luncheon. He tells me that some obviously unfriendly questions were asked. He considers that Reagan handled himself very well and made a very favorable impression on some liberal Republicans who had previously viewed his candidacy with considerable coolness." This report was filed—and ignored by the Democrats.

There was a triumphal visit to a Republican state convention in San Francisco, when Reagan's reception drew hundreds more party workers than those of his rivals. Without making a speech, he was the center of attention. Salvatori, Tuttle, Rubel and the rest of California's conservative Republicans had themselves a candidate.

⊠ CHAPTER EIGHT

CAMPAIGN I:
THE ENEMY CAMP

ON DECEMBER 10, 1965, John Luce, the young press assistant in Governor Brown's northern California political organization, drove down the peninsula south of San Francisco to hear Reagan, who was expected to announce his candidacy and begin his campaign the following month. Luce is a talented writer, a tall, loose-limbed man with long blond hair. His colleagues, their hair more conventionally styled, called him "the surfer," and in truth he looks as though he would be happier on the beach than in a hotel dining room listening to a political speech. Duty, however, brought him to a luncheon meeting of the San Mateo County Chamber of Commerce at the Villa Hotel. It was a chance to size up the adversary, probe for weaknesses and send a report back to Sacramento where the governor was preparing to make his announcement in February. Luce listened and filed his report. It was not one of the top-level policy papers of the Brown campaign, for Luce was not on the board of high strategy. But it was an incisive summary from a trusted worker, and as such it reflects perfectly the

Democratic state of mind in 1965 and the complacency with which the party leaders viewed Reagan.

"He will fall apart when he gets attacked from the floor and is asked leading questions, hounded and the like," wrote Luce. His opinion was shared by Brown and the strategists who advised him—a misconception they held until it was too late. They also agreed with another of Luce's observations: "His attacks on LBJ and Governor Brown . . . won't make it with those who don't think the President is a dictator and those who realize the necessity of close state and federal cooperation. The real issue always boils down to what Reagan would do as governor, and given the present situation and our close working with Washington, he could do nothing."

Luce and his superiors were wrong. Reagan, his mind sharpened by years of arguments in union meetings, would not collapse easily. Nor was the question of California's relationship with Washington important any more. People no longer cared whether Pat Brown could speak to Lyndon Johnson on the telephone. In fact, they were beginning to blame Johnson for many of their troubles—the Vietnam war, taxes and inflation. But in January, 1965, Edith Singer, a secretary in the governor's office, sent Brown's press secretary, Jack Burby, a magazine item saying that Reagan would probably run for governor. " 'Bring him on' is our motto," Burby scrawled on the bottom of the note.

Brown was as confident as his advisers. "I feel young and fresh and I have a young team around me." He added: "I can refer you to my wife. She'll tell you I'm young and vigorous."

By nature Brown is an optimistic man, convinced of the goodness of his fellow human beings. His nickname is Pat —and it suits him admirably, a plain name for an unpretentious man. He is slightly rotund, with dark-brown hair receding from his high brow, clothes a little baggy, shoes tending to be scuffed late in the day. There was no regal air of command about this governor. He was forever telling stories about his social blunders. One of his favorite pictures showed him spilling coffee over himself while John F. Kennedy, whom he revered, laughed uproariously. It hung in his office for everyone to see, along with political cartoons picturing a confused Pat Brown looking owlishly out at the world through his horn-rimmed glasses. When he met someone, he always said, "I'm Pat Brown," just in case he wasn't recognized. Sometimes he wasn't. A few months after he had been sworn in as governor, Brown wanted to swim. The pool closest to the governor's mansion was across the street at a motel. Carrying his swimsuit and towel, the governor of California courteously introduced himself to the clerk at the desk, explained his situation and asked if he could use the pool. The clerk didn't believe him, but the manager finally allowed him to use the pool. Mrs. Brown was upset at the loss of dignity and asked some of Brown's old friends to build him a swimming pool at the mansion.

His notable achievements in his eight years of office were obscured by his greatest flaw, indecisiveness that had prompted even some of his own supporters to call him "a tower of jelly." Because of his trouble in making a decision, national politicians had lost respect for him, and he was doomed to remain in state politics. He wanted to be remembered as a compassionate governor, but, if anything, he was too compassionate. He liked to listen to both sides of a story, and, unfortunately, he saw merit in each. When he was governor, some of his appointees to an important state board were discovered to have accepted favors from men with criminal connections. Brown fired them but then granted them time to explain their case in a hearing open to the press. After hearing their stories, he admitted in public that the men had made a good case for themselves, and he withdrew their dismissal. His action added to the public's impression that he was an indecisive governor.

He had been one of California's good governors, however, and some of his accomplishments would make life better for future generations. "Most governors are lazy," said a reporter who had come West in 1966 to cover the National Governors Conference in Los Angeles. "But one thing about Pat Brown, he works hard." His greatest achievement was the beginning of construction of the great water project. In office for less than a year, he successfully campaigned for a $1.75 billion bond issue to finance it. "It is all very well to work for all the other necessary programs," he said. "But without water, California is without a future." He had put through a master plan to control the jumble of university branches, state colleges and junior colleges being built in the state, and as a result, California's system of higher education was a model for the rest of the country. He also campaigned for bond issues to pay for the new campuses and to finance new prisons and mental hospitals. In 1964 he sacrificed much of his personal prestige in a vain fight against Proposition 14, the ballot measure that nullified the open-housing law. Brown also proposed and later signed the state's first fair employment practices act in 1959.

But by the end of his second term, the public-opinion polls showed that voters were tiring of his familiar face. "The people don't appreciate my greatness," he would say, half jokingly. He had chances to step down, but refused. When the important job of attorney general became vacant, Brown was urged to appoint the most promising young Democrat in the legislature, then assembly majority leader Jerome Waldie. Waldie had so impressed James Moser, the television producer, that he had patterned the hero of *Slattery's People*, his television series about a state legislator, after him. Waldie would have then had two years before the public eye as the chief law enforcement officer of the state and been available as a candidate for governor. But Brown objected that nobody would vote for Waldie because he was from Antioch, a small city in northern California. Instead he appointed his old friend, Thomas Lynch, the district attorney of San Francisco, a capable man without ambition for higher office. A solution would have been to step down in favor of assembly speaker Jesse Unruh. But Brown's friends and advisers in the party despised Unruh, and if Brown had given way to the speaker, Unruh would have ejected them from party control. Brown's wife asked him not to run. But the governor, supplied with public-opinion polls by power-hungry friends, insisted there was no one else.

Brown's first obstacle was to win the Democratic nomination, and for the first time he was facing strong opposition. Mayor Sam Yorty of Los Angeles would make heavy inroads in the bedroom communities with speeches aimed directly at the fears stirred among whites by the Watts riots. In Sacramento one noon, Yorty won a tremendous ovation from a businessmen's club with a racist comment about the Sacramento national guardsmen sent to his city during the Watts riot. "What a difference," he said, "between these fine young men and the people they were sent to control." Don Bradley, Brown's campaign manager, while writing off Yorty as an ineffective candidate, admitted that the mayor was cutting into Brown support in the Los Angeles suburbs. Bradley's strategy, which later proved to be wrong, was to coast through the primary. "We're really working on November," he said.

Brown started his primary campaign on a rainy February morning when, with his wife, Bernice, at his side, he was

driven down to the capitol. He walked into his news conference room, and with characteristic good cheer, he predicted
he would win. Brown was happiest when campaigning, and
perhaps that was the reason he ignored his wife's wishes
and ran again. He liked to shake hands, to mix with the
crowd. "The old adrenalin starts pouring through your veins
when you get into a political campaign," he said. "I don't
know what there is about it, but I love it." The news conference began a day-long trip in which he repeated his announcement in five more cities—Chico, San Francisco, Los
Angeles, San Diego and Fresno. The trip would cover almost
the length of the state, extending about two thousand miles
in twelve hours. It was aimed at obtaining maximum local
television and newspaper coverage, without buying time
on all the stations.

Accompanying Brown were the men and women who
would be at his side the rest of the long year. There was his
wife, attractive and sharp-witted, watching over her husband
with love, amusement, and occasional impatience. Jack
Burby, his press secretary, was at his side. He was a calm pipe-
smoker now, but would be chain-smoking cigarettes and
soothing his aching stomach with Gelusil tablets before the
year was over. Burby lacked Nofziger's taste for political
blood. There was also a contrast between the travel secretaries
for the Brown and Reagan campaigns. Brown's secretary,
Tom Hickey, unlike Van Court, did not carry a gun. In fact,
he disliked guns and went to great lengths to avoid them. In
the summer of 1965 Hickey accompanied the Browns and the
Burbys on a trip to Greece. Brown suddenly began worrying
about his safety in Greece and ordered Hickey to bring a
gun to protect the party. Hickey asked Burby, who was older
and had been with Brown longer, what to do. "Ignore him,"
said Burby, more worried about a pistol in the hands of a

man who didn't know how to use it than an attack by Greek terrorists.

Also on board was Don Bradley, the designer of Democratic campaigns in California for years. Like a rodeo rider who demonstrates his faith in himself by putting up an entry fee he forfeits if he loses, Bradley likes to show his faith in his own ability by putting money on the candidates he believes will win. He is a skilled manager but has too many enemies. He was one of a group of Democrats, many of them with their roots in San Francisco, who had attained influence in Sacramento and Washington during Brown's years in office. There is an advantage to being associated with the governor of California. Bradley, besides assisting Brown, had been employed as President Johnson's campaign director in California in 1964. Along with Democratic national committeeman Eugene Wyman and other party leaders, Bradley advised Brown on policies and appointments and thereby had indirect power through the governor's office. Bradley would not cooperate with Speaker Unruh, nor Unruh with Bradley. Unruh had his own political organization, based in Los Angeles County, and he wanted the influence and power now held by Brown and the men around him. Because the two segments refused to work together, Brown would be deprived of the full support of Unruh's organization.

Another member of the Brown team was Hale Champion, the finance director. He had risen from press secretary to executive secretary to director of the finance department, the most important appointive job in the state. Champion is calm, talkative and resourceful. These qualities proved useful in 1965 when two gunmen sneaked into his house before dawn and kidnapped him, his wife and their infant daughter. The gunmen, running away from the murder of a sheriff's deputy, held the Champions prisoner all day, driving them across the state and into the mountains before releasing them late at night. Champion and his wife talked constantly to the gunmen during the ordeal—calming them and preventing the situation from exploding into violence. Champion was one of the main architects of Brown's 1962 campaign against Nixon, but now he was tired of politics and planned to move on to something else even if Brown won again.

This first trip of the campaign was designed to display Brown's record, and there was something he was proud of at each stop. But it turned out to be no triumphal tour. It rained all morning in the north, and at the first stop, Chico, there was only a small group of rain-soaked reporters and party officials awaiting the governor. It was a depressing indication of the small crowds and unenthusiastic receptions that would follow. Brown talked about his record in Chico and about the water project main dam located about thirty miles to the east. "When you come up here and look at that great dam, then you realize we're moving ahead in California," said Brown. That was to be the basic theme of his campaign in the primary—his record—and in this farming community, people should have been impressed. But they weren't. They blamed him for the cancellation of the program allowing Mexican nationals to harvest California crops at lower pay than American laborers were demanding. They were angry over the rising cost of welfare. They were eager to come out and cheer for someone new. Yorty took some of Brown's support in this area in the primary, and Brown lost overwhelmingly to Reagan here in the general election.

The plane headed south toward San Francisco, and Brown's spirits rose when he stepped off the plane, as they always did when he reached this city. More reporters, a few friends and his daughter, Mrs. Kathleen Rice, holding her new baby, met him. Pat Brown was a San Franciscan, a handicap in California's new politics, where the population and power are now in the south. A San Francisco Democrat such as Brown is as distinctive in western politics as an Irish Catholic Democrat from Boston is in the East. San Franciscans of Brown's era don't even talk like other westerners. They have their own big-city accent and can't, for instance, pronounce their R's. A "thousand dollahs," they say, or "fouh bits"—the San Francisco term for fifty cents that goes back to gold-rush days when forty-niners paid their bills with bits of gold dust.

At the next stop, the Los Angeles Metropolitan International Airport, there was a reminder of Brown's most serious problem, the Negro revolution. Greeting the governor were two legislators and a few other party officials including Billy Mills, a Negro Los Angeles city councilman whose district contained part of the south central area. This was the scene of the Watts riots of 1965 in which 34 people died, 1,032 were wounded and 3,952 were arrested. From this week of terror came the question that would dog Brown the rest of the year—and puzzle President Johnson the following year as he contemplated running for another term. It was how to reconcile the Democratic party's commitment to expansion of social programs with the new need of promising the nervous white majority protection from violence in the hungry Negro slums. Mills was a graduate of UCLA, young, intelligent, ambitious for political power. He had attained a measure of it in an alliance with two other Negro politicians, then Assemblyman Mervyn Dymally, now a state senator, and Gilbert Lindsay, another city councilman. Mills would be elected Los Angeles County Democratic chairman with Unruh's help. "This is my town, Governor," said Mills. "It had better be my town, too," said Brown.

Their meeting was brief and friendly, but Mills and other Negro political leaders were not happy with Brown. They wanted prominent places in his campaign and insisted that he run on a strong equal-rights platform, something that would have pleased the black minority but angered the white majority even more. Mills, two months later, sat in his city hall office and said that the old Negro loyalty to Brown was waning because the governor was more interested in winning votes in the white suburbs. As he talked, it was clear that old ties were being forgotten and that many members of the Negro community would not work for Governor Brown in 1966, or for President Johnson if he ran two years later. Neither would they vote for Reagan or any other conservative Republican. Instead, many of them would look toward the new-left coalition of peace advocates and Negro rights workers that was beginning to form to oppose Johnson in 1968. The governor, Mills said, must stand behind the Negro demand for equal rights, even though the whites objected. "I believe politically you don't abandon your friends," said Mills. "I wouldn't assume all the Negroes will vote for me on the basis of what I did on Proposition 14. If I were a white politician, I would stick by my guns and run on my record."

Brown was estranged from the Negro community even more when he endorsed three antiriot bills in the legislature, but failed to propose any substantial assistance for Watts and other Negro slums. He carried the Negro districts against Yorty in the primary and later in the general election. But as Mills and other Negro leaders had predicted, the enthusiasm was missing and the turnout wasn't as high as expected.

From Los Angeles, Brown flew south to San Diego, and this city revealed the utter hopelessness of Brown's idea that his record and his promise of federal assistance would carry him through. San Diego has benefited from the bounty of the government as much as any city in the state, but it is conservative. It voted for Goldwater against Lyndon Johnson in 1964 and would support Reagan against Brown in 1966. San Diego is a contradiction. It is the home of a big Navy base. Under Brown, the state began a new University of California campus and a medical school. A state college is also located there, as is the university's famous Scripps Institute of Oceanography, making San Diego a center in underwater exploration. Electronics and aerospace industries are beginning to eliminate the unemployment created by layoffs at the Convair plant. State beaches and parks are nearby. Brown, standing in an aircraft manufacturing firm's hangar, surrounded by the locally produced hardware of the space age, gave his message of prosperity and returned to the city several times to tell it again. But San Diego wasn't listening. Here was evidence that government-provided prosperity doesn't buy elections.

Over the mountains and back into the central valley the plane went, to Fresno, a rich agricultural city in the middle of vineyards and grainfields. The ranchers were registered Democrats around here, but they were angry because they believed Brown was sympathetic to the unions trying to organize their farm workers, and they believed he permitted too much welfare spending. The valley would puzzle Brown for the entire campaign because it was traditionally Democratic, and he knew it was slipping away.

After dinner it was cold and dark in Fresno. The tired traveling party boarded the plane for the flight back to Sacramento. On the plane, Brown wearily talked of the campaign ahead. "It's been rather a hard day," he said, "but I feel very confident of my own position." He said he would avoid attacks on any of his opponents—a vow he forgot later. "I don't intend to campaign against anyone from now till

November," he said. "The best defense is a good offense. I intend to take the offensive on my record from bell to bell."

To his surprise, Brown ran badly in the primary. He defeated Yorty by 1,355,262 votes to 981,088, a dismal showing compared to Reagan's strong victory in the Republican primary. Afterward, Brown complained that his staff had not equaled Reagan's public-relations job. He was unhappy about a decision to withdraw television ads during the last few days of the primary campaign to save money for the general election. He called for help from an old friend, Frederick Dutton, a lawyer and University of California regent, who was his executive secretary at the beginning of his first term. Dutton had left Sacramento to join John F. Kennedy's Administration and now practiced law in Washington. By July he was in Los Angeles, in charge of the office Brown had set up at the headquarters of the National Governors' Conference in the Century Plaza Hotel. To visitors it seemed that there was a new spirit to the Brown campaign. Dutton talked about arrangements he had made to bring in Unruh. The speaker was made a member of a new advisory committee, and he, in turn, loaned the Brown campaign his top assistant in Los Angeles, Sam Hartog.

But Champion and Bradley had been on the scene before Dutton, and were well entrenched in their positions. Staff members soon told stories of friction between Champion, Bradley and Dutton. In August, Bradley and Dutton quarreled in Brown's Sacramento office over the selection of a state chairman. Dutton advised Brown to accept Unruh's choice, Mrs. Carmen Warschaw. Bradley insisted on a liberal assemblyman, Charles Warren. Dutton threatened to walk out of the campaign, but Brown quieted his two advisers. He went before the convention and gave a half-hearted endorsement of Mrs. Warschaw, while praising Warren in another indecisive performance, and it angered all factions of the party. Warren won, and Mrs. Warschaw, a domineering millionairess who was called "the Dragon Lady," loudly pulled out of the Brown campaign. It was another sign of Democratic disunity—and another blow to Brown.

Through much of the summer, Brown remained in Sacramento, playing golf with his wife in the mornings. As usual, Mrs. Brown won, but she said he was improving. In the afternoons he would look over papers from the office and sit in the hot Sacramento summer sun by the executive mansion swimming pool. On Labor Day he formally opened his campaign against Reagan at a rally on the Alameda County Fairgrounds, not far from the vineyards set among the pretty valleys and rolling hills southeast of San Francisco. Only twelve hundred people were in the half-filled outdoor theater, for the day had passed when union members spent their holiday at a public picnic. Now they went to their mountain cabins or took their boats out on the bay. Nearby, a phonograph played records of Pete Seeger singing "We Shall Not Be Moved" and other old-time union songs. But the music was just a sad reminder of the militant labor movement of years gone by. There was no militance in these bored men and women, even though Brown tried mightily to stir them up. "I am here to ask for my contract to be renewed, and I ask with my hand and heart." He talked of his record—"six new state colleges, three university campuses, the greatest freeway system in the world, seven balanced budgets and only one tax increase." The audience applauded dutifully, but they lacked the enthusiasm Brown was looking for.

So it went for the rest of the campaign. Misfortunes multiplied. Support was not forthcoming from some of the most liberal Democrats, usually among the party's most dedicated workers and generous contributors. It was an early manifestation of the antiwar troubles that would face Johnson in California in 1967, when thousands demonstrated outside the Century Plaza Hotel when he came to speak in midsummer. Brown supported Johnson's stand in Vietnam in 1966 and the liberals opposed it.

One of the most serious defections came from the ranks of the California Democratic Council, which, in 1967, would join with militant Negroes to form a peace and equal-rights national convention delegation to oppose the President in the 1968 California Presidential primary. The council, an organization of about 40,000 political volunteers, had been founded in 1953 by Democrats who, fired by the spirit of Adlai Stevenson's first campaign for the Presidency, wanted to rejuvenate the tired Democratic party in their state. For years the Democrats had held the registration majority, but had elected only one governor in this century, Culbert Olson. He had served from 1939 to 1942 and then was routed from Sacramento by Earl Warren. An important function of the California Democratic Council was to make endorsements in Democratic primary elections. In 1958 all of its candidates, including Brown, won the party primary. It again endorsed Brown without reservation in 1962, but in 1966 many of its members were disenchanted because of his position on the war. In one of the first errors that would affect his campaign, Brown, on the advice of State Controller Alan Cranston, supported an independent-minded newspaper publisher, Simon Casady, for CDC president in 1965. Within months Brown regretted it. Casady, an uncompromising opponent of the war, traveled through the state attacking the President and Democratic congressmen who supported Johnson in Vietnam. "When you treat the President with contempt, me with contempt, the congressmen with contempt, you have forfeited the right to lead a Democratic organization," said Brown. He had Casady removed at the CDC endorsement convention in February, 1966, but it was at high cost. The more militant antiwar members rudely booed Brown and walked out in the middle of his speech.

Brown continued to talk about his record from September through November, but this constructive approach was submerged by the virulence of his anti-Reagan attacks. Brown charged that Reagan was an extremist, but with little success. Staff members traced the background of some of the men and women who supported Reagan and found among them members of the John Birch Society and others who contributed to the society. "Are they just plain citizens seeking good government?" a Democratic campaign publication asked. "Or are many of them of a special breed—extremists from the far-out right who find in Reagan their man on a horseback?" But Brown was never able to convincingly demonstrate that Reagan himself was a supporter of the Birch Society. The liberal San Francisco weekly paper, *Sunday Ramparts,* concluded that while Reagan was conservative, "The Democrats have been unable to show genuine connections to the John Birch Society, to any other rightist organization or even to decidedly right-wing opinions." There was a guilt-by-association manner to the strategy, one that recalled the methods of the late Senator Joseph McCarthy.

With three weeks to go, Brown conceded that he and Reagan had not yet had a "confrontation on the issues. I'll plead guilty to that." Admitting the failure of his attacks on Reagan, he said: "I've failed on occasion to talk about the central issues facing California. I'm not going to let that happen again."

When Vice-President Hubert Humphrey came to California to campaign for Brown in late September, he confided to newsmen that the governor should use a more positive approach. Humphrey had been sent out to draw crowds and help the sagging Brown campaign. Some of the impact was taken out of his trip by a small group of antiwar demonstrators who interrupted his speech at a state college in the San Fernando Valley—the vanguard of later, more numerous demonstrations. Despite this detraction Humphrey focused attention on the Brown campaign for a while and gave it a lift. Brown was counting even more on a visit from Robert Kennedy. Kennedy came late in October and campaigned with Brown in the southern and northern parts of the state. With Kennedy at his side, Brown drew his biggest crowds; he later said that if he won, the credit would have to go to the senator. But they were Kennedy crowds, young people more interested in joining a Kennedy crusade. Beside him, Brown looked dull.

Brown also expected a boost in October from a visit by President Johnson. But the President canceled the trip because of an operation for corrective surgery.

The worst setback came on September 27, 1966, when Matthew Johnson, a sixteen-year-old Negro boy fleeing from police in a stolen car was shot to death in the Negro slums of San Francisco by a white policeman. Violence, burning and looting in protest of the killing quickly began in the Hunters Point and Bayview sections. Brown was first told about the situation at 7 P.M. while at dinner at a friend's house near San Diego. He acted quickly. By 10:40 P.M., one hundred California highway patrolmen had been ordered to help San Francisco police, and by midnight Brown had called out the national guard. Although he and his staff were worried, he continued with campaigning in San Diego, answering reporters' questions about the riot. "My last concern is whether it will have any effect on the campaign," he said.

Brown said that he was determined to put down violence. "As long as I'm governor all the laws will be enforced to the best of my ability, and I intend to use all of my strength to protect property," he said. But he could not bring himself to denounce the residents of Hunters Point, where half of the young men were out of work. Instead, he was sympathetic. "We do have difficulties with race relations throughout the United States, and somewhere along the line, we have to have an answer to living together." In midafternoon of the next day, Brown decided to fly to San Francisco. Only four people were in the Grizzly II for the flight north—Brown, Burby, Hickey and a reporter. Brown, slowly realizing the immensity of the blow his campaign had suffered, looked out the window at the storm clouds and the ice forming on the wings of the plane. He was slumped in his favorite seat, toward the front of the plane, his coat off. Finally he talked of the riots, puzzled at why they happened in "the most affluent nation in the world." He also talked about how he was now disliked by Negroes as well as whites. He had met with fifty Negro leaders recently, he recalled, and "all they said was, 'You sold us out, Governor.'"

Brown wondered aloud if he should tour the riot zone. Hickey told him that Mayor John Shelley of San Francisco was there the night before and had been hit by a rock. Burby insisted that it wouldn't be safe for Brown to tour the area. The governor leafed through a newspaper, filled with stories of the violence, and paused at a picture of the police carrying away the body of the dead boy. "This is what does it. This little boy."

In San Francisco he hurried to the Hall of Justice, where Mayor Shelley and Chief of Police Thomas Cahill assured him that the situation was under control. He made arrangements to visit the area in the morning and then drove to North Beach for dinner at the restaurant owned by his friend Joe Vanessi. After his morning tour of Hunters Point, he headed south to resume his campaign. At the scene of the uprising, a few people had been injured, eighty arrested and one thousand two hundred national guardsmen were on duty. San Francisco was quiet on September 30, but the violence had been the major news story in the state for two days, and the threatening racial issue had again been brought before the public.

Looking back on it, some of Brown's advisers pinpointed the riot as the time when all hope for victory vanished. While not specifically blaming the San Francisco violence, Brown later said: "I thought on October 1, when we failed to make a breakthrough in the polls, that it would be very difficult. Before that I had great confidence in the record. But when we had been campaigning awfully hard in September and began to get some newspaper support, and we were making no progress with the right-wing extremist issue, then I knew we were in trouble."

There was a month to go, and the governor was too proud a man to admit defeat. His pride carried him through the next thirty-five days. He wanted to be remembered as a great governor. The thought of losing to Reagan made him furious, and his jaw would tighten in anger and his fists would clench whenever he thought about it. "Why, oh why, my friends," he would ask, "would you turn this state over to a man who has never fought before a city council or a board of supervisors? To me it is preposterous. *Believe me* when I tell you that."

Those who watched him could see the man's determination

as he requested—and sometimes demanded—support. Public-opinion polls showed him behind, and as the weeks passed, old friends deserted him. The lieutenant governor, a meek-mannered, undistinguished man, Glenn Anderson, who had twice been carried to victory on Brown's coattails, now stayed away from him, hoping to salvage his own victory. "Where the hell's Anderson?" Brown would ask. Even the attorney general, his old friend Tom Lynch, seldom—if ever—was on the platform with Brown. Only the controller, Alan Cranston, remained loyal. In the last week of the campaign, he took ten thousand dollars from his campaign treasury, handed it to his assistant, Jack Johnson, and told him to take it personally to Brown. Abandoned by almost everyone else, Brown was deeply touched. Although defeatism had taken over his headquarters, the governor would not give up.

At a night rally at San Bernardino, his spirits soared when the crowd was bigger than expected. The electricity failed, and Brown said: "They can cut off the electricity, but they can't shut up the greatest governor California has ever had." Later, back among the valley farmers, he said: "I'm entitled to be reelected. It is ludicrous that the Republican party would nominate a man without experience."

The days were strenuous and long. The airplane trips stretched over the state and the only relaxed part of the day was in the late evening, with the last speech given. Then the reporters covering the campaign—the regulars from the Associated Press, United Press International, the Los Angeles *Times,* the Los Angeles *Herald Examiner,* the Sacramento *Union,* and visitors from the East—would climb on the plane after Brown. Aboard the plane, Brown would tell the reporters that it wasn't over yet. "I'm going to do a little Harry Truman work and I think the glamour of this man is going to fade," he said—hopefully invoking the memory of Truman's upset win over Thomas E. Dewey in 1948.

But Reagan's glamour didn't fade, and as the election neared, all of the bounce would vanish from Brown at the end of the day. Now he was tired and wanted it to end. Late in October he sipped Scotch on the Grizzly II and looked across the aisle at his wife. "Tired old governor," he said. "Tired old wife."

⊠ CHAPTER NINE

CAMPAIGN II: THE WINNER'S STORY

NORWALK IS ONE of the bedroom communities that stretch in a dreary row along the Pacific Coast south of Los Angeles. It is a formless city, encompassing ten square miles of suburban tract houses, one looking very much like the next. Without tradition, it is a new city incorporated in 1957 for a reason that seemed particularly appropriate for the times —a revolt against big government. Businessmen and residents of these subdivisions believed that the Los Angeles county board of supervisors, their governing body at the time, was too far away to understand their problems; they couldn't get a street repaired without a long hard fight with the county bureaucracy. "The larger your government becomes, the more cumbersome it becomes," said a resident of Norwalk in a statement that could have come from one of Ronald Reagan's campaign speeches.

Norwalk is not a city of the rich. The houses are modest, costing about $16,500, and are generally built on sixty-by-one-hundred-foot lots. Only a few of the residents are in medicine, law or other professions. The overwhelming majority are skilled or semiskilled laborers, with an average yearly income of $6,200. Many of them work on the Apollo project at the nearby North American plant or in other government-supported industries. Government spending is important to Norwalk in another way. Metropolitan State Hospital for the mentally ill employs fourteen hundred of its residents. It is, by every traditional indicator, a Democratic city, and, not surprisingly, three out of four voters are registered as Democrats.

But by 1966 registration no longer meant much to these blue-collar, working-class suburbs around Los Angeles. Anger at the county in the mid-fifties had turned into a revolt against the government in Sacramento and Washington, and these people wanted a change. After the incorporation of their community, taxes were still too high and paychecks dwindled in the face of a bewildering array of taxes by the county, the fire district, the recreation district, the school district, the state and the Federal Government. When Norwalk residents discussed taxes, they would inevitably condemn the expensive state welfare program, supported by tax money, and this in turn brought the discussion to the Negro revolution. Norwalk itself is a white city. Only three of its approximately twenty-four thousand families are black. In 1963 Brown and the Democratic legislature had offended these suburbs by enacting into law the open-housing bill that prohibited discrimination by property owners against Negroes and other minorities in the sale, leasing or rental of property. A year later Norwalk showed how it felt about the law and voted for the statewide ballot measure that nullified the open-housing law. The people, in the words of a Democratic strategist, were "the non-minority wage earners here from the Southwest or South. The party is too liberal for them." The proposition was subsequently overturned by the state supreme court and later by the United States Supreme Court. Neither decision was popular in this area, and the rulings did much to reinforce the common dislike of the judiciary, another remote branch of big government. A short distance to the south a big sign overlooking the freeway proclaimed "Impeach Earl Warren," and in these suburbs were found chapters of the John Birch Society, which sponsored the right-wing crusade against the Chief Justice of the United States. George Wallace, the segregationist ex-governor of Alabama, found supporters in these areas when he was trying to qualify his American Independent party for California's 1968 Presidential primary election.

In April, 1966, Reagan toured these suburban communities, and the reception was enthusiastic wherever he went, especially in the shopping centers. These were the Main Streets of a society that lived by the automobile and freeway, and every afternoon and evening such centers were crowded with shoppers. Political reporters considered the reaction of the crowds almost as sound a test of public opinion in the area as a scientific poll. At the Lakewood Shopping Center, where dozens of stores were built along a long, wide mall, customers from both the working-class communities such as Norwalk and the more affluent subdivisions in Orange County to the south awaited Reagan. Although his visit was in a relatively light midweek shopping period, Reagan was surrounded by more than five hundred people yelling "Good luck" and "Give 'em hell about the unions." Standing on a concrete ledge near some trees in a planter box, Reagan grinned modestly and said: "I guess there's no secret about what I'm doing here."

On the face of it, they were yelling for the wrong candidate.

Yet in spite of their modest incomes and dependence on government contracts for jobs, these people are conservatives. Why? Theories abound: They have made some money, and they are frightened of losing it. They are lonely, insecure, rootless people, moving from suburb to suburb, from job to job, and they are reaching back to old-time values for stability. Or perhaps they are influenced by the wealthy established families of the area. Maybe, because so many are transplanted from the South and Southwest, they are conservatives or even bigots at heart. Whatever the reason, they voted for Nixon for governor in 1962 when most of the state backed Brown. And in 1964 these people came very close to giving Goldwater a majority in their area.

Later in 1966, when Brown came here, he was surrounded by teen-age members of an ultraconservative political group who shouted their opposition to him. He managed to finish his speech and leave unharmed, but one reporter, to protect himself from the crowd, locked himself in the Pacific Telephone communications car to phone in his story without interruption from the young people. When United States Senator Robert Kennedy, campaigning for Brown, visited Lakewood, the teen-agers and some of their parents were even more vicious. Earlier in the year Kennedy had become involved in an argument with Samuel Yorty, the mayor of Los Angeles, over Yorty's handling of Negro slums. Yorty, who ran against Brown in the Democratic primary, was admired in this area for his strong defense of the police during the racial violence in Watts the year before, and when Kennedy appeared, the teen-agers waved signs praising the mayor and telling Kennedy to go home. Obscene slogans were scrawled on many of the signs, and the senator had difficulty speaking as the mob milled about him. Bobby Kennedy was no hero to the youngsters at the Lakewood Shopping Center.

After the Lakewood appearance, Reagan stopped at a smaller shopping center and talked to about one hundred women and a few men. It was still midafternoon. The women, standing near their station wagons filled with children, listened intently. At night he spoke to a packed crowd at a dinner that followed what was becoming the typical pattern for a Reagan appearance—show business personalities to warm up the crowd, followed by the candidate's speech. Reagan made no secret of his movie background. In fact he advertised it. He was introduced by Andy Devine, the froggy-voiced comic sidekick in Gene Autry cowboy movies, who said: "I don't know why an actor can't get into politics. What's wrong with an actor who wants to do something for his country and state? I haven't run into a crooked actor yet, I'll tell you that." The Voices of Faith Choir sang the "Ronald Reagan Pep Song" to the tune of "California Here I Come": "Ronald Reagan, here we are. You're the one we're hoping for." The Voices of Faith weren't seen again on the campaign, but Devine, Edgar Bergen, Chuck Connors, the television cowboy star, and other Hollywood people became fixtures. Connors was so popular with the audiences that some people suggested he run for the United States Senate. Flattered, the tall actor finally said he couldn't afford to leave show business.

With much fanfare Reagan was at last brought out, and he told stories about his days in the movies and about his work in the Screen Actors Guild. He even reminisced about broadcasting the Cubs' games. It was a show, and the audience enjoyed it all, the jokes and the serious part. Welfare and unemployment insurance were Reagan's targets that night, and when he finished speaking, people crowded around him, as they had earlier in the day. Finally the rally was over, and Reagan left Lakewood and returned home.

It had been a typical day for the candidate, and in the eight months that followed, neither his routine nor his speech would substantially change. It was a simple campaign, designed by Bill Roberts and Stu Spencer to display their candidate's best qualities and hide his weak points. His greatest weakness was inexperience, but the strategists quickly turned this to their advantage. Roberts, the principal campaign manager, knew that Reagan could not match Brown's knowledge of state government. "We decided not to show brilliant knowledge, which he did not have," Roberts said later. "We tried to operate on the level that he is not a professional politician, that he is a citizen politician, Joe Doakes running for office." The use of the term "citizen politician" was masterful strategy, for, as Roberts realized, "the term professional politician does not conjure up a good image with the general public." Reagan's boast that he was a citizen politician, Roberts said, "was one of the best ways he could compete with Brown on knowledge of the issues. It was a defense measure but later on it turned into a real asset. At the end, Brown was defending himself against being a professional politician."

Roberts had a quick grasp of the issues. "I'd say that our three main ones in this campaign were, first of all, morality, then taxes, spending, that whole ball of wax; then the eight years of incumbency." He also knew how to avoid an issue. He was aware that his opponents would try to link his conservative candidate with extremist right-wing groups such as the John Birch Society. He knew that Reagan would be asked to repudiate support from members of the John Birch Society. Richard Nixon had done this when he ran for governor in 1962, and as a result, he lost the support of much of the party's conservative wing. Roberts did not want this to happen to Reagan. Thus Reagan stopped short of repudiating the Birchers and avoided offending ultraconservatives who wanted to join his crusade. But out of respect to moderates who disliked and feared the Birchers, Reagan expressed strong disapproval of Robert Welch, the founder of the society. "I wanted a strong enough statement disavowing Welch," said Roberts. He opposed telling "a whole segment of the party to go to hell" because it would deprive his candidate of financial support and the help of some of the party's most enthusiastic volunteer workers.

The most significant contribution the Reagan campaign made to American politics was the shrewd use of television. Reagan's tendency to tire easily forced the strategists to rely more on television than personal appearances. "He doesn't hold up well," said Roberts. "Give him three or four days of three or four meetings in a row and he gets real irritable." Roberts and Neil Reagan put together a series of television spot announcements that took the place of many of the traditional personal appearances. They were unique because of their simplicity—just Reagan standing or sitting in front of the camera, talking to the viewers. Expensive sets and clever writing were avoided. "We had to stay away from Hollywood productions," said Roberts. "To Reagan it was an extreme danger. People would have said: 'Oh, for Christ's sakes, Darryl F. Zanuck stuff.' We did it in a very simple manner and cut costs." A University of California film producer, Ernest Rose, agreed that Roberts had succeeded. He said Reagan's television films were "almost intentionally awkward, crude and bumbling." The spots were essentially illustrated lectures with what seemed to be "an intentional effort not to make [them] slick and commercial."

Personal appearances were an essential part of the campaign, however, for they helped raise money and build up the enthusiasm of party workers. But they did not serve the traditional purpose of directly winning the votes of hostile or unconvinced voters.

Spencer-Roberts' success in displaying their candidate to advantage was revealed the night of January 4, 1966, when Reagan announced that he was running for governor in a televised speech. Stu Spencer said that the speech was basically written by Reagan and reworked and revised in cooperation with his advisers. It was a good speech that dealt knowledgeably with all of the major state problems, and it convinced thousands of viewers that Reagan was not, as his opponents insisted, an empty-headed actor mouthing someone else's lines. Just as important, the speech was carefully given a moderate tone to show that he was not another Goldwater. Instead, Reagan held up the vision of a better California and asked his fellow citizens to help him attain it. "As of now," he said, "I am a candidate seeking the Republican nomination for governor. . . . California's problems are our problems . . . it won't matter if the sky is bigger and bluer out here if you can't see it for smog, and all our elbow room and open space won't mean much if the unsolved problems are higher than the hills." His speech was hopeful. "Our problems are many," he said, "but our capacity for solving them is limitless."

The speech also contained something for the Goldwater fans and for the working-class residents of Norwalk and similar communities, a well-aimed appeal for morality and law and order. This, along with the moderate tone, would become a basic part of the campaign. "Our city streets are jungle paths after dark, with more crimes of violence than New York, Pennsylvania and Massachusetts combined." Immediately after his discussion of crime were these words about Berkeley: "Will we meet [the students'] neurotic vulgarities with vacillation and weakness, or will we tell those entrusted with administering the university we expect them to enforce a code based on decency, common sense and dedication to the high and noble purpose of the University? That they will have the full support of all of us as long as they do this, but we'll settle for nothing less." And finally, there was the condemnation of welfare, heavily self-righteous: "Working men and women should not be asked to carry the additional burden of a segment of society capable of caring for itself but which prefers making welfare a way of life, freeloading at the expense of the more conscientious citizens."

Now he needed a bigger staff to run the campaign. Even the most experienced candidate needs trustworthy assistants—men who provide him with the material and the advice for the long campaign, schedule events, arrange trips, assure him of a place to sleep while on the road. A campaign in California is like a Presidential campaign, for the population centers that must be covered are over a wide area: a morning in Los Angeles, lunch in San Francisco, an afternoon rally in Oroville one hundred and fifty miles to the north, dinner in Oakland across the bay from San Francisco; four speeches or more in a day, hundreds of hands to shake, dozens of party leaders to recognize with a smile and a familiar word. Like Dwight Eisenhower, also a stranger to politics when he ran for high office, Reagan needed guides through the forest.

By January, an important addition had been made. It was Lyn Nofziger, the press secretary, who would eventually become the most important of Reagan's advisers. Nofziger, forty-one, is a short, balding, plump man. His clothes are rumpled, and when he doesn't diet, his stomach appears in danger of bursting through his shirt. He has been conservative since his youth. Just after World War II he testified before the California legislature's Joint Fact-Finding Com-

mittee on Un-American Activities that one of his teachers at
Canoga Park High School in 1941 and 1942 "was always
on the side of the left. She argued one side with some of the
kids and some of us argued the other side. There was no
impartiality on her side." Nofziger looks like a jolly fat man,
an impression he reinforces with constant puns. He has,
however, intense ambition and unlimited capacity for work.
He had pulled himself up from the obscurity and low pay of
a suburban newspaper near Los Angeles to a job as national
political reporter for the Copley papers and finally to this
position—adviser to the most promising political candidate of
the year.

Nofziger looked at the world with perpetual suspicion, always afraid that someone would derail his candidate, and
thus himself. As a Washington reporter, he was thought by
his colleagues to be industrious and competent, but he was
not one of the famous journalists of the Capitol. Those who
knew him were always surprised at his power and effectiveness
as Reagan's press secretary when they came to California. On
his part, Nofziger was guarded with reporters, handing out
news he thought would help his candidate and blatantly
withholding anything that would put Reagan in an unfavor-
able light. He believes most political reporters are too liberal,
especially those from the East. When he covered the Goldwater campaign, he used to pass out buttons marked "Western
Tory Press" or "Eastern Liberal Press," depending on how
he felt about a reporter.

Entering the Reagan campaign at about the same time
was Philip Battaglia, a successful attorney. He started as
southern California chairman, a figurehead position, but in
the end would be the state campaign chairman and, finally,
Reagan's executive secretary and "good right arm." To Battaglia, life had been a struggle to succeed, to acquire wealth,

power and social position. At the age of thirty-two he was a partner in one of Los Angeles' most respected law firms, Flint-McKay, and a member of the University of Southern California's board of trustees.

Other staff additions were two college professors, Dr. Stanley Plog of the University of California at Los Angeles and Dr. Kenneth Holden of San Fernando Valley State College. These two men would be the brain trust, the intellectuals who supplied the layman candidate with all of the information he needed to convince the electorate that he was capable of being governor. They would write the position papers and research the complicated state problems, some of which Reagan scarcely knew existed. Spencer and Roberts, who picked the two, did not tap the traditional campaign sources of intellectual advice. For Plog and Holden were behavioral scientists—men who combined the traditional disciplines of psychology, sociology, statistics, political science and other social sciences to find out why men behaved in a certain manner. In their spare time they owned a small research firm, the Behavior Science Corporation of Van Nuys. Some of their assignments were prosaic, such as setting up a complete psychological testing service for a school system. But others dealt directly with subtle relationships between people. They would be assigned by a troubled business to go into a plant or office, interview the workers and supervisors, find out how they got along together, and deduce from their behavior the reason for the business problem. Perhaps a supervisor was insensitive to the compaints of his workers. He would be shifted. Perhaps an executive was not, in the opinion of Holden and Plog, psychologically sound enough for promotion. He would be told. When the stock market slumps, businessmen look for economic causes, but Holden said: "We think it's largely psychological." Plog and Holden are both psychologists. Holden has his doctorate from Ohio State University. Plog's is from Harvard.

Plog and Holden first met Reagan at the candidate's house. To someone with Holden's neat academic mind, the scene at Reagan's home was distressing. "He didn't have a secretary, and he was assimilating stacks of material on state issues, clipping newspapers and magazines. It was a monumental task." Quickly Holden and Plog, ever the behavioral scientists, analyzed their prospective client. Some of Holden's observations: "Charismatic personality. Knows his position and the position of others. . . . He is not a map reader, he is not a reactor. Reagan knows who he is and what he stands for. His library is stacked with books on political philosophy. He can take information and he can assimilate it and use it appropriately in his own words."

Holden and Plog talked with Reagan about the campaign. "He liked the cut of our sails and we liked the cut of his," Holden said. They joined the Reagan team, and Holden proudly claimed it was probably the first time in American history that a major political candidate has taken on intellectual advisers from a firm specializing in approaching the voters in psychological terms. "We looked at the campaign as a problem in human behavior, a very complex problem." The idea was to find out why the voter would mark his ballot for Reagan or for someone else. The Behavior Science Corporation decided that it would try to pinpoint the issues that concerned the voter and offer Reagan methods of approaching them. As an example, Holden and Plog, along with Reagan, became aware shortly after the campaign began of the voters' intense interest in the University of California. Reagan, at that period, always concluded his speeches by asking for questions from the audience, and there was always a question about the university. It soon became clear to

Holden that the voters were especially unhappy about President Clark Kerr's handling of the student demonstrators, and that Reagan would have to offer a constructive alternative that would not be attacked by the Democrats as political interference with the university. Holden came up with the idea of proposing an investigation of the university by a non-partisan commission headed by John McCone, former chief of the Central Intelligence Agency. McCone was a Republican, but Brown would have difficulty criticizing him since he had enthusiastically chosen McCone the year before as chairman of the commission that investigated the Watts riots. Holden recalls that Roberts was unenthusiastic about the plan, but Holden flew to San Diego where Reagan was resting and sold the candidate on the idea. Reagan used it for campaign speeches, but the commission never materialized. Another of Holden's ideas was turned down—that Reagan be flanked by university professors when he proposed the commission, including two Nobel prize winners who supported his candidacy.

The main job of Behavior Science was to supply the candidate with information—books of it. Holden and Plog singled out eighteen main problem areas and began gathering information, for neither man was, himself, an expert in any field of state government. One of the most complex issues was school finance, a field fully understood only by a few school administrators. Plog and Holden invited such educators from the San Fernando Valley to their office and asked them to talk about their problems. The two psychologists put the information in a growing pile of black books. These books—there would be eight of them before the campaign ended—contained five-by-eight-inch cards containing basic facts. From these books Reagan would take the information for his speeches, which he would write on three-by-five-inch cards. In addition, Behavior Science gave him position papers on issues that "he could react to and sharpen up his own philosophy."

Either Holden, Plog or an assistant—and the black books —would accompany Reagan on every campaign trip. If Reagan didn't know the answer, the behavioral scientist and the black books would be consulted. And if the answer wasn't available on the road, a phone call would be made to Behavior Science's office in Van Nuys, where an assistant would look it up. This technique permitted Reagan to counter the skepticism with which his candidacy was greeted and to become a convincing candidate. He would adopt a similar method with the mini-memos after he took office.

As important as the staff was, help also came from outside the Reagan organization early in the Republican primary that preceded the general election campaign. In California the parties choose their candidates in open primaries, and for the Republicans these races were so bitter in past years that the party was rendered incapable of winning the general election. The Republican state central committee, trying to avoid name calling for once, adopted a rule that had the effect of preventing Reagan's opponents from questioning his scanty qualifications before the primary. It was proposed by the state chairman, Dr. Gaylord Parkinson, and so important was the rule to him that he called it the eleventh commandment—"Thou Shalt Not Speak Ill of Other Republicans." The rule was received as enthusiastically by the party as anything handed down by the Lord at Mount Sinai. Tired of defeat and of the fighting between conservative and moderate Republicans, the party organization wholeheartedly supported Parkinson. The result was to destroy the hopes of Reagan's main opponent, George Christopher, the former mayor of San Francisco. Christopher wanted to raise the experience issue, but every time he called Reagan inexperienced, he was accused of violating the commandment.

For Christopher the primary campaign was a disaster. He was a bulky, rough-featured man who had two remarkably successful terms as a mayor, but was little known in southern California and was a poor campaigner for the age of television. He was effective and even dominating in a small group, but he had little feeling for the language, and in speeches he became entangled in such sentences as: "I am cognizant of two philosophical thoughts which perhaps pertain to this election." He was the candidate of the moderate Republicans who supported Rockefeller against Goldwater in California in 1964 and were trying to regain control by backing a successful gubernatorial nominee. Christopher was their second choice. Their first was the state's senior senator, Thomas Kuchel, but he disappointed them by refusing to run. For a while there was a frantic scurrying for an attractive candidate to oppose Reagan, who was backed by the old Goldwater organization. The minority leader of the assembly, Robert T. Monagan, was suggested. He was forty-five, an aggressive, athletic-looking man with a plain but effective speaking style. But he was from the small northern California city of Tracy and it would take a long, expensive campaign to make him well known in southern California. Monagan had the enthusiasm, but not the money, and by December Christopher's supporters were asking all the other moderates to put their financial contributions in the former mayor's pot. When Reagan won the primary, Monagan and some of the others joined his campaign. But they were never trusted by the men who originally supported Reagan.

Christopher's campaign suffered another blow from a surprising source, Governor Brown's campaign organization. Polls had convinced Democratic strategists that Christopher, a moderate whose philosophy was not too much different from Brown's, would be able to cut deeply into the Democratic votes in the general election and defeat the governor if he won the Republican primary. The polls said that Reagan was more popular than Christopher within the Republican party, which had grown more conservative, but that Reagan would have difficulty in attracting Democratic votes in the general election. In this case the polls were wrong, but politicians, always groping for certainties in an uncertain business, used them to guide their decisions. One poll in April showed Christopher ahead of Brown 54 percent to 34 percent, with 12 percent undecided. Reagan, on the other hand, led Brown only by 44 percent to 41 percent with 15 percent undecided.

Brown's campaign organization looked into Christopher's past. He had become wealthy in the milk distributing business, and in the process he was convicted of violating milk price stabilization laws in 1940. He paid a fine and afterward always maintained that the violation was a conscious protest against laws he thought were too restrictive. The record of the conviction, along with an unflattering police photograph, had been used against him unsuccessfully when he ran for county supervisor and then mayor of San Francisco. The Brown organization employed a former San Francisco newspaperman, Dick Hyer, to investigate Christopher's background, and then in the last two months of the primary campaign began leaking the information to newsmen. On May 9 and May 10, Drew Pearson distributed columns discussing Christopher's milk control law violation, and Brown's aides admitted to a reporter that they had supplied the information to the columnist.

With the help of the Democrats and the eleventh commandment, Reagan's chances for the nomination looked good. Only once did he falter, in an argument over civil rights. In March, 1966, he and Christopher appeared before the state convention of the National Negro Republican Assembly in Santa Monica, attended by the few Negroes who, for reasons that are hard to understand, still clung to the Republican party after it had nominated a Presidential candidate in 1964 who voted against the United States civil rights bill. Sharing the platform with Christopher and Reagan was William Penn Patrick, one of the minor candidates. Ben Peery, a Los Angeles businessman who was a black conscience of the Republican party, rose to ask a question he had asked at G.O.P. meetings in the past. To Reagan, he said: "How are Negro Republicans going to encourage other Negroes to vote for you after your statement that you would not have voted for the civil rights bill?"

Reagan is not a bigot, but he is unusually sensitive when anyone questions him about race relations. He is defensive about the subject even at the best of times, and he was even more so at this meeting, for he had been trying to win support among the black community without success and was frustrated by his failure. Christopher also irritated him. The mayor's criticisms of Reagan, limited by the eleventh commandment, had been mild, but Reagan and his wife kept track of all of them until they were magnified out of proportion. And he was sick with a virus that weakened him for most of the primary campaign. Reagan gave his standard reply—he favored the aims of the bill, but it was "a bad piece of legislation." He defended Goldwater's vote against the bill, saying: "If I didn't know personally that Barry Goldwater was not the very opposite of a racist, I could not have supported him."

It was Christopher's opportunity, and he rose to take

Utterly absorbed, Reagan attends a 1939 Screen Actors Guild meeting with his first wife, Jane Wyman, who divorced him later (she said his union activities bored her). George Murphy, in Reagan's row, seems similarly inclined.

What did his future hold? A decline in his movie career and the end of his first marriage awaited Reagan after his discharge from the Air Force in 1945. With Reagan are returning veterans (l. to r.) Wayne Morris, Gig Young, and Harry Lewis (Paula Drew is the fortune teller).

Although he now recalls that he was once a "bleeding-heart liberal," Reagan was a friendly witness during the turbulent House Un-American Activities Committee hearings in 1947, eager to tell how he helped defeat the Communists in a struggle for control of the Screen Actors Guild.

Those who know Reagan recognize the pursed lips as a sign of disapproval. He was not impressed when, with his second wife, Nancy, and Bill O'Connor, a Los Angeles attorney, he met Adlai Stevenson during the 1952 Presidential campaign.

Reagan, the conservative crusader, whipped up enthusiasm among Barry Goldwater's supporters outside the San Francisco Cow Palace before Goldwater was nominated at the 1964 Republican National Convention.

Housewives—called "the hormone vote" by one campaign strategist—
were entranced when Reagan spoke at a backyard rally during a visit
to one of California's white middle-class suburbs before the 1966 election.

Victory night for California's new Governor.

Reagan and Governor Edmund G. Brown expressed sincere contempt for each other during the election campaign, but they managed a smile and handshake when Reagan visited Brown's office in the state capitol before his inauguration.

Reagan listens with apparent distaste as Clark Kerr, the president of the University of California, leaned down to chat before the meeting of the university regents at which Kerr was fired. Regents chairman Theodore Meyer is seated at Reagan's left.

College students and professors protesting Reagan's education economies booed him when he unexpectedly appeared at an anti-administration rally on the capitol steps.

The smiles of Reagan and his shirt-sleeved communications director, Lyn Nofziger, looked forced as they left a stormy news conference dealing with accusations of a homosexual ring in the administration—and body-guard Arthur Van Court (far left) and Press Secretary Paul Beck weren't smiling at all.

advantage of it. "Contrary to my opponent, I would have voted for the bill if I had been in Congress." He added that "the position taken by Goldwater did more harm than any other thing to the Republican party, and we're still paying for that defeat. This situation still plagues the Republican party, and unless we cast out this image, we're going to suffer defeat."

Weeks of tension took their toll, and Reagan stepped up and said: "I want to make a point of personal privilege." He shouted: "I resent the implication that there is any bigotry in my nature. Don't anyone ever imply I lack integrity. I will not stand silent and let anyone imply that—in this or any other group." He slammed his fist into his hand, mumbled a few words and stalked out of the hall, followed by concerned assistants. One newsman reported him as saying: "I'll get that S.O.B."

It was the first time the candidate had become unstrung. Reagan got into a car and was driven home. Holden was afraid the campaign would be destroyed by a moment's anger. Very upset, he recalled he persuaded Nofziger to follow Reagan home and bring him back. He called the Reagan house and talked to the candidate, who had just entered the door. Holden advised him to come back, and Reagan finally agreed. Accompanied by Nofziger, he returned to the convention and told the president, the Reverend Lawrence C. Thomas, that his anger wasn't directed at the delegates.

Christopher tried to use the incident as evidence of mental instability. "Mr. Reagan, of course, has been ill, and I extend my sympathy in this moment of his emotional disturbance," he said. But Reagan's quick return to the meeting took away much of the sting. "Frankly, I got mad," he said. He felt Christopher had inferred he was a bigot. "There was no outright charge . . . I felt in the manner of answering, there were inferences that placed me over in that category. It was the sum total of the afternoon. I'm not a politician. There are just some things you can't take as a man." A newsman brought up a central issue: He wondered if the incident would raise questions about Reagan's "emotional stability under stress." He asked if Reagan was emotionally fit for the campaign ahead. It was a blunt question, but Reagan merely smiled and said "yes." Hollywood columnists, he recalled, had said he was a "Boy Scout and a square," and he told the reporters: "Fellows, you can't have it both ways. You can't be a wild-eyed kook and a square."

Christopher, shackled by the eleventh commandment, remained an underdog without an offense right up to the election day. His defeat was worse than he expected. He had hoped for strong support from the northern counties, but Reagan carried fifty-three of the fifty-eight counties in the state, and Christopher did well in only two, his home county of San Francisco and in San Mateo, which adjoins it to the south. Reagan's margin was overwhelming—1,417,623 to 675,683.

From then on, Reagan and his advisers were confident of victory. "To me, it was a matter of staying alive from the primary to the general," said Roberts. "Most of the issues were ours to pick and choose." For the next few months it was necessary only to avoid mistakes and stick to the pattern established early in the year. Soon Reagan would be so certain of winning that he would begin to put together his new administration.

In the north there was a homespun quality about the campaign, mostly because of the campaign plane, a twenty-two-year-old DC-3 called The Turkey. Mervin W. Amerine generally used it for carrying live baby turkeys from his San Joaquin Valley ranch to market, but after the primary he offered it to Reagan—along with his services as pilot. If Amerine had worked on the Warners' lot when Reagan was making B movies, he would have been cast as a pilot. He was tall, calm and handsome, a man who had been flying for twenty-eight of his forty-three years. His plane was reliable but slow. Like all of the sturdy DC-3s, it wasn't pressurized and the ride was sometimes uncomfortable. Whenever the plane landed, all those aboard would yell, "Gobble, gobble, gobble," with Reagan, sitting in front behind the pilot's compartment, joining it.

The real battleground was the south. Thirty-eight percent of the voters lived in Los Angeles County—2.96 million people—and they, along with the voters in neighboring Orange and San Diego counties, would to a large extent determine the election. A bus rather than an airplane was the symbol of the southern California campaign. A comfortable Greyhound bus was loaded each morning with sweet rolls and coffee for breakfast; soda, beer, sandwiches and fried chicken for lunch, and whiskey and gin for the long drive back to headquarters. It was a self-contained home with a lavatory for the long days on the freeways. In the mornings the bus would leave Reagan headquarters and bring the six or seven members of the traveling press, the staff and the candicate to the first event of the day, which was sometimes a coffee hour with women or a stop at a television station to tape a show for future viewing. After that would be a noon stop for a speech at a luncheon. In the afternoons there would be a rest stop at a motel. After Reagan's last blow-up over civil rights, the afternoon stop was seldom missed. His nap over, the candidate would rise refreshed for a dinner speech, which would end the day. By 10 P.M. he was usually in bed.

For reporters his campaign was a pleasant change from

traveling with Governor Brown, who was out every day from 7 A.M. to midnight. But from the way Reagan talked, his public never guessed that his schedule was limited. When campaigning in the south, he spent many of his evenings and nights at home, but whenever he and Mrs. Reagan appeared together at a luncheon or dinner, they would hug each other on the platform and remark to the audience how long they had been separated by the campaign. It was a sour sight to the traveling newsmen from northern California who had been away from home for two weeks at a time.

His campaign was aimed at the white majority. Seldom was a stop made in a Negro community, although Reagan made a conscious effort to win the Mexican-Americans away from the Democrats. *"Ya basta,"* he cried—"We've had it." He was followed by a mariachi band when he went into Mexican-American communities, and the violins, trumpets and guitars made his appearance exciting. He concentrated on a sore point, charging that Brown had neglected these people in appointments and in social programs. In October, Mervyn Dymally, then a Negro assemblyman from the Watts area and later a state senator, said the Mexican areas "are usually nine-to-one Democratic, but Reagan will make some dents in it."

He was surprisingly successful with the labor vote, demonstrating that the leaders of organized labor had lost their old-time hold on the rank and file. Standing in the yard of a plant, among union members, he said: "Even though I knew the upper crust of labor is opposed to my candidacy, I wasn't prepared for the extent they would lie about my record." With great effect, he told about his days as Screen Actors Guild president and about how he had opposed the right-to-work initiative that was backed by William F. Knowland, the Republican candidate for governor in 1958. He was warmly applauded when he said: "As long as we say a person must belong to a union, we must protect the union membership with a secret ballot." That position was opposed by organized labor.

"We've tried to support you a little bit," one union member told him. Another—with an "I'm a Democrat for Reagan" sign pasted across his bare stomach—said: "I'm shaking the hand of the next governor of the state of California."

The campaign was going so well by early October that Reagan's strategy board decided to offer some help to the Republican candidate for lieutenant governor, Robert Finch. Finch was one of the more accomplished politicians in the nation. He had managed Richard M. Nixon's campaign for the Presidency in 1960, which came close to winning. Two years later he advised Nixon, his close friend, to stay out of the California governorship election, but Nixon ignored him. In 1964 Finch was in charge of George Murphy's successful Senate race. The candidates for governor and lieutenant governor do not run together as a ticket in California, as the President and Vice-President do. Traditionally each man fends for himself. Finch, in the primaries, would not choose between Christopher and Reagan. He was concerned with winning his own nomination. In the general election he was by himself much of the time, always trailing the incumbent, Glenn M. Anderson, but slowly making headway. By instinct and philosophy Finch was part of the party's moderate wing, and as Reagan swept ahead of Brown, moderates began asking why he wasn't helping Finch. Reagan, in fact, was not spending much time with any of the other candidates. Finally the move was made. "We want Mr. Finch," Nofziger said. "We would like to make as many joint appearances as possible." From then on Finch was included in many Reagan campaign events.

In November Finch would poll more votes than Reagan and go to Sacramento heralded as one of the strongmen of the administration. But he was never completely welcomed in the inner circles. His philosophy of government was too liberal and his old ties to Nixon made him suspect by Reagan men looking toward the Presidency.

During the last two weeks of the campaign, Reagan, who had before sat in the back of the bus writing his speeches or studying, relaxed. It seemed that the crisis was over; the rest of the campaign was a triumphal march to the capitol. In these last weeks there was even some hilarity in the winner's circle—merriment that was part of traveling with a winning team. In San Francisco one afternoon, the party was met by Miss Sue Warschaw, who had been assigned by the Brown campaign to heckle Reagan and tape-record his speeches. She had water pistols to "put out the prairie fire" with which Reagan usually ended his speeches and gave the weapons to the press covering Reagan. The reporters battled each other with water the rest of the afternoon and on the commercial airliner that Reagan and the campaign party took back to Los Angeles that night. But by then the water guns had been filled with gin, and those who were aboard the plane recall that Reagan determinedly read a book, trying to appear that he wasn't part of the group firing gin-filled water guns in the cabin of a United airliner.

The Reagan team was confident and their confidence was well founded. Soon the campaign would be over, and the next stop would be Sacramento. On election night it ended quickly. Reagan and his wife were driving to their party at a hotel in Los Angeles when a radio newscaster announced that Reagan was the new governor. "It can't be over," Nancy said. "We're not at the party yet." He had won easily, by a margin of 993,739 votes. That night there were victory parties at the Biltmore and Ambassador hotels in Los Angeles. It was at the Ambassador that Brown was dealt the final blow. Hurrying over to congratulate Reagan was Mayor Sam Yorty, who by refusing to support Brown after losing to him in the primary had become a leader—and a symbol—of the Democrats who had left their party and gone over to Reagan.

CHAPTER TEN

THE CREATIVE SOCIETY TAKES OVER

COLD RAIN FELL on Sacramento in November and December of 1966, a chilly reminder of the oppressive financial problems that faced the new governor. The Creative Society was moving in and change and retrenchment were the order of the day. Although the inauguration was not until January 1, temporary headquarters were set up six blocks from the capitol in a building that appeared eminently suited for the well-groomed, extremely confident examples of youthful corporate success who had taken leave of their businesses to assist Reagan. Their offices were in the International Business Machines Building, a square structure with a glass front and no frills, a product of the no-nonsense business world. It was to this world, rather than to the men and women who had chosen government for a career, that Reagan turned for advice after the election.

He needed advice badly. In the next few months Reagan would be required to deal with a budget deficit of about a quarter of a billion dollars, plus a state debt from the previous year. So staggering were the requirements of governing a state of 19.7 million people that it is a wonder anyone wanted the job, and after a year in office, Reagan's customary good cheer would sometimes be replaced with testiness. His task was more difficult than that of his predecessors, for he had pledged unequivocally to reverse the directions of the past. Seldom have campaign promises been advertised as loudly or an administration taken over with as much ballyhoo. Reagan's pledge was to examine every one of the state programs with a businessman's eye for economy and efficiency, and then to make deep and lasting changes in them, squeezing out the fat and politics of past years and leaving the state lean, hard and more efficient. It was inevitable that some of the promises would not be kept.

In his campaign he had also made another promise—to keep politics out of his appointments. He said: "As governor, I will make all appointments to state offices on the basis of experience and qualifications and not on the basis of personal loyalties or political obligations." But of the first two hundred jobs he handed out, only twelve were listed as going to Democrats. Republicans received one hundred thirty-nine, and the party affiliation of the others was not disclosed. He criticized Brown for awarding defeated Democratic candidates with judgeships and other jobs, something Brown often did. When three Democrats were running for a state senate seat, Brown cheerfully stood beside them at a rally and assured the crowd not to worry about the two losers—because he would give them a job. Reagan often cited the incident in his campaign, but when he became governor, he found jobs for a number of defeated Republican candidates, including the defeated G.O.P. candidate for attorney general, Spencer Williams, the only Republican to lose in the statewide election in 1966. He was given the assignment of secretary of human relations.

There was, in the Reagan administration's first year, a wide gap between the promise and the deed, a seeming determination to promote his national reputation rather than solve the problems that were left to him by Governor Brown. Pledged to economy, he signed a record $5.08 billion budget. Nevertheless, when he traveled around the country a few weeks later, winning friends for a possible bid for the Presidency, Reagan talked as if his economizing had succeeded completely. He said he had given Californians what they wanted when they voted "against the idea that we can, as a state or nation, afford anything and everything simply because we think of it." Then, to inevitable applause, he would list his economies. Viewed against the mammoth government of California, most were stopgap efforts, the product of an administration attuned more toward public relations than the hard work of permanently trimming down programs—temporarily freezing the hiring of state employees and halting the construction of a $4 million state building. Big reductions were made in spending for higher education and mental health, but they were done in a hasty manner. Services were reduced, but no lasting reforms were achieved.

In the minds of some of Reagan's advisers, Sacramento appeared to be merely on-the-job training for the Presidency. Early in the administration Henry Salvatori, in an interview with Doris Klein of the Associated Press, gave a hint of the new team's priorities. "People criticize Ronnie for having no political experience," he said. "But he has a great image, a way to get through to people. Look at the Goldwater experience. His philosophy was sound, but he didn't articulate it moderately. The governor has a similar philosophy, but he can express his thoughts. Look at John F. Kennedy. He didn't have much of a record as a senator. But he made a great appearance—and he had a beautiful wife. So does the governor. Nancy Reagan doesn't have to take a back seat to anyone. And the governor has plenty of time between now and the nomination to make a record as an administrator. But I don't believe people in other states really care much about what's happening in California anyway."

Reagan and his young staff, led by Battaglia and Nofziger, moved into the IBM building with the attitude of men who would quickly clean up the mess in Sacramento and move on to something else. They were, commented one old government hand, convinced they were the sole repository for goodness in the world—that everything that had gone on before was bad and everything the administration did would be right. So new to government were they that a guidebook was prepared in October by Assembly Minority Leader Monagan and his staff. It was a thick book, a sophisticated civics course containing an outline of the historical development of the role of the governor; a list of all the positions in the governor's office, with salaries; and a summary of the legal requirements of Reagan's relations with the legislature, including the date on which he must submit his budget.

Battaglia, as executive secretary, and Nofziger, as press secretary, had a great deal of power in the new administration. They had the governor's ear. They were jealous of their position and of anyone who might usurp it. Nofziger was more rumpled than ever, but also more industrious and enjoying his new position. His arrival was always welcome, for he alone among the staff retained his sense of humor. Battaglia was the most dedicated to improving the state government. He put all of his considerable drive and talent to work, confident that success in Sacramento would bring him to the high place in the world he had always sought. Battaglia had taken a cut in salary to join Reagan, and like others in the administration, he loved to boast of it. He had been reluctant to go into state service, for he was convinced that government was filled with political hacks, a view shared by almost all of the governor's appointees. Another assistant, Thomas Reed, thirty-two, son of a wealthy businessman, lectured reporters one day on the type of men the administration wanted—young people like himself who had made large amounts of money in the rough and tough world of private business and were now willing to make their talents available for a time to the government. Another of Reagan's aides was William Clark, the cabinet secretary and the originator of the mini-memos. One day in Clark's office, his eyes suddenly wandered from his guest to a rear wall. The visitor looked back in surprise, and Clark explained in an aristocratic manner that "the civil servants" had hung some of his pictures on the wall and that the arrangement was now so pleasant that it distracted him. In his way of speaking, the term "civil servant" became a synonym for handyman or maid.

Another important member of the team was Dirk Eldredge, thirty-four, a computer systems marketing representative from IBM. A month after Reagan's inauguration he would leave Sacramento and return to IBM—the first of the important staff people to return to the businesses from which they were on temporary loan. Eventually others would leave— among them Battaglia, Reed, Jack Lindsay, a legislative liaison man, and Richard Quinn, an assistant executive secretary. By December, 1967, only Nofziger, Clark and a few others were left of the staff that worked with Reagan on the campaign.

As vital as the governor's personal staff was the "kitchen cabinet," the wealthy financial backers whose advice Reagan respected and often followed. It was a diverse group, and the only common denominator was wealth and maturity. The latter quality made their advice more important in Reagan's mind than that of some of his staff members who, while wealthy, lacked the experience he respected. Henry Salvatori was one member of the kitchen cabinet. So were A. C. "Cy" Rubel and Holmes Tuttle. Seven others were among the favored ten. Through the campaign and into Reagan's administration, they were viewed as mystery men by Democrats—ultraconservatives who exercised undue influence on the governor. Salvatori scoffed at that—there was no mystery to him. Always accessible, he liked to talk frankly of the role that he and the others played in the administration—adviser and counsel to Reagan, who, he insisted, always made up his own mind. To Salvatori, the wealth of the unofficial cabinet members was a virtue, for they were so rich that they asked no special favors in Sacramento. It made the Reagan administration unique because "not in the history of America has an administration come in without a single obligation. None of these fellows were after anything." The roster of the kitchen cabinet turned up names representing all sorts of Republican party beliefs. Two of the most influential had supported Christopher in the primary. They were Arch Monson and Leonard Firestone, Jr., of Los Angeles, the president of Firestone Tire and Rubber Company of California, who was Christopher's southern California finance chairman and a supporter of Senator Kuchel.

Most, like Salvatori, Tuttle and Rubel, were deeply conservative and among the original Reagan backers. They were Jaquelin Hume of San Francisco, the president of Basic Vegetable Products, Incorporated, one of the first members of the Friends of Ronald Reagan; Edward Mills, an old Goldwater supporter and also one of the first behind Reagan;

Taft Schreiber, vice-president of Music Corporation of America, had been vice-chairman of Reagan's statewide campaign committee. The two others were Reagan's personal attorney, William French Smith, who had been active in the Republican party, and Leland Kaiser, a San Francisco investment banker who had been neutral in the primary because of his job as treasurer of the Republican state central committee.

These men remained in the background and the day-to-day duty went to the staff members. The young men who assisted Reagan were, in a sense, the junior varsity, painfully knocking heads in the misery of daily practice—hoping one day to attain the dignity, solid wealth, social position and prestige of a Salvatori or a Firestone. Sometimes they must have wondered if it was worth it. There was, for example, the day Reagan was prematurely sworn in as governor—by accident—an event that almost took some of the glow off the elaborate formal inaugural ceremony being planned.

Weeks before the ceremony, the secretary of state's office had mailed Reagan a copy of the oath of office—a two hundred-fifty-word pledge of loyalty to the government and an affirmation of nonassociation with subversive groups. It was the custom for the governor to sign the oath only after he was sworn in, but Reagan mailed it back to the secretary of state, signed although not notarized. Bert Clinkston, a deputy secretary of state, called Reagan's office in Sacramento two weeks before the inaugural and asked an assistant if the governor-elect wanted to delay his signature until the ceremony. No, replied the assistant, unaware that the signature, once notarized by Clinkston, would automatically make Reagan governor at midnight, January 1. Reagan would sign it in his office now, for the inaugural ceremony would be too hectic a time.

"When I got there," Clinkston recalled, "I assumed that

he had been briefed, but nevertheless, I told him: 'This is the document that will make you governor.' Then we went ahead with the oath." Reagan repeated it aloud and then signed the paper. The witnesses were Van Court and Friedman, the security men. Nofziger was furious when word of the unscheduled oath-taking leaked out, for Reagan's insistence on a midnight inaugural had made the timing of the swearing-in a major news story and the subject of many jokes. "Clinkston came over with the oath of office and left Ron with the belief he was just signing a loyalty oath," Nofziger said. "No one thought it was a swearing-in procedure. But he did raise his hand and affirm what had to be affirmed. He actually did what Clinkston asked him to do, but it was not fully explained to him."

Reagan went ahead with his formal swearing-in anyway, even though Clinkston's superior, Republican Secretary of State Frank M. Jordan, said: "Whatever he does now is just a formality." A mistake wasn't going to stop the estimated ten thousand people expected in town for the five days of events to celebrate the G.O.P. victory. These were the Republicans who had grumbled through eight years of the Brown administration, men and women who hadn't had much of anything to rejoice about since Eisenhower's second victory in 1956. This was their chance to yell, to forget the losing battles for Nixon and Goldwater. With money left over from the campaign, economy was forgotten for the festivities—a series of events which lasted from the swearing-in at 12:01 A.M. on January 1 until the last of the celebrants struggled home from the inaugural ball, which was held Thursday, January 5. About $100,000 was set aside for temporary redecoration of an ugly barnlike building at the State Fairground, but even piped-in heat couldn't warm the place, and the women were forced to wear their fur coats over their new gowns. Five bands played at the ball and Walt Disney Studios designed the inaugural program. But the week was not all revelry. On the morning before the ball Reagan and his wife attended a prayer breakfast, and he asked for God's help in the job ahead. He said: "Belief in the dependence on God is essential to our state and nation. This will be a very integral part of our state as long as I have anything to do with it."

While plans were being made for the inaugural, the new administration had to master the government. On November 28, while Reagan and Nofziger were in Los Angeles at the southern California interim headquarters in a cottage on the grounds of the Ambassador Hotel, Battaglia, Eldredge and others first learned of the dimension of the financial problem they faced. They sat down in the conference room of the finance department in Sacramento with Hale Champion, Brown's finance director. Accompanying the Reagan group was Caspar W. Weinberger. He was an attorney and a former assemblyman who first opposed Goldwater and then Reagan, but he joined the Reagan campaign after the primary. Battaglia learned on him heavily for advice in this period, much to the disgust of some of the more conservative advisers. Champion informed them of the budget deficit. At the end of the current year, June 30, 1967, there would be a slight surplus, but in the following year anticipated spending would exceed income by about $250 million. This was not a surprise. As the legislature's financial adviser, A. Alan Post, reported: "For a number of years, current cash income has been less than outgo, but the problem has been temporarily solved. . . . In effect, this has postponed major tax increases. Such increases, however, are necessary for the [next] budget year." Reagan would have to propose a tax increase to cover the deficit. For several years Governor Brown had pushed through new programs, but had failed to provide enough taxes to pay for them on a long-term basis. Now, as Reagan said, the day of reckoning had arrived.

Champion shocked his successors with more news. Not only was a deficit imminent, but the state was in debt. Every year state officials transferred, or borrowed, money from certain stable funds in the government to use in the general fund, which is supported by tax revenues and pays for daily operating expenses. This borrowing is necessary because much tax revenue does not come in until June or July, while expenses remain constant throughout the year. But because of Brown's insistence on postponing a tax increase in past years, this year there would not be enough money to borrow. It was a serious problem, one calling for an even bigger tax increase than Reagan had anticipated. After the meeting one of Reagan's aides said he was reminded of William Buckley's remark when he was asked what he would do if he was elected mayor of New York—Buckley said he would ask for a recount.

Champion's news was gloomy, and by the time Reagan and his assistants transmitted it to the public, it looked even worse. With his knack for overdramatizing whatever he was involved in, Reagan flew to Sacramento, conferred with Battaglia and Weinberger and then announced that California was in the middle of a financial crisis. "I didn't realize it would be this bad," said Reagan. Recalling what he had said of the Brown administration's financial policies during the campaign, he said: "I could have doubled what I said and not been wrong. All I've said about postponing the day of reckoning was true." He added: "I'm a born optimist. I had my fingers crossed, hoping I was painting a picture darker than it was. I wasn't. California is confronted by a very serious financial situation." Democrats did not agree. They said the current situation had been anticipated by Brown and the legislators, and remedies had been planned. "I am concerned that statements exaggerating this deficit and distorting our need for cash seriously jeopardize our ability to sell bonds at a reasonable interest rate," complained the chairman of the senate finance committee, George Miller, Jr. As it turned out, the cash debt was $194 million—not the $750 million Reagan had predicted at one point. And the deficit for the following year was much smaller than he anticipated.

According to Champion, the new administration got more bad news two weeks later when he told Reagan's advisers that California was facing a potential deficit in the Medi-Cal program which pays for medical services for the needy. But, curiously, it was not until February that the administration took public notice of that deficit and began planning to deal with it.

November marked the beginning of Reagan's battle with the budget, a long war that had some comic aspects. He was limited by laws which made it all but impossible to cut some spending. In other instances his economies were held back by political considerations such as Champion encountered three years before when he tried to save money by charging farmers $6 million in fees for the services they received from the state. So powerful were the agricultural interests that the bill never got out of the committee. Reagan found such obstacles everywhere. Battaglia, Eldredge and other advisers met with Reagan's task force of Republican legislators, and the administration officials suggested cutbacks in welfare. The senators and assemblymen rejected the idea as politically impossible. Reagan had pledged to cut down welfare and in his speeches had conjured up visions of unwed mothers— Negroes, in the minds of many of his listeners—relaxing in sin, in front of a color television set, while living on welfare payments. But now it was bleak November, and the reality was somewhat different. There were many different types of welfare, and the question of whose benefits would be cut was hard to answer. Did Reagan mean to affect the 275,235 men and women over sixty-five who, because of the law, are not eligible for social security and live on their $98.88 old-age security payments? None of these people, certainly, were living in luxury. The administration found that welfare also meant aid to the blind, a program that supplied its people with an average of $124.92 a month. There were 83,294 people receiving aid to the needy disabled, who averaged $101 a month. Welfare in California was even given to a few victims of violent crimes. The state paid $64.18 a month to six people under a new Democratic program passed the year before to help innocent victims of crime on the streets. The unwed mothers who caused so much controversy in the campaign were included in the largest category, aid to families with dependent children, whose beneficiaries received about $46.09 for each person in the family. That is $184.36 a month for a family of four, and nobody was getting rich on that in America in 1967.

Even if Reagan had thought these payments were too high, cutting them was almost impossible. Of the $1.039 billion spent for welfare in California between July 1, 1965, and June 30, 1966, $493,576,990 came from the Federal Government, and Washington limited the state's power to reduce the welfare program. It was, as Battaglia admitted in those days, very complicated. The biggest portion of the state's spending went for education—$1.7 billion. If there was, as the administration believed, fat in every layer of government, why not cut this? The law forbade economy cuts in state aid to local education in a special provision that was designed to prevent just such reductions. The law required state support to local schools to increase as the population went up, and the formula demanded that the state add $40 million more in 1967 to the $1.1 billion already set aside for local elementary schools and junior colleges, just to meet the needs of a growing population, 4.9 million of whom were between the ages of five and seventeen.

In the opinion of most economy-minded legislators—Democrats and Republicans—there was no way to make immediate substantial reductions in the cost of California government. All that could be done was to make existing programs more efficient, eliminate a few luxurious schemes and put a brake on the growth of government. Reagan was advised by senior government officials to take a long, careful look at government and then make major internal reforms that would not produce immediate results, but have major budget-cutting effects in future years.

There were those in Sacramento with solutions, but these men—knowledgeable Republican legislators and others—were not acceptable to the governor, who had campaigned against professional politicians. Assemblyman John G. Veneman is a Republican rancher from Modesto, in the heart of the San Joaquin Valley where farmers rejected Governor Brown because, in part, they were unhappy over welfare. It must have been a disappointment to Reagan when Veneman said: "I don't see any major cuts in welfare, I just don't see it. Most programs are geared to federal programs, and to say we're going to make major cuts is a little impractical. If we hold the line, we'll be accomplishing quite a bit." At best, Veneman's advice was considered suspect by the administration. He had been one of the most vigorous critics of Reagan during the primary, and his main interest in the election was acting as campaign chairman for Lieutenant Governor Finch.

Reagan seized upon an unlikely place, the state of Ohio, as an example for California to follow. In Ohio four years before, Republican Governor James A. Rhodes had taken over a state that he considered a hopeless financial mess. He cut appropriations by almost 10 percent, dismissed five thousand state workers and put a task force of businessmen to work trying to find ways of cutting government costs. Hotel management men went to prisons and state hospitals and suggested more efficient methods for these institutions, using their own experience of providing for overnight guests. It was a dramatic, easy-to-understand way of reducing the costs of state government, and in the past, Rhodes's finance director, Richard Krabach, had offered advice to Republican governors Dan Evans of Washington and George Romney of Michigan. He now was willing to help Reagan.

In mid-December, Battaglia, Reed and Nofziger flew with Reagan to a meeting of Republican governors in Colorado Springs, Colorado, heard Krabach, and as Reed recalls it, decided to go ahead with the Ohio plan the following week. It was the easiest, most direct way of solving the pressing fiscal problems—but not, in the opinion of government employees working with finance, the most satisfactory. In the first place, Ohio was the wrong example for California. The level of its services was below that of California; it had none of the problems caused by the size and diversity of California, or by its population; Ohio was not committed to as high a level of state support for public schools or to tuition-free higher education. Ohio State University, with its five-hundred-dollar-a-semester tuition, did not have the academic prestige of the University of California.

Interested in learning more about the new model for the administration, the Sacramento *Bee,* a newspaper that had strongly opposed Reagan's election and been among his most bitter opponents ever since, sent a reporter to Ohio to learn about the state. "California is so far ahead in development of modern state services, I would have thought Ohio would turn to you for experience," he was told by Dr. James Robinson, professor of political science at Ohio State University. "If you want to be thirty-seventh in education, forty-ninth in mental health and forty-second in public welfare, follow the Rhodes plan," said a Democratic state senator, Charles J. Carney of Youngstown.

The Brown administration liked to brag that California was number one, although in some categories the boast wasn't true. But state services in California were significantly better than those in Ohio. California's welfare payment of $46.09 a month per person for families without fathers was fourth in the nation. Ohio's $30.21 was thirty-first. The *Bee* also found that Ohio pays only 25.2 percent of the income for local schools, which compares poorly to the 38.7 percent in California. The more money the state pays to a local school district, the less the local property taxpayers must pay. What is more important, state aid equalizes differences between rich and poor school districts. This means a great deal to the resident of a poor or middle-class area with a low tax base. It is not so important to wealthy neighborhoods, where the tax base is high. In 1966 Paul Briggs, Cleveland's superintendent of schools, illustrated what this means in testimony before the United States Civil Rights Commission. He said his city could spend only $418 a year per student, while nearby Shaker Heights, which he called "the seventh wealthiest city in America," spent $883.

So impressed were Reed and Battaglia with Ohio's plan and with Krabach that they asked him if he wanted the California finance director's job. He expressed interest but said he would accept only for a short time, the first one hundred days or so. Reagan was looking for someone more permanent. He had first offered the important position to A. Alan Post, the respected legislative analyst, and had been turned down. Now he was looking outside the government for some ideas. His choice would be one of the most important decisions of his administration. The finance director, who is paid $30,319 a year, prepares the budget and has a great deal to say about the day-to-day government operations through his control of spending. The unofficial advisers had been placed on a task force to find men for some of the top jobs of the new administration, and their first assignment was to find a director of finance. It took more than a month. "If Mr. Reagan was seeking a $15,000-a-year man, there would be no trouble," a spokesman said at the time. "The trouble is he is seeking a $100,000-a-year man."

The subcommittee, with attorney William French Smith acting as executive vice-chairman, asked for help from some of the management consultant firms that assist industry in filling top jobs. The four firms were Price Waterhouse and Company, Booz Allen and Hamilton, John McKenzie and Associates and Cresap McCormick and Paget. Several business executives were asked but turned down the offer. Attorney Smith was impressed with Gordon Paul Smith, an executive of Booz Allen and Hamilton. Gordon Smith was an energetic bantam, five foot five, who, like Reagan, had a photographic memory. He was a supersalesman in a new industry, that of private consulting firms who advise governments on complex projects. Does a city need a new airport? It signs a contract with one of these consulting firms, which then determines whether the city can afford the project and how it can best be financed and built. Gordon Smith said he was interested in the job. Although he said he was earning three times as much as the finance director is paid, he thought he would like to enter public service. Attorney Smith called Salvatori, who invited the new prospect to his home that evening for an after-work drink. Salvatori liked him, and the next day he had him to breakfast with Tuttle and Schreiber. Smith, now a favored choice, was added to a final list of prospects, and Reagan picked him.

Smith's knowledge of government was greater by far than any of Reagan's personal staff members. But according to Reed, Smith did not provide the answer the Reagan administration chose for its fiscal woes—the Ohio-style budget cuts. He was not appointed until December 15, a few days after the weekend of the governor's conference when Battaglia, Reed and Nofziger talked with Krabach. By the time Smith moved into the finance director's office and settled behind the pleasantly antique desk Champion had used, said Reed, the decision had been made and Smith had only to carry it out. Policy was to be made in the governor's office, not in the finance director's office as had been done under Brown. That usurpation of power was later to irritate Smith, who always claimed credit for the 10 percent cuts, and almost forced him into resigning.

The job now was to put the 10 percent cuts into effect. The administration quickly ran into difficulty because such across-the-board reductions were unsuited for government in California. Hale Champion, Brown's finance director, is a prejudiced witness, an ousted official eager to defend his record. But in this case his criticism of the 10 percent cuts has some validity. He was asked if he would have used that approach if he were a finance chief with a mandate to economize. "I would never make across-the-board cuts," he said. "There are different departments, doing different kinds of jobs. A 10 percent cut hits an efficiently run department and destroys it." The across-the-board cuts were doomed for another reason. Only one state fund was short of money, the largest one, the general fund, financed by general taxes. Other important services are financed by other funds, supported by special taxes. Gasoline taxes, for example, are set aside for the highway construction program, and this substantial revenue must be used only for highways. Thus a 10 percent cut applied to the highway department could do nothing toward solving Reagan's immediate financial problem because, by law, the money could be used for nothing else. It only would have the effect of slowing up needed road construction.

Despite its weaknesses, the announcement of across-the-board 10 percent cuts offered Reagan definite public-relations advantages. It allowed him to submit a budget lower than Brown's final request of the year before. That first $4.62 billion budget was hailed by Reagan as an example of the administration's determination to cut costs. In the budget's 1,007 pages, every department's spending program had this notation: "Less 10 percent reduction." The department of the youth authority, efficiently run and hard put to handle the more than 6,000 youthful offenders in institutions and the 15,741 on parole, was slashed 10 percent. The same standard was used for some of the most inefficient and unimportant departments. Administration officials explained that these were just goals, that another budget would be set up later with more money for departments that proved they needed more. They were correct. Two months later Reagan submitted a second budget of upward to $5.06 billion, and the 10 percent cuts he had hoped for had gone down to an average of slightly more than 6 percent. The legislature increased the budget, but Reagan trimmed it down again to $5.08 billion by cutting their appropriations. "I just want to say that this administration came in on an economy platform," said Reagan, "and we do not take the promises we made lightly."

The budget that received the most attention from the public was the first one—with the 10 percent cuts. This helped establish Reagan's image as an economizer. Even though the original low figure was discarded, a booklet boasting of Reagan's achievements in his first eight months of office dutifully referred to it and said the governor had made "the largest cut ever made in a state budget."

There were some budget plans that seemed more attuned to attracting publicity than reducing state expenses. Some were absurd. On February 6, 1967, Battaglia, on behalf of Reagan, sent out a memorandum asking the state's 169,000 civil servants to work on two state holidays, Washington's Birthday and Lincoln's Birthday. Battaglia explained that it would give them a chance to catch up on work at no extra cost to the state—joining Reagan and other top administration officials who planned to come in on the holidays. Only 2 percent showed up. State officials said privately that Battaglia didn't have the authority to issue such a memorandum, that only the finance director could make the request. The same objection was made to another Battaglia memorandum, banning out-of-state trips unless he specifically authorized them. Friends of Finance Director Smith said he became increasingly unhappy with Battaglia during this period.

Other cuts were more serious. In March, 1967, Reagan eliminated 3,700 jobs in the mental hygiene department, cutting deeply into the ranks of psychiatric technicians who care for the patients and maintenance workers. Treatment clinics in four cities were closed. Reagan said the population of the hospitals had dropped from 34,191 to 27,130 in four years while the staff had remained the same. But Dr. Robert Spratt, superintendent of Napa State Hospital for the mentally ill, indicated he thought Reagan had missed the point. He said that the decline in the number of patients had permitted intensive care of more patients. "It was always recognized," he said "that as the number of patients decreased, the staffing would not be reduced so that eventually all patients could receive intensive treatment. We've never reached that point, and now the cut in staff will have to come from the intensive-treatment wards." What would happen, he said, was that the hospitals would become custodial institutions, and in the long run it would cost the state more.

At DeWitt State Hospital, the home of 1,053 mentally retarded and 704 mentally ill, a psychiatric technician told how the budget cuts affected the ward where she cared for mentally ill women. "We have two people on duty today to take care of thirty-two patients. There were supposed to be three, but one person is gone." Last year, she said, "we used to put dresses on them and fix their hair and care for them like people should be cared for. Now when we get them out of bed we leave them in their nightgowns."

As in other departments, Reagan's achievements in the mental health department were overly publicized economies that struck government like a dull axe, saving money in the short run but falling short of making lasting changes. He closed no hospitals for the mentally ill, but reduced the staffs in all of them. Legislative analyst Post, just as dedicated to economy as Reagan, had proposed a more lasting reform —he suggested closing down the two most inefficient hospitals and expanding local mental health clinics so more of the ill could move out of the hospitals and be treated close to home. Post's plan—which Reagan rejected—might have saved more money in the long run by cutting down the hospital population sharply. By decreasing the institutional staffs Reagan saved money in a single year, but took no permanent steps to reduce the numbers of patients in the hospitals.

Throughout the state government maintenance was postponed, car purchases put off, construction canceled, and other steps taken to show an immediate reduction in the budget. But one day the cars would have to be bought and the new buildings put up, and so there was no long-range saving. The fundamental structure of government had not been changed. There were no internal reforms, and so there was no guarantee that when Reagan left office, spending would not zoom again.

The Creative Society had become bogged down in worrisome details. The public was unaware of this, and Reagan himself was convinced he was carrying out his pledges. On April 4, 1967, he was good-natured when he was asked by reporters to comment on his first hundred days. "I had been led to believe there was a honeymoon period," he said, "but evidently I lost the license on the way to the church because I haven't had any honeymoon for a hundred days. I would think that probably the greatest characteristic of the one hundred days has been the surprise of a number of people who almost accused me of breaking political union rules in that I did attempt to carry out campaign promises.

"I didn't know that you weren't supposed to do that."

CHAPTER ELEVEN

A CITIZEN POLITICIAN MEETS THE PROFESSIONALS

GASLIGHTS FLICKERED on the walls of the garish red and gold room that houses the state senate of California. It was an unusual arena for the biggest triumph of Ronald Reagan's first year as governor, but this was where victory came, amid the gaudy splendor reminiscent of a luxurious Gay Nineties house of prostitution. Only the desks and state seal woven into the red and gold carpet were evidence that this room was a solemn chamber of state government. And they were hardly noticed among the red shutters, the red and gold marble columns topped by gold leaf and the big senatorial chairs covered in bright blue. The politicians who were members of the inner circle of the senate had spent $100,000 of the taxpayers' money two years before to redecorate the room to their own tastes, which ran to shiny silk suits, two-tone shoes. and martini and steak sandwich lunches paid for by special-interest representatives. It looked like proof—in living color—of Reagan's campaign charge that,

"They've been in power so long, these professional politicians, that we're beginning to see a degeneration of moral
standards."

This was the den of the enemy, and it was here that Reagan
would send his lieutenants in July, 1967, to bargain and
trade for passage of the most important bill of his administration, a measure he needed to make his first year a success. It
would levy the largest tax increase in the history of any
state, increasing taxes $944 million in 1967 and $1.01 billion
in 1968. Passage of the tax bill would provide a test of
Reagan's fitness for high office. Success would give him
leisure to travel and participate in national politics. Failure
would keep him at home trying to raise money to pay for
the running of the government, dogged by the local difficulties that have overcome other governors. The tax bill
was especially important to Reagan now because of the
troubles that had overtaken the rest of his legislative program. Many of the bills he had requested had been rejected
by the Democratic-controlled legislature. Even some of his
own Republicans had deserted him and left bills buried in
committee. A few weeks before, Nofziger had correctly stated
that a defeat on the tax bill would hurt Reagan's national
reputation.

Part of the administration's difficulties was expressed correctly one lunch hour in Posey's Cottage, a restaurant a
block away from the capitol, when a red-faced, beefy senator,
Randolph Collier, looked up and said: "They won't get
eight votes for the [tax increase] bill." They needed twenty-
seven in the senate, the two-thirds majority required for a
financial bill. The main problem was the Republican party's
failure to win control of the senate and the assembly when
Reagan was elected governor. As big as his triumph was, it
did not carry along enough candidates to take over the legis-

lature. If all the votes given to the Republican legislative candidates in November, 1966, had been totaled, they would have exceeded the Democratic votes. But these representatives are elected from districts, and a Democratic reapportionment had drawn the individual districts so skillfully that the Democrats still managed to hold on to the assembly forty-two to thirty-eight. In the senate, reapportionment allowed the Democrats to remain in control twenty to nineteen, despite the midsession death of one of the most influential Democratic senators, J. Eugene McAteer of San Francisco. But Democrats held back from using this majority to openly challenge Reagan. His victory of almost a million votes frightened them. Instead they decided to fight a holding action, preserving the liberal programs they had created under Governor Brown and limiting Reagan's retrenchments.

By simple mathematics, Reagan needed Democratic votes if any of his programs were to become law. Without Democratic support he would have nothing to show for his first year as governor. But for most of the legislative session he had refused to negotiate. And until his need for the tax bill, he had not come to terms with the most powerful man in the legislature, Jesse Unruh, the Democratic speaker of the assembly. That was another reason for Reagan's troubles.

At forty-four, Unruh was one of the most pre-eminent state legislators in the United States. During the 1960 Presidential campaign he had been John F. Kennedy's man in California, and after Kennedy's assassination he gave his loyalty to no one else. With Brown defeated, Unruh waited for a chance to move on to higher office. But sometimes he looked back on his childhood as the son of a poor Texas sharecropper, afraid, a friend said, "that he'd wake up one day and find out he was going around without underpants again." He was built like a football guard, a powerful-looking man with a thick neck and broad shoulders. When he had come to the legislature thirteen years before, he had weighed about two hundred eighty pounds and was called "Big Daddy" after the domineering father in Tennessee Williams' play *Cat on a Hot Tin Roof*. He quickly acquired power in the legislature and in the political life of southern California. As speaker he had jealously fought Brown, convinced he was more qualified to be chief executive. The fighting hurt both men and left Unruh with the reputation of a bully. With the determination of a poor boy who would not be denied fame, he worked to repair his image, dieting away almost one hundred pounds, swearing off political brawls and building a legislative program upon which he could one day run for higher office. He acquired polish, grace and skill and now lectured at Rutgers, Yale, Berkeley and other campuses. But occasionally he would slip into an auditorium and hear a cowboy band. Western-music fans cheered him as one of their own when he was introduced at a concert in Sacramento.

Unruh ruled the assembly with the same sort of strength and guile that Lyndon B. Johnson had used in the United States Senate in the fifties. In the next few months, the relationship between Reagan and Unruh would often resemble Johnson's relationship with another Republican chief executive, President Eisenhower. Like Johnson, Unruh was afraid to challenge the popular chief executive publicly. Sometimes he would even work with him. But in private he yearned for the governorship and cursed the fate that had given it to Reagan.

In the past few years Unruh had spent much of his time trying to improve the image of the professional politicians in the legislature. Neither he nor the other legislators liked Reagan's attacks on professional politicians. For despite the senate's gaudy decor and the remnants of lobbyist control, the

California legislature had become one of the nation's best in recent years. In 1966 a *Saturday Evening Post* article on state house corruption had singled out California for praise, saying that the legislature "has shown ability and willingness to initiate."

Only two decades before, the stench of corruption was heavy in Sacramento. It was still the era of the "cinch" bill, a peculiar measure directed against a specific industry or group. Once he had introduced it, the author would wait patiently for the industry to pay him off, and then he would drop the bill. In those days, the assembly public morals committee took its orders from the most famous of the California lobbyists, Arthur L. Samish, the fat representative of liquor, beer and race track interests. Meeting in a hot, overcrowded little room, with its members underpaid and ill-informed, the committee waited for instructions from Samish's messengers before making decisions. So powerful was Samish that he even mocked California's popular and respected governor, Earl Warren. Warren might be governor of the state, said Samish, but "I am governor of the legislature." Samish's boasting finally resulted in an investigation, and he was sent to jail for income tax evasion.

The legislature had cleaned up and gained self-respect since then. It had added, for example, a new twist to the inevitable conflicts between the executive and legislative branches. Instead of merely obstructing the governor's programs, it proposed alternatives. The assembly, tired of Governor Brown's inaction, investigated the complexities of treating the mentally retarded and then pushed through a reform plan. An assembly committee found that elderly people were being forced into mental hospitals without trial on often erroneous grounds that they were senile. The executive department wouldn't act, so the committee drew up a "bill of rights" for the mentally ill; they pushed it through and Reagan signed it. A few years earlier, while Governor Brown and industry were congratulating themselves on a booming economy, the assembly ways and means committee took a skeptical look. With the figures in their own research, they found that the state was too heavily dependent on defense spending and gloomily, but correctly, stated: "Space and defense industries are ill fit to convert output to civilian demand."

Unruh believed in equipping legislators with a capable staff, so they would no longer have to rely on lobbyists for much of their advice. He supplied assemblymen with more help to free them from the time-consuming job of answering mail from their constituents. Fringe benefits were improved. With Unruh's help the legislature became so independent that the assembly sent its own lobbyist to Washington to round up federal support of its projects. Finally, in 1966, the voters recognized the legislature's new status and voted the senators and assemblymen a $10,000-a-year pay raise in exchange for legislative acceptance of the nation's strictest legislative conflict-of-interest rules.

These men did not forget Reagan's past criticisms, and although he tried to mix with them, he found it difficult to participate in the back-slapping camaraderies of politicians. They found him pleasant, quick-witted, humorous—and remote. "He makes an effort to be one of the boys, but never lets the bars down," said someone who had watched him at the regular parties he and his wife gave for small groups of legislators. "Meanwhile the legislators are running around acting like legislators, drinking, baring their souls, talking."

Another reason for Reagan's problems was the old division between moderate and more conservative Republicans, a split that was evident among G.O.P. legislators. The moderates did not agree that the Creative Society was the only answer to California's problems, and while they carefully kept their disagreements to themselves, they were reluctant to help the governor.

Reagan was not, however, without advantages. The first was his big vote, the evidence of a popular mandate. Another was the nature of party politics in California. The Democratic control of the legislature was, in a sense, a mathematical deception. In Sacramento, as elsewhere, the representatives paid more attention to the wishes of their constituents than to the orders of party leaders. In California, party leadership was weak. "There is no Democratic party in California," Unruh once said. Hiram Johnson and the progressive reformers had wrecked party strength when they threw out the political bosses in 1910. The direct primary replaced conventions. And to weaken the party structure even more, candidates were permitted to "cross file": that meant they could seek the nomination of their party and the other party at the same time. Many times, candidates would win both the Democratic and Republican nominations. This blurred party lines and gave an advantage to the candidate best known to voters, the incumbent. Democrats eliminated cross filing in 1959, but official party organizations remained weak, unable to exert pressure on legislators. In the assembly, Unruh could influence votes, but even he had to respect the pressures from local districts. A Democrat coming from a suburban district whose residents—concerned with taxes, Negro militancy and crime—voted for Reagan in 1966 would not quarrel publicly with the governor. To do so would invite the possibility of defeat.

Reagan knew his political problems could be overcome, and his tax increase approved, if he could come to terms with Unruh. Unruh not only had control of the assembly, but he held a balance of power in the senate. Some senators were his friends, and had been helped by campaign contributions he had directed their way. And, strangely enough, Unruh's ambition forced him into an alliance with Reagan. For Reagan and Unruh had something in common. Both understood that political advancement in California depended on the votes of the growing white middle class of conservative suburbanites. Unruh needed an issue to win these people away from the Republicans, to make them realize that their economic interests—a determining factor in their vote—rested with him, not Reagan. Unlike Reagan, he could not appeal to them with veiled criticisms of the civil rights movement or promises of a drastic reduction in welfare costs. That would have been contrary to Unruh's basic beliefs, and would have lost him the support of minorities in the Democratic party. Instead, he decided to appeal to the pocketbooks of the middle class. He would shape the tax bill to his own taste, make sure the governor was blamed for the big increase —and take credit himself for whatever was popular in the plan. His approach was devious. In exchange for his support he would force Reagan to eliminate a big surplus in the bill, a surplus Reagan had hoped would take him through his entire administration without another tax increase. Unruh would have the surplus put in a special new fund to finance reductions in local property taxes—and then take public credit for creating the fund. In addition, Unruh had a suspicion that the administration had underestimated its spending, and that in the following year Reagan would either have to ask for another tax increase or try to get back some of the surplus money Unruh wanted to put in the tax relief fund. In short, he was putting together what he hoped would be a time bomb under the Reagan administration.

Shortly before the vote on the tax bill, Reagan and Unruh

talked for an hour in Reagan's office. This was not a meeting place of Unruh's choosing. He liked to deal in his own office, safely seated behind his desk, in a room decorated with Kennedy mementos and souvenirs of trips to the Orient and Europe. But the protocol of government required him to go downstairs, be ushered into Reagan's office and sit across from the governor. It was Reagan who seemed irritable. He made a strong statement in favor of his version of the tax bill. He insisted on paying back a $194 million debt from the Brown administration. He also wanted to put a tax on such services as shoeshines and auto repairs, but Unruh told him: "Your tax on services is so incredibly bad that I'm tempted to keep it in the program, but in the interests of good government, I'll take it out."

In the middle of the conversation Reagan interrupted and gave Unruh a lecture on the economy of the nation and the state. It seemed unnecessary to Unruh, who operated an economic consulting business as a sideline. But he listened politely until someone changed the subject and the conversation returned to the tax bill.

Unruh and Reagan finally agreed on terms for a bill. Unruh promised to speed the bill through the assembly, and then help Reagan round up votes in the senate. There was an unexpectedly tense moment in the assembly. Democrats refused to vote for the tax increase until every Republican voted first. One first-year Republican refused, and it took personal persuasion from Reagan to change his mind.

The assembly vote was a preliminary step before the real drama—the fight in the senate. This was where Reagan's aides would meet their greatest test. They went upstairs to the senate chamber, following the same path Reagan had taken six months before on the day he delivered the budget message. The intervening months had taught the four assistants much about government, and they were ready for the administration's most crucial day. Battaglia—now with so much influence that some of Reagan's other friends jealously called him "Governor Battaglia"—led the group. He was followed by Vernon Sturgeon, an aide who, until his defeat the year before, had been a favored member of the senate. There was also Jack Lindsay, an assistant with the looks, enthusiasm and lack of sophistication of a junior chamber of commerce president, and Paul Beck, the glowering, dark-complexioned press secretary—a former reporter who always seemed guiltily ill at ease when confronting his ex-colleagues of the press corps in the heat of daily battle. They greeted the sergeant at arms and walked into the chamber. Unruh soon joined them. He walked down the hall and through the big wooden doors that guarded the colorful room. Reagan wasn't in the capitol. After sending his troops into the fight, he had flown south to have a bladder stone and a nonmalignant growth on his lip removed.

In the need for victory, the Reagan men forgot all the old campaign promises of no political deals. Where once the administration scorned legislators' appeals for patronage, they now listened. Through his aides, the governor asked recalcitrant senators if they wanted to make a deal. Several, rebuffed for months, were delighted, and Battaglia, standing quietly in back of the senate chamber, talked to them. One senator was told that Reagan would now sign his appropriation bill, despite the administration's economy goals. Two more were told that, by coincidence, the men they were backing for judgeships would now get the appointments. Power was also used. The legislature's only member of the John Birch Society, John Schmitz, whose conservative constituency provided some of Reagan's most enthusiastic and wealthy supporters, refused to vote for the tax increase. Brought into a side room by Battaglia, Schmitz was told that every one of his bills would be vetoed if he refused Reagan a vote. He wouldn't surrender.

Despite Schmitz' refusal, the bill passed and was flown to Reagan's hospital room where he signed it the next day.

Reagan's political maneuvering was resented in the senate, where Battaglia was ordered off the floor just before the vote. And Unruh so offended the old-guard senate leadership by the way he went from desk to desk calling in old debts that Chairman George Miller of the senate finance committee later said: "I am sickened by the presence of this little Nero on our floor. Let him restrict his wheeling and dealing and politicking to his own den and befoul his own aisles." Looking back on it, one of the participants in delicate negotiations remarked: "It was the first time the Reagan administration showed any signs of any normal wheeler-dealer ability."

The victory was, in a sense, a triumph of Reagan's innate political ability over the rigid, cumbersome system he had set up for running the government, a system better suited to a conservative, slow-moving corporation. All of his information, for example, flowed through the cabinet secretary, who turned it over to Reagan in the mini-memos. The governor examined them for the first time in half-hour sessions, and that finished the work. "One of the ground rules is we leave nothing on his desk as we go out," said Cabinet Secretary William Clark. "More often than not, he puts what has become the trademark around here—OK-RR—on the bottom of the memos. I take the originals and they are filed away in our minute books." As Clark saw it, business should be conducted during office hours and not over dinners or at cocktail parties. Icy, methodical, fond of making rules and sticking to them, Clark didn't believe in the after-hours conferences and give-and-take that are part of politics and government.

In one important case earlier in the legislative year, information was so slow in reaching the governor that his administration almost met with disaster. The issue was a bill liberalizing a ninety-five-year-old law that permitted abortions only to save a woman's life, and no issue caused a bigger dispute during Reagan's first year in office. So badly did he handle it that he ended up doing the impossible—he antagonized both the doctors and churchmen who were supporting the reform and the Roman Catholic Church which opposed it. For a while he seemed to be doing his best to kill the reform and please the opponents who were writing him at least one hundred letters a day. But in the end he angered the Catholics by signing it, and when the fight was over, he had only one souvenir—a picture of himself putting his signature on the bill after a day of confused indecision. As a critic commented, the widely printed picture would quickly go on the bulletin board of some Catholic churches at election time.

Although abortion reform had been an issue in California for years, it became more important in 1966 when a state board charged nine respected San Francisco physicians with unprofessional conduct for aborting women who had contracted German measles in the early months of pregnancy. The ailment can result in the birth of a deformed child. Before the action, many legitimate physicians had been performing abortions in German measles cases, with the unofficial approval of their hospital surgical boards. The fight for reform of the law was taken up by one of the young men who had been responsible for the improved quality of the legislature, Senator Anthony C. Beilenson, a Democrat from Beverly Hills. He had introduced the reform in the past, but had been laughed at as a dreamer. Now, with the charges pending against the San Francisco doctors and the enactment of abortion reforms in Colorado and North Carolina, his chances looked brighter. But first Beilenson needed Republican support, for Democrats were split.

As it turned out, Republicans would not back the bill either. Reagan informed senate Republicans that he would not support it because he did not approve of the German measles section aimed at preventing the birth of a potentially deformed child. He said: "I cannot justify morally . . . taking of the unborn life simply on the supposition that it is going to be less than a perfect human being, because I don't see very far . . . from that to some day deciding after birth that we will sort out those people who should be allowed to live or not, and I don't see any difference between that and what Hitler tried to do." He approved, however, the provision allowing abortions to prevent pregnancies caused by rape or incest or to prevent a birth that, in the judgment of a panel of physicians, would gravely impair the mental or physical health of the mother. Beilenson agreed to Reagan's changes, and Republicans were free to vote for the bill. It narrowly passed the senate.

When the liberalization law reached the assembly, Reagan unexpectedly started another fight. On the morning of the assembly debate he said he had new objections. The deal he had made with Beilenson was now off, and he would not support the bill unless new changes were made. Opponents, expecting assembly passage, were suddenly given new hope. Their last-minute attempt to kill the bill appeared to be succeeding. One of the opponents had, through Battaglia, placed in the governor's hands a legal opinion declaring that there was a loophole in the bill. Possibly, the opinion said, abortions could be used to prevent the birth of a potentially deformed child, despite the Reagan revisions. A doctor could evade the intent of the law by convincing a supervising panel of physicians that the birth of such a baby would injure the mental or physical health of the mother. The information in this legal opinion should have reached Reagan days before. But it came late and was a complete surprise to him.

How did Reagan explain his ignorance of the implications of the bill? "For one thing," he told reporters at his weekly news conference, "I've been out of the city and I've only just received an analysis from the legislative counsel." Television cameras, as usual, were recording the weekly meeting with newsmen. Reagan usually sparkled during these sessions, but this time he was not prepared. "These are fast-moving days," he said, "and I have been—I left the city Friday morning, and I've been involved in other activities. I haven't been vacationing. I've been pretty busy and just arrived back. . . . There are some five thousand bills or so up there, and we have had frequent meetings and do keep as close contact as possible, and I don't think there has been any lapse at all." Obviously there had been a lapse in the information given the governor by his staff; when the possible loophole in the bill had been debated in the senate two weeks before, Reagan either had not heard of it or had not understood its implications. The blame had to fall upon the governor's isolation from outside contacts and news and the inherent inadequacy of the mini-memos.

Beilenson was furious at Reagan's latest hesitations. So was the Republican who was his floor manager for the bill in the assembly, Craig Biddle. Further amendment would have the effect of killing the bill. The senate was required to approve the amendments, and there was little chance that senators, having voted for the bill once, would risk criticism by voting for it again. The issue was too controversial.

But as it turned out, the assembly paid no attention to

Reagan. Biddle opposed Reagan's changes and informed his fellow assemblymen that Reagan had promised him "he would sign it in its present form." In a rare open Republican break with the governor, he told the assembly it was its duty "to pass legislation of this house" no matter what the governor said. Biddle and other Republicans joined Democrats in approving the bill forty-eight to twenty-nine without the amendments Reagan had asked for. When Reagan signed it, he smiled dutifully for photographers while Biddle and Beilenson stood next to him. He jokingly threatened not to sign the bill before he finally wrote his signature at the bottom. To refuse would have caused a deep split between him and the Republican legislators who had voted for the bill. With the bill now law, they were satisfied.

Reagan had liked to criticize his predecessor, Governor Brown, for being indecisive, but Reagan's own wavering on the abortion bill showed that he too had difficulty in making up his mind on an emotional issue. For the first time he was faced with a problem that did not fit the neat partisan pattern to which he had grown accustomed. The debate cut across party lines, and with his surprise objections, Reagan antagonized both conservative Republicans and liberal Democrats. Several special-interest groups who had been following the bill were angry and disappointed. The matter was, however, more a topic of conversation in the capitol than anywhere else—something for insiders to speculate about. Public opinion polls showed his popularity high, and none of the legislators who complained privately about him would challenge him in public. The mistakes might hurt him later, but for the present even Unruh held back from fighting Reagan in the open. The strength of his mandate was shown a few months later, when every single Republican legislator

stood behind him and defeated Democratic attempts to over-
turn his vetoes of more than $30 million in appropriations—
including money for some Republican projects.

Reagan faltered on the abortion bill, but he showed he
could deal with political realities on the tax bill—which was
vital to the success of his first year in office. He could compromise with his enemies. He would boldly announce a
controversial program, quietly modify it in the face of
criticism and then hail the compromise as a complete victory.
He was described as " a man who charges up a hill in the
daytime and retreats under the cover of darkness"—a description that irritated him. "You can't win," he said. "You set
your feet in concrete and say: 'Here I stand or fall'; then you
are being stubborn and unreasonable. You try to indicate the
world is a fallible place. You do your best and you make
decisions on certain facts, but you try to keep yourself with
an open mind."

The adoption of the philosophy of the "open mind" was
an important development in Reagan's political career. His
willingness to negotiate with his foes on the bill that was most
important to his administration and his ability to get it
through the legislature provided arguments for his supporters
who contended he was not another Goldwater; he was not
bound to a rigid conservative philosophy that he would not
modify. Reagan's new ability to compromise made him
appear more moderate—and more acceptable as a potential
candidate for President.

CHAPTER TWELVE

SOME HUMAN ISSUES

Forty-fifth Street in Sacramento—where Ronald Reagan lives—is more than one hundred miles from the death chamber of San Quentin Prison, but in April of 1967 this street became a part of the intense drama of California's first execution in four years. The houses here are showcases, with broad yards graced by sweeping lawns and beautiful gardens, and shaded by tall trees. Surrounded by the flat Sacramento Valley, the builders of the homes had turned elsewhere for architectural inspiration. One of the homes is an imitation of a pink Mediterranean-style mansion, flanked by baby palm trees. Another is made of gray stone and looks like a castle. One is a southern mansion with tall columns in front, resembling Tara, Scarlett O'Hara's home in the movie *Gone with the Wind*. The home the Reagans had leased is in the style of an English Tudor country house, of bricks painted white. A garden extends back to the next block, and a big swimming pool is the centerpiece of the back yard. Although U.S. 50, the crowded transcontinental highway, is nearby, Forty-fifth Street is isolated from the rest of the city by the high cost of its homes and by tradition, which reserves it for the old, established families of Sacramento. It is a patch of wealth amid blocks of middle-income homes—inward-looking, rich and Republican. No Negroes live there.

This street was built for ease, comfort and peace and quiet. But on the night before the execution, demonstrators were there, one hundred men and women walking up and down the street, carrying signs and candles in silent protest of the governor's refusal to grant clemency. Barricades were at either end of the street, placed there earlier in the evening by police intent on stopping automobiles of the curious. The governor had some supporters, too. They were young people of college and high school age who heckled the marchers and tried to crowd them off the sidewalk, but policemen separated the groups. Neighbors watched from their front lawns in disapproving silence.

Demonstrations before executions are not new in California. Governor Brown faced them when he reluctantly allowed men to die in the gas chamber. He upheld the death penalty law even though he didn't share Reagan's belief in its value. Brown often tried to persuade the legislature to repeal the death penalty and was regarded by the public as one of the state's most outspoken opponents of capital punishment. He was a former district attorney of San Francisco and was attorney general of California before becoming governor, but he believed the death penalty did not deter crime and felt that only the poor went to the gas chamber. Those with more money could hire skillful lawyers to save their lives. Reagan believed that executions prevented some crimes and he made the death penalty a political issue in his campaign against Brown, pointing out that there had been no executions in four years. Most had been postponed because of court decisions, although Brown granted clemency in some cases. Reagan implied—and many voters believed—that Brown was to blame for all the delays, and when condemned men overflowed their quarters in San Quentin State Prison and new cells were built, Reagan complained that the executions had been put off so long that there was a need for an "urban renewal project on death row."

Thus, even though Brown had allowed murderers to be executed, his reputation was that of a man too soft to let a killer die. Reagan's decision to allow this execution was a symbolic act to the voters, an indication that Brown's grudging acceptance of the death penalty would be replaced by a willingness to use it as a direct answer to crime in the streets.

The demonstrators outside Reagan's house were hostile. They thought the governor, in allowing the condemned man to die, was carrying out the wishes of the middle-class white constituency and that the execution was a symbol of bigger changes that were on the way. They feared radical changes in social policy, with crime and violence being treated as serious offenses against the law instead of symptoms of deeper social ills. The demonstrators were correct. Social policy had been changed, and there was a tough attitude against crime. Generous aid to Negro slums had been slowed. Reagan was attempting to repeal or modify the open-housing law to calm white fears of Negroes moving into their neighborhoods. A campaign had been launched against welfare fraud, with the administration hinting that it was a widespread offense.

Reagan had repeatedly made it clear he would use the death penalty. He stressed the point strongly early in his term in a meeting with five officials of the American Civil Liberties Union of southern California, a session that provided a rare view of the intensity of his feelings. The five men were escorted into the governor's big meeting room rather than his private office. At the outset, Reagan said he was familiar with the issue and had, in fact, debated it while a young man in school. One member of the group said he was concerned by some of Reagan's campaign statements that had indicated he would rely on the court's verdicts in death penalty cases. Reagan replied that the statement was incorrect, that he would overrule the courts if the facts warranted it. Then the conversation turned to a general discussion of the worth of the death penalty. To counter the arguments of the civil libertarians who opposed capital punishment, Reagan related the details of one of the most macabre cases in California criminal annals and then asked his visitors how they would treat the killers in that case without the death penalty. One of those at the meeting recalled listening in surprised silence while the governor graphically described the crime, which involved the sexual mutilation of the male victim.

There were no sexual aberrations involved in the case of the man whose execution was now being protested on Forty-fifth Street. It involved a crime particularly relevant to the times and to the smoldering war between blacks and whites in the big cities. It was the case of Aaron Mitchell, a Negro who had killed the symbol of authority in the city, a white policeman. Although the condemned man had lived in Sacramento, his surroundings were far removed economically from Forty-fifth Street. He was a laundry worker whose criminal record dated back twenty years and included sentences in state prisons in Missouri and Colorado for auto theft, larceny and assault. In 1963, while on bail from a robbery charge, he slipped through the rear entrance of a neighborhood bar and restaurant with a sawed-off shotgun slung around his neck on a string. He ordered the customers—there were about twenty-five of them—into a corner of the barroom and then fired the shotgun into the ceiling. As the gunsmoke and noise filled the room, Edward Liccardo, one of the owners, sneaked into the kitchen, called the Pacific Telephone operator and told her to summon the police. Mitchell meanwhile ripped out an extension phone, unaware Liccardo was on the other phone. He told the owners to open the safe. They argued for about two minutes and then patrolman John Bibica came in the front door. Mitchell first headed for the front door toward Bibica and then retreated into the kitchen. He saw patrolman Ronald Shaw coming through the back door and yelled: "Drop your gun, I've got you covered." He snatched Shaw's revolver as patrolman Arnold Gamble approached the kitchen door. Mitchell, using Shaw as a shield, moved forward. Witnesses at his trial testified that Mitchell fired four shots from Shaw's revolver. Three missed, but the fourth tore through Gamble's chest and killed him. Gamble had fired four times, and both Mitchell and Shaw were hit, the policeman in the leg.

Mitchell ran out the door, followed by officers Reese and Bibica. Reese fired six shots and Bibica five. They found Mitchell in a shed, wounded four times in his abdomen and chest and once in his right albow. On May 31, 1963, Mitchell was sentenced to death. In 1966, after his case had moved slowly through higher courts, he asked Governor Brown for clemency. Brown unhappily refused the plea, intent on carrying out the law he opposed. But his decision against Mitchell was not remembered by others, and Reagan, campaigning for governor, continued to accuse Brown of refusing "to execute the sentence of the courts."

The complexities of the law gave Mitchell another chance. The state supreme court accepted a second appeal and ordered a new trial. He was sentenced to death again and once more asked the governor for clemency.

This time there was a new governor. Reagan's adviser on

capital punishment cases was Edward Meese III. Meese was a serious young deputy district attorney from Alameda County, across the bay from San Francisco, who had helped direct the police at the University of California the night protesting students were arrested for refusing to leave the student union during the Free Speech Movement demonstrations of 1964. He is hard-working, able, and, in the words of an associate, "a man who has no doubts about the solid virtues of American life, who is convinced there is a right and a wrong." It is a belief he shares with Governor Reagan.

On Tuesday, April 11, Reagan looked at the case for a final time, leaned across his desk to Meese and said: "I think it will be my decision not to intervene." Later that day, Reagan, more solemn than usual, explained his reason to reporters. "In this particular instance the man, the father of two children, who was killed was a policeman. I think that if we are going to ask men to engage in an occupation in which they protect us at the risk of their life, we of society have an obligation to them to let them know that society will do whatever it can to minimize the danger of their occupations. I think any policeman is entitled to that. There are no bands playing or flags flying when he shoots it out with a criminal on our behalf."

Meese attended to the details of carrying out Reagan's decision. He telephoned Mitchell's attorneys and Lawrence Wilson, warden at San Quentin. Later he returned to the governor's office. It was a moment he would long remember. Reagan was upset, talking earnestly to Nofziger. He had agreed earlier to fly south to Anaheim for a civic ceremony and throw out the first baseball for the opening of the California Angels' new stadium. Now, with the condemned man awaiting death, he didn't want to leave Sacramento. But assistants told him that appearing at the new stadium was part of his responsibility as governor, and finally Reagan said: "All right, you tell them I'll go down." He ordered his chartered jet to stand by to return him to Sacramento as soon as the ceremony was finished. Meese said: "I'll meet you at the airport." Reagan replied: "Don't inconvenience yourself. If there's anything new, come out."

Meanwhile, Mitchell, through his mother, had sent a hand-written last appeal to United States District Judge Alphonse J. Zirpoli. As he gave his mother the note, Mitchell said: "Mama, maybe it's too late." She asked her son to sing for her. He sang a spiritual, "I'm Willing to Run All the Way." He told the family minister, the Reverend Samuel Callier of the Faith Temple Church of Deliverance, who had accompanied Mrs. Mitchell, that he felt right with God. Sorrowfully, she delivered the appeal to Zirpoli in San Francisco, but he refused her, saying that only the governor could act now.

Reagan returned home from the baseball stadium before 10 P.M. He had an assistant telephone to the capitol, where Meese was waiting in his office, to find out about Mitchell's condition. That afternoon, after his mother had left, Mitchell had slashed his wrist, and although the wound was not serious, the suicide attempt had been nerve-wracking, dramatizing the agony of the condemned man and making the whole execution process seem more brutal. Meese had talked to Warden Wilson and was able to report that all was under control.

As usual, Reagan went to bed early that night, facing for the first time the pre-execution ordeal so dreaded by his predecessors. On such a night in 1960, Governor Brown sat alone in his study and pondered the case of Caryl Chessman, awaiting death for committing sex crimes against his kidnap victims. Brown's advisers told him to let Chessman die. His conscience insisted that he spare the man, who was not a killer. Brown compromised and gave Chessman a reprieve until the legislature could vote on abolition of the death penalty. When the legislature refused to end capital punishment, Chessman was executed. In later years Brown often talked about the awful burden he carried that night.

Reagan later told a close friend about his emotions the night before Mitchell was to die. He had gotten up and thought about Mitchell. Outside, the marchers still paced back and forth in front of his house. He glanced down at them and asked himself if there was anything more he could have done in the case or if there were any facts he had not considered. Alone with his conscience, he concluded he had done all he could and he returned to bed. "There is no question about it," he said later, "this is one of the worst features of the job. But it must also be just as bad for the judges involved, for the jurors, for all the others who have had to participate in this. It is not an easy task to be the last resort and have to deny clemency."

When morning arrived, the gas chamber was ready. Fifty-eight witnesses, many of them reporters, waited in the beige room that adjoined the "smoke house," as prisoners called the chamber. They heard Mitchell groaning and screaming in his prison cell, twelve feet away. At 10:01 A.M., three guards escorted him into the chamber. He was limp and still groaning. "I'm Jesus Christ," he shouted—words that Warden Wilson said Mitchell often used. "He was quite religiously oriented," Wilson said. Straps were placed around Mitchell's arms, chest, abdomen and legs. One guard patted him on the knee twice as if to reassure him. His head slumped down and then he looked up at the witnesses. At 10:04 A.M., potassium cyanide tablets were dumped into a vat of acid. His chest was racked by spasms; his head bent forward; he exhaled as if he had a dry cough and then his body slumped forward against the straps. At 10:16 A.M. Mitchell was pronounced dead, and Warden Wilson notified Meese by telephone.

Reagan had been waiting in his office. At 10 A.M. he had buzzed Meese on the intercommunications system and asked if there was any word. At 10:18 Meese walked down the hall to Reagan's office and said the execution had been completed. The governor sat silently for a minute and then said "O.K." For a few minutes, neither man said anything. Then some of the tension disappeared and they chatted casually. Before Meese left the office, Reagan once again remarked: "This is about the toughest decision anyone will ever have to make."

It had been a painful but important milestone in Reagan's career. So significant was the execution to the administration that it was listed in the administration's promotional booklet. It told how he "refused to interfere with court decisions on capital punishment except in those cases . . . where clemency appeared appropriate." An adviser was more specific. In telling of Reagan's achievements, he said the execution provided evidence of Reagan's insistence on law and order. Law and order, in the sixties, was a loaded political term to whites who were afraid of Negro defiance of the law. To them it seemed to mean "stamp out Negro militance and violence." In that context the execution of Mitchell touched one of the emotions involved in the white-backlash reaction to Negro riots.

Reagan himself said he never believed there was a white backlash, although his very denial contained criticism of Negro militance. He said backlash may be "nothing more than the concern people have for what has seemed to be on the part of some extremists in the civil rights movement, the taking to the streets the issue of violence, of demonstrations, instead of an orderly process of appealing wrongs through legitimate channels. Now to call this a white backlash, I don't think is fair. I think this is a backlash, if there is such a thing, against this breakdown of law and order. I don't think it is addressed to any particular minority group." His statements appealed to the fears of the white community. "Certainly," he said, "when no city street is safe for our women after dark, we have the right to insist that the victim of crime has rights at least equal to those of the criminal in protection under the law." As for racial disturbances, he said: "I think they have to be met and controlled, and whatever force is necessary to preserve law and order must be exerted." When racial violence broke out in Detroit in July, 1967, Reagan said: "It is very apparent in Detroit right now that these are no longer riots connected with civil rights in any way. These are riots of the lawbreakers and the mad dogs against the people."

Administration policies in other areas were highly approved by whites who resented the Negro drive for equal rights. One of the most sensitive areas was the attempt by more prosperous Negroes to move out of the slums and into more pleasant neighborhoods occupied by whites. At stake were two rights. One was the right of a man to freely spend his money for the property he wished to buy—and obtain the state's protection if someone interfered with him. The other —considered more important by Reagan—was the right of a property owner to dispose of his property as he wished. The state open-housing law, however, protected the right of a citizen—black or white—to live in any home he could afford. Reagan had promised to work for repeal during the campaign. "We all have the responsibility to work to end discrimination and insure equal opportunities for all, including the opportunity for a man to enjoy all the bounty he is able to earn," said Reagan. "But I am opposed to trying to get this with legislation that violates basic tenets of individual freedom."

As one of his first acts as governor, Reagan chose as real estate commissioner a man who backed the campaign for the initiative to nullify the housing law, Burton E. Smith, the former president of the California Real Estate Association. Reagan's position, however, was ambiguous, for he had also supported the Republican party's state platform which asked for either modification or repeal. When the legislature convened in January, Reagan's position remained unclear. William T. Bagley, a Republican assemblyman who had opposed Reagan's nomination but supported him later, introduced a bill to merely modify the law. But Republican John Schmitz of conservative Orange County, a member of the John Birch Society, introduced a bill for repeal. For Reagan a choice between modification and repeal was difficult. To side with Bagley would have angered the real estate association and the Republican party's right wing. But to join those favoring repeal would have been a blow to his tenuous peace with the party's more forward-looking elements.

The decision was just as difficult for the legislature. The senate, with new members from white middle-class suburbs of southern California, was in a mood to repeal the law. And supporters of repeal of the fair housing act had the help of the senate's president pro tem, conservative Democrat Hugh M. Burns, who had fought the Rumford act four years before. At one point the repeal bill was almost approved by a committee, and only an appeal to Burns' pride in the senate prevented it. Senator J. Eugene McAteer of San Francisco told Burns that every major newspaper would carry front-page stories that the senate of California had voted for a bill by a John Birch Society member to repeal the open-housing law—and the senate would be held up to the nation as an example of bigotry. The argument worked for a time, but later Burns took over the authorship of the bill himself, and the senate passed it. At the same time, the assembly passed the bill to modify the law.

Now the pressures within the party were felt in the governor's office. By this time Reagan was in a hospital in Santa Monica recovering from the bladder stone surgery, and Executive Secretary Battaglia had assumed command in such a strong-minded way that others on Reagan's staff were irritated. He made no secret about the fact that he was opposed to repeal and wanted some sort of compromise that would leave the law weakened, but still on the books. F. Jackson Pontius, lobbyist for the real estate association, was working for repeal, but to his bewilderment, he found that there was no friendly ear in the governor's office. Battaglia, as he had done so often before, refused to listen to the conservatives and telephoned Reagan at the hospital, urging him to back the compromise. Reagan agreed, and Battaglia began to apply the same pressure that had helped push the tax bill through the senate a few days before. This time he failed. Pontius and other lobbyists used their influence in the senate, and Republican senators informed Battaglia they would not support the compromise. More troubles beset the assistant. The Republicans who insisted on outright repeal made an alliance with liberal Democrats who didn't want any change in the law at all. As a result, the compromise backed by Reagan was defeated.

Reagan's identification with the unsuccessful compromise on the law had been an attempt to find a path through the baffling racial tension of California—to offer help to the Negro while remaining true to his conservative principles and retaining the support of his middle-class constituency.

But his plan had failed, and from then on he directed his words to the prejudices and fears of the white community. In September Reagan traveled to a California Real Estate Association convention and renewed his friendship with these die-hard foes of open-housing laws. He said: "We may not be able to get the act repealed, but if we can keep all of our people together, we can make that beginning." He talked about discrimination during his out-of-state speaking tours. He told an audience in segregated South Carolina: "There is no law saying the Negro has to live in Harlem or Watts." In the same city, he remarked: "Everybody is entitled to equal rights, and it is the obligation of the Federal Government to enforce these rights. Maybe in some cases, though, the problem is solved for some at the expense of taking away the constitutional rights of others." In racially tense Chicago, he conceded that the Negro community has "proved its citizenship, but they have to make a choice and quit listening to false prophets. You settle one thing with them [militant Negro leaders] and they will be back with another point. Some of them think they have found a pretty good thing."

This was a frank appeal to the white backlash, made during a time when whites and blacks in the United States were pulling apart. As the months passed, Reagan invariably rejected the middle course. In September, 1967, militant Negro students at San Jose State College protested against racial discrimination in fraternity and sorority houses and against discrimination encountered by Negro athletes. With tension high, the college president canceled the college's opening football game and then, after days of negotiations, announced a settlement of the dispute that included an order to the fraternities and sororities to stop discrimination. Negroes and whites praised the settlement as proof that honest discussion between black and white could avoid violence.

Reagan, however, criticized the president for canceling the football game and said he had bowed to threats of violence. He agreed with the extremely conservative state superintendent of public instruction, Max Rafferty, who said he would have called out the Marines to make sure the game was played.

Reagan's philosophy toward welfare also reflected the popular prejudices of the day. Governor Brown had expanded state welfare payments to the handicapped, aged and to the most controversial category of all, unwed mothers and their children. There was a feeling in the minds of many voters that welfare was costing too much—and was going to people who refused to work. Since many of the Negro slum dwellers received welfare payments, the antiwelfare mood was inevitably part of the anti-Negro feeling. Reagan's criticisms of welfare always got a warm applause—even when they were based on errors in fact. "Great numbers of people are coming to California simply because they know that in twenty-four hours they can be taken care of by the rest of us," he said during the campaign. Welfare, said Reagan, was based on the theory of giving a man an income "just because he was born." His statement was erroneous. There was only one category of welfare that had no eligibility requirements, and that was aid to the blind, providing assistance to 12,000 in 1966. The biggest category, aid to families with dependent children, including aid to unwed mothers, required a recipient to live in California at least a year before receiving aid. After a few months in the governor's office Reagan recognized his error. "We have some pretty good and sound residency requirements here," he said. "My criticism during the campaign was a lack of enforcement, particularly by way of county relief."

Reagan vetoed seven federal War on Poverty programs, and

one of the first actions of his administration was cutting back one of Brown's answers to racial strife in the Negro urban slums—antipoverty centers that placed such services as welfare and unemployment under a single roof, so the recipients wouldn't have to spend the day scurrying between widely separated state offices. Reagan offered another approach. He believed that private business, properly channeled, could single-handedly solve the problems of the black ghettos. Governor Brown had also believed that business must help, and following the Watts riots, his employment department cooperated with the Management Council for Merit Employment, set up by the Los Angeles chamber of commerce to find jobs for Negroes after the violence had ended. This unique program was headed by H. C. (Chad) McClellan, a former president of the National Manufacturers Association, who bought a small paint company in 1927, became a millionaire and sold out in 1962. Brown believed that McClellan's group provided only part of the answer. Reagan said it could do much more.

McClellan had offered a promising way out of the seemingly incurable unemployment in the Negro slums. And it was true that the expensive welfare programs of the Democrats had failed to help much. McClellan was a surprising poverty fighter—seventy years old, no friend of welfare, unhappy with the high taxes that took business profits. But at the request of the chamber of commerce, he began putting together a group that would find jobs for chronically unemployed Negroes in the Los Angeles riot area—the south central section of the city. His preliminary findings detailed the failures of years of public assistance. "We discovered that unemployment in the riot area—about 25,000, we judged—represented two or three times the unemployed average for our county as a whole and that county welfare costs were more than $400 million annually. We became convinced that virtually all welfare recipients would prefer a decent job to relief. Many, perhaps half, of the Negro unemployed were readily qualified to meet industries' minimum job entry requirements, but others would need pre-job training."

With a $90,000 budget, supplied by private foundations, the council accomplished much. McClellan persuaded dozens of Los Angeles employers to send recruiters to the Watts state employment center within a few weeks after the riots. The newly located center made it easier for the state to find jobs for the unemployed, for business got a better impression of the applicants on their home ground. By November, 1966, fourteen months after the riots, 201 firms cooperating with McClellan's program reported they had hired 17,903 people from the riot area.

Reagan, while running for governor, praised McClellan's plan as the way out of unemployment in the slums. He always referred to it as his alternative when he attacked welfare and thus gave a constructive tone to his criticism. "I am wholeheartedly in support of practically all of the social legislation we have ever had," he said. "I am violently opposed to some of the methods we have chosen, because they have not brought the good they were supposed to bring. I don't think there is any real good to humanity or compassion in adopting some kind of welfare that perpetuates poverty and puts people on the public dole." The nation's goal, he said, "should be elimination of the need for welfare."

But there were those who thought McClellan's approach hadn't worked. Budd Schulberg, the novelist and screen writer who organized the Watts Writers Workshop, wrote that the people in the riot area "would like to see a list of the jobs Chad McClellan's committee claims to have filled.

They wonder if people are not being run through the statistic machine three or four times as figures are based merely on what each company reports." If there were 17,000 permanent jobs, they insisted, one would be able to see the positive effects on the community. And it was a fact that unemployment was still alarmingly high in the ghetto. In the hard core of this city-sized slum, the unemployment rate was 12 percent, as compared to the 3.7 percent unemployment average in the United States. More significant were the findings of a Department of Labor study which was conducted after the Watts riots. This study revealed that one out of three in Watts was "sub-employed," or had a serious employment problem. It concluded that "unemployment—or sub-employment—in the slums of Los Angeles is so much worse than it is in the country as a whole that the national measurements of unemployment are utterly irrelevant. . . . The situation there is that about a third are unable to earn a living."

The wreckage of Watts and racial violence in other parts of the state testified to the failure of old methods of state aid to the needy, and winning private industry's cooperation was a major accomplishment. But Reagan destroyed the effect of this accomplishment by continual statements casting doubt on the worth of public welfare. In his speeches the poor became the enemy, trying to take away the hard-earned savings of the middle class. An antiwelfare tide was in the country, and Reagan was interested in riding it. Economy was more popular than assisting the needy, and the governor, in well-publicized moves, trimmed his welfare program to fit the limits of his stringent economy rules. While agreeing that job training was the answer to reducing the growing welfare rolls, he refused to spend much money for it. He would not recognize that only government had the resources to train and find work for the hard-core unemployed—the bitter young men in places like Watts where the Department of Labor study found that unemployment was "primarily a story of inferior education, no skills, police and garnishment records, discrimination, fatherless children, unnecessarily rigid hiring practices and hopelessness." Reagan was not even willing to increase spending in the slums for the thing that would strike at one of the causes of unemployment—education. When the representatives of the Mexican-American community asked for increased state aid to schools in the urban slums, he turned them down in a bitter meeting that showed how deep the split was between Reagan and the poor. Fifteen Mexican-Americans met with Reagan in his office in Los Angeles in mid 1967. Some had traveled to Sacramento from Los Angeles the month before, but, through a mixup, were informed there was no room on the governor's schedule. At the meeting they asked him to support a bill that would give urban schools an additional fifteen dollars a pupil in state aid. "The governor said the state has no money for such school aid programs," reported Gonzalo Molina, one of those in the session. "We suggested he adopt a withholding system for income tax payments, and he said he would never approve such a plan, that it would create very serious accounting problems." At that time, mention of income tax withholding made the governor angry, and this meeting was no exception. Molina said that Reagan "became quite upset and pounded the table, but later apologized." Lyn Nofziger thought Molina exaggerated Reagan's anger. The governor, he said, spoke "sternly and strongly, he raised his voice—but I wouldn't say it was shouting." He added: "When a guy keeps bugging you about withholding where your position is pretty well known, well, [you have] a reason to raise [your] voice." Besides, "We had them down for fifteen minutes on our schedule and they stayed forty-five minutes."

It was the same on other human issues. The sound and fury of Reagan's oratory—for the benefit of the men and women who provided his political base—captured all the attention and obscured his accomplishments. It was not noticed by the public, for example, that Reagan canceled the execution of another killer, Calvin Thomas, who had thrown a fire bomb into the home of a girl friend and killed her baby. The prosecutor had asked Reagan to refuse clemency, but Meese looked over Thomas' record of epilepsy and brain damage and told Reagan: "I think this is one where you might want to consider clemency." Reagan replied: "I've been thinking that, too," and spared the man's life. He also granted a temporary reprieve to another killer who was needed to testify at the trial of an accomplice. There was not going to be the "blood bath" in California under Reagan that some of his opponents had feared.

What was important to Reagan in the first year was to create an image of ending what many Americans felt was growing social unrest, violence and public subsidies to those who disobeyed the law. As a result, he offered no real solutions to urban problems, particularly those of the black ghetto. His mandate from the voters had been to reverse a trend, and his goal was to convince the rest of the nation he had done so.

CHAPTER THIRTEEN

THE VANISHING LAND

WHEN REAGAN became governor, California was still uniquely beautiful, even though man was callously violating nature every day. Around the basin occupied by Los Angeles, mountains untouched by bulldozers rose above the smog, and there were still bighorn sheep roaming wild in the Angeles National Forest. In the High Sierra, Lake Tahoe stretched clear and blue along the mountains for twenty-two miles, the largest mountain lake in the nation. At most places, swimmers could still see the sandy bottom, even though murky signs of pollution were visible. Tall garish hotels produced sewage and destroyed the landscape; gambling casinos, billboards, pizza parlors and neon signs cluttered the south shore of the lake. Like Tahoe, California had retained its beaty, but decay was setting in. Countryside was being surrendered to a population growing at the rate of 600,000 a year. There were almost ten million vehicles crowding the highways, each spewing out noxious waste into the air. Man had reduced the size of San Francisco Bay from almost seven hundred square miles to about four hundred by filling in portions of it, destroying in the process the natural shoreline habitat of fish and wild birds. Swimmers playing in the surf along the lovely southern California beach of Santa Barbara could taste oil in the water, spilled into the ocean while being loaded onto tankers.

"California is a unique, bright land and somehow or other we must keep her so," said California Tomorrow, a private conservation organization. But it asked: "How polluted can a bright land become and still be bright?"

"It is possible to stop, here in the West, the destruction of the land that is called California," wrote Raymond F. Dassman, a zoologist and biologist. "California can be a model that all the world would admire. It can set an example that all the other regions would try to follow."

This was the challenge of California, and Reagan first met it in the state's most important conservation battleground—the cold, foggy counties two hundred miles above San Francisco. Here was the northern home of the last great stands of the redwood, the tallest tree known to man. Some of them were growing before the birth of Christ. Once they had covered much of the coast of California, reaching from what is now the Oregon border, south through San Francisco to below Monterey and Big Sur. Most of them were gone when Reagan took office. Only about 750,000 of the original 2 million acres remained, for redwood is a durable, all-purpose building material of consistently high value. The giant trees still covered the mountains of the north coast, however, sometimes reaching unbroken from the sea to the mountain peaks. But except for 50,000 north-coast acres in state parks (part of the 115,000 acres of trees under state ownership), the redwoods were falling to the logging companies at the rate of a billion board feet a year.

It was a one-industry economy up in the north-coast

counties—lumber. People there approached the land with the nineteenth-century outlook that resources were limitless and were placed on earth for man to exploit. Local government, the newspapers, radio and television all reflected the viewpoint of the big lumber companies that controlled their one industry. The north coast rejected the idea that the redwoods were a national treasure. To the people there, the trees were payrolls, money to keep the economy running. So strong was the influence of the industry that when the League of Women Voters in Eureka warned that a proposed $30 million paper pulp mill would cause air pollution and pour potentially poisonous waste water into the bay, city councilmen scoffed. "If there's anything that's discouraging, it's the little old lady in tennis shoes crying. . . . Let's wait and see what they are going to do, if they are going to pollute the air. They are going to bring in $30 million here; we should be thankful to them."

The north-coast residents were so determined to protect the lumber industry that they supported a proposed freeway through the last remaining untouched beach on the California coast, Gold Beach. Walking down the beach was like visiting a forgotten California. No buildings or roadways blocked the view of towering bluffs rising directly from the beach. Off to a side was Fern Canyon, which looked almost primeval with perpetually green growth climbing the steep canyon walls. Gold Beach was one of three possible sites for the freeway. A second site would have cut through the heart of the memorial groves in the state redwood parks. A third—the only one acceptable to those who wanted to preserve the resources of the state—ran up a ridge outside the park and through cut-over land owned by lumber companies. But the lumber companies opposed it because after its construction a steep climb would slow their lumber trucks.

Local governments opposed it too. Only pressure from conservationists from other parts of the state prevented the highway from being built through the beach or the redwood groves—pressure that was intensely resented in the north country. "They can sit in their chairs in the Bay area and sip their sherry and say 'I know there is a redwood wilderness,' no matter how many people are thrown out of work," complained lumber company executive Bernard Agrons.

Now the north coast's energies were directed against proposals for a redwood national park—a plan to protect at least some of the remaining redwoods from the loggers. The area found a ready ally in Governor Reagan, for he was bound by his conservative philosophy and his campaign promises. "The economic needs of the lumber industry should be considered," he said. "A tree is a tree—how many more do you need to look at?" Expanding on that, he went on to say that there are 115,000 acres of redwoods preserved in parks in California now. "If this 115,000 acres were stretched in a line and a road run through the middle," he said, "one could drive for two hundred miles and see nothing but redwoods on both sides. . . . We have made adequate provision for redwoods."

Executives of the lumber companies had long been aware of Reagan's sympathies. Darrell Schroeder, vice-president and general manager of the Miller-Rellum Lumber Company, was Del Norte County chairman of Reagan's campaign. After Reagan became governor, and Miller-Rellum property became involved in the park controversy, he insisted that the company be given a like stretch of government-owned redwoods in return for any timber land it lost to the park. The government land had been held in trust by the forest service for a park, and United States Agriculture Secretary Orville Freeman did not want to turn it over to the loggers. In addition to his commitment to help business, Reagan was obligated by belief and campaign promises to side with local governments in such disputes—and in this case local governments followed the lead of business. "As governor," he said while campaigning, "I would work to return to the cities and the counties those powers usurped from them in recent years by the state."

But on the redwood issue Reagan found himself pitted against the gadfly of the conservation movement in the United States, the Sierra Club. John Muir, its founder, had persuaded the Federal Government to intervene in California's local affairs in 1864 and make a national park out of the Yosemite Valley and the nearby giant sequoias, trees that exceed even the coast redwoods in age. They were threatened by loggers, ranchers and miners in the High Sierra. Now the Sierra Club was asking the government to intervene again. But even the Federal Government was feuding with the club. So vociferous was its opposition to proposed federal dams in the Grand Canyon that the day after it had published newspaper ads opposing them, the United States Internal Revenue Service warned that the club might lose its tax-deductible status for violating rules against taking part in political activity. The Sierra Club's redwood park plan authorized the Federal Government to purchase 77,000 acres of redwoods in Humboldt County, around the city of Eureka. Combined with the 13,000-acre Prairie Creek State Park, it would result in a 90,000-acre Redwood National Park. Among these trees would have been 33,000 acres of virgin redwoods, the original growth. But at the same time, the Sierra Club plan would have taken all of the holdings of the Arcata Redwood Company and put the firm out of business.

Here was the issue—the conservationists on one side, the

company and the local residents and their government on the other. The lumber industry, through its redwood park and recreation committee, said that if the park were created, "every business in the redwood region would suffer. Thousands would come off our congressional district's tax rolls. Drastic unemployment and higher taxes would result." But the conservationists added up all the remaining trees and concluded that if the present rate of cutting continued, the industry would be forced to cut back its operations in a few years anyway, reducing employment. A Bank of America study in 1965 concluded that employment in the northern lumbering counties would be down 25 percent in 1975 even without a park.

The Sierra Club park plan was unacceptable to the Federal Government. President Johnson asked for a smaller park farther to the north, encompassing two present state parks and 29,000 acres of the Mill Creek redwood area, a partially logged-over section that contained only 7,000 acres of virgin redwoods. But Reagan wouldn't even accept this modified plan; he stood with the lumber companies. He favored a plan that would link state redwood parks and other state land and leave most of the lumber company land alone. And he insisted on the land trade that would give Miller-Rellum land now under the control of the forest service. Finally, even California's senior senator, Republican Thomas H. Kuchel, agreed to that trade in his own compromise park plan. And the Sierra Club, modifying its demands, also agreed to support the trade and to back Kuchel's plan for a 64,000-acre park.

But Reagan also had other demands. He insisted that the park not deprive north-coast residents of their jobs; the state must receive "full, fair and equal value" from the Federal Government for the state parks turned over to it; the Federal

Government must encourage the economy of the area by accelerated public-works projects; counties in which the park would be located must receive federal payments to replace the property taxes they lost by the Federal Government's taking over private land; "harassment of the lumber industry must stop"; and—last on his list—the interests and goals of conservation groups should be respected. Of Kuchel's compromise plan, he complained that the 14,000 acres of privately owned land that would be taken over by the park was too much. The plan, he said, could "seriously damage the lumbering industry."

By the end of the year, the redwood park had still not been authorized by Congress. A Democratic state assemblyman said Reagan was asking impossible conditions from the Federal Government to kill the park plan. And Representative Jeffrey Cohelan said Reagan's lumber company supporters were engaging in delaying action to win time to cut the most valuable timber. "The lumber companies apparently feel that one of the ways they can beat this proposal . . . is to scar the area so badly it would no longer be desirable," said Cohelan. The Senate finally approved Kuchel's compromise, but final passage was not certain.

Reagan sided with local government again on the issue of stopping the pollution of Lake Tahoe, six thousand feet above sea level in the Sierra Nevada, about three hundred miles east of San Francisco. Once, when the lake was hard to reach, there were forests of pine and fir coming down to the water. But the transcontinental highways over the Sierra were improved after World War II, and people found their way to the spectacular lake. Hotels, motels and subdivisions were built on meadows and hillsides. Creeks were clogged with dirt and refuse from construction. This, along with sewage seeping from cesspools and inadequate treatment plants, began to pollute the lake. Neither the state governments of California and Nevada nor the five counties surrounding the area would act to curb the construction that was ruining the lake. What was needed was a regional government to enforce controls on sewage disposal and development.

Tahoe resembled the north-coast area in that it was a one-industry area. The industry was the vacation business, summer and winter. Like the businessmen of the north coast, the residents around the lake were willing to sacrifice long-term values—preservation of the lake's beauty—for short-term gain. They did not believe that the lake was in immediate danger of pollution, despite the testimony of scientists from the state department of public health and the United States Public Health Service.

Early in 1967 Reagan and his family drove up to Tahoe for an inspection and a visit with Nevada's new Republican governor, Paul Laxalt. After the visit Reagan said that conservationists had exaggerated when they warned it would be too late to save the lake if action were not taken that summer. In fact, he was so little concerned with the threat of pollution that—in the interest of economy—he tried to delay a $2 million loan to a Tahoe sewer district for a sewage disposal system, but later agreed to lend them the money.

The lack of concern didn't last. In 1967 the threat of federal action—if local and state apathy continued—pushed the state into moving. After doubts and delays, a bill was passed setting up a regional planning agency for the Tahoe basin. It had Reagan's support. Local government, however, was given a majority of votes on the agency's board. But the fate of the clear blue lake was still in question. Those who were concerned about its preservation doubted the willingness of local people to curb development, since they had never shown any inclination to do so before. It seemed to many conservationists that the lake was still in the hands of those who were spoiling it.

In his campaign, Reagan had made clear that there would be a change of management of the state's resources if he were elected. There were signs of it before his inauguration. Among those he called on for advice was A. Ruric Todd, Sacramento lobbyist for the Pacific Gas and Electric Company. Disliked by conservationists, P.G. & E. had dammed wild rivers for power plants and tried to build a nuclear reactor at Bodega Head, a rugged outcropping a few miles north of San Francisco, a place of lonely beauty and the home of rare marine life. Despite protests from the Sierra Club and other such groups, the company began to work on the plant, abandoning the project only after the Atomic Energy Commission questioned the safety of such an installation, constructed on the earthquake fault that crosses the area. But a big hole excavated for the reactor remained at Bodega Head as a souvenir.

A new era of cooperation was beginning between the utilities and the governor's office, which had often been unfriendly under Governor Brown. The P.G. & E., like other utilities in California, was subject to regulation by a powerful agency appointed by the governor, the public utilities commission. Reagan appointed to the commission a University of California professor who specialized in the study of the relationship between private utilities and government and who was a faculty member in a university-directed management program for P.G. & E. He was joined by another appointee not unfriendly to private utilities, a former state senator who had been a well-liked member of the senate club in which utility lobbyists held power. "I think it would be nice if we had some men on the PUC who understood the rudiments of private business and free enterprise," said Reagan.

Conservation seemed a blind spot for Reagan in many ways. During his campaign he suggested that the state take an inventory of all the state parks and trade or sell those that were not needed. He was unsure about the state's geography. In December, 1965, before he announced for governor, he took a campaign trip up the Sacramento Valley and commented admiringly on the scenery. "Is that what they call the delta?" he asked. It was a serious error to those who knew California's geography. Reagan was told it was the Sacramento Valley and the delta was more than one hundred miles away. The location of water projects confused him. "Here I am on the wrong river again; you've really got me," he said one day while being questioned about a local flood control project.

His campaign for governor did not emphasize conservation. An eight-page position paper he issued gave his views on crime, public education, academic freedom, taxes, government spending and labor management, but there was not a word about saving the state's resources. And after his inauguration, part of his own staff put itself on the side of the subdividers who were buying up open space in the Mother Lode country north of Sacramento. This area, where the forty-niners came in search of gold, had become a forgotten part of California when the gold mines closed, but now, with the city dwellers looking for open recreation land, a new gold rush had been started by land speculators and developers. Battaglia, Nofziger and four other of Reagan's aides became part of a group that paid more than $1 million for two thousand acres of land in Nevada County, near one of the prettiest towns in the area north of the river in which gold was first discovered in 1848. Their land adjoined a development in which the subdividers had created a lake around which they were planning to build homes and a golf course. The value of the land owned by Reagan's aides would increase if the lake development were successful. There was a danger that local officials might bow to Reagan's staff in zoning matters to improve their standing in Sacramento. But Nofziger said: "If anyone asks for so much as a local zoning ordinance, I'll scream." He promised the investment would have no effect on state decisions. Reagan, while not participating in the deal, approved of it. He had had successful land dealings of his own. He had sold his own ranch in the mountains north of Los Angeles for $2 million, and he loved to tell about the profit he made on it.

When conservation organizations were criticizing Reagan for his refusal to accept their redwood park plan, an assistant jokingly summed up what seemed to be the administration's attitude. He said a redwood tree had fallen on a man at a state park and added: "Now maybe they'll start a society to protect people from redwood trees."

Forests and open spaces, in short, were a side issue with Reagan. He was more interested in cutting down the cost of state government. But his first year was not quite the resources disaster that conservationists had expected. Because he was more concerned with other matters, he allowed his administrators wide latitude, and instead of destroying the state's resources, they surprised critics with several imaginative ideas. Reagan introduced his first resources appointee one morning when he walked into the news conference room across from his office followed by a tall, gawky, middle-aged man in a rumpled suit. He was Norman B. Livermore, a fourth-generation Californian who had just resigned as treasurer of the Pacific Lumber Company to accept a new job, that of administrator of the state agency that controls all of California's resources—the rivers, the forests, the lakes, the wildlife and mineral wealth. He was a Republican. His brother was the Republican county chairman in San Francisco. Livermore's lifetime had been spent in the lumber business. On the surface, it looked like another surrender to the lumber industry. But Livermore was also a member of the Sierra Club. He had grown up in the Sierra and led mule trains along its rugged trails. "I've spent a thousand nights in the Sierra," he said. "Being up there gives one a chance to be by himself away from telephones, and the camaraderie around the campfire is one of the greatest things of all." As a lumberman he had gone against his colleagues by opposing the freeway through Prairie Creeks Redwood State Park. But he also admired man-made works and respected private industry. He liked to visit Jebediah Smith Redwood State Park, for on one side are the "primeval, almost religiously inspiring coast redwoods. And on the left is a saw mill. They're both necessary." He conceded: "I am a living contradiction." He had once visited Glen Canyon Dam on the Colorado River, a project opposed by the club, and said: "It's an exceedingly dramatic dam. Stand on that dam facing south and to your east is the highly spectacular Lake Powell. The dam is one of the biggest works of man. On the right, look down that fantastically wild and beautiful gorge, and you've got purity. You feel strongly about both." The out-of-doors, he said, should be open to lumbermen as well as hunters, fishermen and hikers.

Livermore quickly told the lumber industry that he wanted stricter enforcement of laws governing their logging operations and that he was unhappy with the way they had been carelessly clogging streams with debris. "The lumber companies have a long way to go in scenic forestry," he said.

"The leaders in the industry will admit they have been laggards in the past." Reagan, in his campaign, had defended the past conduct of the lumber industry, yet he now backed up Livermore. He backed him up again in another important issue, the preservation of the Middle Fork of the Feather River. This river, in a remote corner of northeastern California, is one of the last wild rivers in the United States. One hundred years ago men did not worry about wild rivers. All rivers were wild. But men built dams to prevent floods, to store water for irrigation and to create hydroelectric power. By the 1960s, most of the nation's great rivers were shackled by dams and reservoirs, and concern was expressed that one day children would never have the chance to see a river running free. Of all the rivers in the Northern Sierra in California, only the Middle Fork of the Feather was still unshackled. So rugged was its canyon that few fishermen and hikers found their way to the river. But good fishermen could take an easy limit of big rainbow trout in a day from the stream. The departments of Interior and Agriculture listed the river as one of seventy-three streams in the nation which should be part of a system of wild rivers protected from dams.

The river was in jeopardy when Reagan took office. An irrigation district controlled by rice growers wanted to dam it. The project would give the district free water, paid for by the sale of hydroelectric power to the Pacific Gas and Electric Company. Under Governor Brown's administration, the state water commission approved the project, as did another state agency, the water rights board. Only the courts or the Federal Power Commission could stop it. Reagan's own legislative aides expected him to side with the irrigation district and do nothing to interfere with a project that would help both the farmers who supported his election and the P.G. & E. But instead, he followed Livermore's advice. He allowed state agencies to fight the project in the courts, and he supported adoption of a legislative resolution asking the Federal Power Commission to refuse to license the project.

Some of Reagan's other appointments were just as surprising as Livermore. Once again following Livermore's advice, Reagan retained Governor Brown's director of fish and game, Walter Shannon, who had alienated the lumber industry with his criticisms of their logging practices. Reagan had been under heavy pressure to appoint someone more friendly to private business. And for parks director, Reagan reached to the San Francisco Bay area and hired one of the most imaginative parks men in the nation, William Penn Mott, Jr. In Oakland, the drab city that sprawls across the bay from San Francisco, Mott had built an imaginative Children's Fairyland when he was parks director there, persuading local businesses and clubs to pay for replicas of scenes from fairy tales. Not wanting any open space to go to waste, he even had flowers planted on boulevard dividers. Building parks, said Mott, is like building a church. "You've got to have faith."

Mott and Livermore were conservative dreamers, and that made their dreams acceptable to Reagan. Never did they seek to violate his administration's economy rules. Under Mott, for example, the fees for state park camp grounds were raised from two dollars to three a night. "I feel the users of special facilities should pay for them instead of putting the burden on the general public." A visitor asked Livermore to name the most important change he had brought to resources management in California. "Economy," he said. "We're working on it all the time. Reducing the out-of-state travel, reducing the window dressing."

The resources economy wave meant a major change in resources policy. Under all the governors since World War

II, the state had concentrated on buying park land, pushing aside delays to acquire open space before it was taken by subdividers. Delays would mean increases in price. As a result of this race against the land developers, by the time of Reagan's election the state park system had grown to almost one hundred ninety parks, each of them capturing a bit of California's uniqueness. Together they were a panorama of the great state. The redwoods were not all that was preserved. Beaches from the Mexican border to northern California were owned by the state. San Simeon, William Randolph Hearst's mountain castle in the central California mountains above the Pacific, was part of the system. State planners had reached into the desert and preserved eighty thousand acres along the Salton Sea. An old gold-mining operation was preserved at Malakoff Diggin's State Park and a lumber mill at another park. Jumping in just ahead of the developers, the state bought valuable beach land along the shores of Lake Tahoe. There appeared to be little limit to the state's buying spree, which was endorsed periodically by the people when they approved selling bonds to borrow money to buy more parks. Now, said Reagan, it was time to slow down the purchases and develop what the state owned. Livermore agreed. "It is time to pause and take stock," he said.

Mott felt that the state could make a "major thrust in developing what we have." He envisioned bringing in more private concessionaires to provide some of the attractive and expensive recreation features to the state parks. But there was the chance that the private restaurants, hotels and shops might be priced out of the reach of most of the Californians who traditionally used the parks. The way was also cleared for the state to sell or lease one of the few publicly owned recreation areas in the High Sierra skiing country. It was Squaw Valley, the site of the 1960 Winter Olympics. Squaw had been a mistake from the start, with the state taking possession of only a stretch of the valley floor while private developers owned the profitable ski slopes. But instead of trying to make the area more profitable for the state, Reagan and the legislature took the easier course of turning it over to the private developers who had a history of charging high prices for skiing in the Sierra.

Economy was so important under Reagan that it became the governing philosophy in resources administration. But what of the challenge of preserving the "unique, bright land"? Cutting down by 90 percent the amount spent for park acquisition and development, Reagan in effect withdrew the state from its long-standing race against the land developers to acquire open recreation space. Each year's delay in the purchase of a park site meant that inflation increased the cost or that the land would be purchased by a private developer. In the past park officials had felt that they first needed the land—and could plan its development later. Reagan, however, decided to delay many land purchases and to cancel plans to buy sites for nine parks. "They don't understand the open-space idea," complained a spokesman for a conservation organization. "Our job is to acquire land while there is still some to be acquired."

Reagan was the guardian of the state's resources—the forests, rivers, mountains and lakes being overrun by timbermen, motel operators, hamburger stand owners and millions of recreation seekers. His job was to balance the needs of local government and local industry against the needs of the majority of Californians who lived elsewhere. But in meeting the challenge of saving the state's resources, Reagan considered himself also the guardian of the rights of local interests, the protector of "home rule"; as a result he was reluctant to offend the local interests and unwilling to admit they were controlled by businessmen who prospered by exploiting the resources of the state. California had many problems in the 1960s, and one of them was to save open recreation space for the people. Reagan was unwilling to sacrifice either his economies or his commitment to home rule. He didn't recall that it was another Republican, Abraham Lincoln, who intervened in 1864 and signed the bill saving the Yosemite Valley from the local interests who were destroying it.

CHAPTER FOURTEEN

CRISIS IN HIGHER EDUCATION

RONALD REAGAN first met Clark Kerr, the president of the University of California, at a dinner party after the election, and the meeting was an ominous sign of what awaited Kerr and public higher education in the state. "He barely greeted me," Kerr remembered a year later, after he had been deposed from the presidency in a coup that startled the nation's academic community.

The host, H. R. Haldeman, a Reagan political supporter and a member of the board of regents which controls the nine campuses of the university, had given the party so the regents could meet the new governor. Reagan's statements during the preceding political campaign had worried friends of both the university and of California's eighteen state colleges. Reagan had made Kerr's stewardship of the university a campaign issue. He had charged that the university administration had been lax enough to allow marijuana to be smoked at a dance on the Berkeley campus and "had abdicated their authority." Faculty members, he suggested, should "be given a code of conduct that would force them to serve as examples of good behavior and decency for the young people in their charge."

Reagan's statements were always enthusiastically received, because part of the resentment that middle-class Californians felt against their government was prompted by the student demonstrations at the University of California at Berkeley and on other campuses. The beards and the hippies had made the university and all of higher education an object of public distrust. No longer were Californians enthusiastic about paying big taxes for public education. Hidden away in the hearts of parents was the fear that their own children might one day go away to college, grow beards and march against authority.

Kerr represented much of what Reagan thought was wrong with public higher education. Kerr was Reagan's complete opposite in appearance, style, interests and philosophy. He had been the president since 1958 and presided over the university during its greatest growth and greatest unrest. Before that he had been a professor and later chancellor at Berkeley, and right-wing elements had always considered this campus a sanctuary for the far left. In 1952, as a professor, Kerr led a fight against a loyalty oath. As president he gave an honorary degree to a Berkeley professor of psychology, Edward C. Tolman, who had resigned years before after refusing to sign the oath.

At the dinner with Reagan, it was obvious to Kerr that the balance was tipping against him. In the last months, Brown had been his most powerful defender. With him gone Kerr was without political support, and his critics on the board of regents were in the ascendency. One of the university regents rose to make a toast to Reagan—"To the man who will bring a big breath of fresh air into the university." Reagan accepted the toast and replied in measured words that he hoped that faculty members would now teach their students to respect the morality of the community. Kerr, a Quaker, later said he thought to himself that youngsters should be taught a morality higher than that of the community.

In the following weeks, Reagan began his offensive against public higher education in California, demonstrating that the university and the colleges were not as free from the political pressures of the day as their founders hoped they would be. The University of California board of regents, while outwardly designed to be free of politics, is actually sensitive to the election results. Sixteen of the regents are appointed by the governor for sixteen-year terms. Theoretically, there will always be a group of regents who were appointed by previous governors—thus preventing the incumbent chief executive from exercising absolute control. But the board also has eight ex-officio members, including the governor—members who are regents only because of other offices they hold. They are the lieutenant governor, who is usually a member of the governor's party; the president of the state board of agriculture, a gubernatorial appointee; the president of the Mechanics' Institute; the president of the alumni association; the superintendent of public intruction and the university president. In 1967 only Assembly Speaker Unruh was a political opponent of the governor.

Kerr's supporters charged Reagan with political inter-ference following the president's dismissal. Kerr, except for a statement on the day of his firing, has remained silent. But almost a year later he broke his silence in a long interview. He is still in Berkeley, like a deposed monarch in comfortable exile. He is the chairman and executive officer of the Carnegie Foundation's commission on the future of higher education, which is studying, among other subjects, how to finance public higher education. He is paid a salary by the Carnegie Foundation, nearly as much as he received as president of the university. In addition, he is paid a sum as a part-time professor at Berkeley. His office is located within walking distance of the statewide university administration building where he reigned as president. It is an unusual office. It has no desk, just a round table with chairs, a blue-upholstered Danish modern couch and a matching chair.

Kerr is a bitter man, for he feels that the university he served so long has treated him harshly. The editor of the alumni magazine had asked him to write an article on his work for the Carnegie Foundation, but then was prohibited by his superiors from publishing it. When Charles J. Hitch became the new president, Kerr asked the university public-relations office to issue a statement he had prepared congratulating Hitch. The university office refused.

Kerr believes that Reagan and a group of regents planned and executed his firing. He says that Reagan was not truthful when he denied it and when he said that Kerr provoked his own dismissal by demanding a vote of confidence. Kerr supports his case with an account of previously undisclosed events that proved to him Reagan's involvement. His story varies from that told by the governor and by Theodore C. Meyer, the chairman of the university regents. Kerr refrained from telling it during the past year because he did not want to bring any controversy to the university. But now he believes that Reagan is running for President, and thinks that the American people should know how "Reagan lied on his record. I don't think he is a trustworthy individual," said Kerr, "and I think if the people of the United States want to consider him for President, they ought to consider his record."

His story has its roots in the Free Speech Movement

troubles of 1964. Kerr's difficulties had come suddenly after six years of success. To him, the university was a living part of society. No longer, he said in his inaugural address in 1958, was the university "a tiny band of scholars situated on the periphery of society." The university's research had provided society with such diverse inventions as the hydrogen bomb and the mechanical tomato picker. Its campuses were all over the state, and Kerr, realizing the coldness of a big university system, had decentralized authority, giving day-to-day responsibility to the chancellors of each campus. His academic plan looked ahead to the year 2000, setting down the guidelines for the expansion of the university. At new campuses at Santa Cruz and San Diego, a bold experiment was in progress to dispel the depressing bigness of campuses like Berkeley and Los Angeles. Students lived and worked in small "cluster colleges" where undergraduate education was emphasized. In his quiet, almost icy way, Kerr was remarkably successful in winning larger appropriations every year from the legislature and in helping to persuade the people to approve bond issues to pay for new buildings.

But even some of those who opposed his firing strongly criticized him as an administrator. His downfall came because the university had become what he described in his inaugural as an intersection crossed by diverse elements of a changing society. Berkeley was the first of the campuses to be hit by the student militancy of the sixties, and Kerr was the first of the university administrators to have to deal with student bodies rebellious over Vietnam, civil rights, and the cold bureaucracy of modern universities. In the fall semester of 1964, militants who had spent the summer in the South with the civil rights movement returned to Berkeley convinced of the virtue of direct action. In September, Alex Sherriffs, the vice-chancellor, insisted that students be forbidden to use the sidewalk in front of the campus' main entrance, Sather Gate, to collect money and gain support for off-campus political activities. At the time, Kerr recalled, Sherriffs was saying that students needed some heavy discipline. But political activity in front of Sather Gate was one of Berkeley's most hallowed traditions. Kerr feels that by overturning it, Sherriffs helped cause a tense situation on the campus. He was later dropped as dean by a new chancellor, Roger Heyns, and in 1967 was hired by Reagan as a special assistant for education.

In a way, Kerr was tricked by his own decentralization policy. He was out of the country when Berkeley officials closed the strip without consulting their superiors on the statewide university staff. Kerr thought the action a mistake and was critical of the campus officials for acting without consulting his office or the students.

Berkeley administrators had always been overly fond of sticking to rules, no matter what the extenuating circumstances, so on September 30, five students were threatened with discipline for breaking the new rule. By October 1, the first of the big Free Speech Movement demonstrations was held to protest the university's action. Some two thousand students surrounded a police car to prevent it from taking away a young man for operating a Congress of Racial Equality table in defiance of the rules. The protests continued the next day, and several hundred police were called.

Famous as a mediator of labor-management disputes, Kerr, with his calm ways, seemed inadequate in the face of this student militancy.

Following Thanksgiving recess, the dispute over student penalties continued, and on the night of December 2, more than eight hundred students crowded into Sproul Hall, the main Berkeley administration building. They were protesting the administration's insistence on imposing penalties on two students, Mario Savio, the fiery leader of the revolt, and Art Goldberg. At 3:35 A.M. Governor Brown dispatched more than six hundred police, and 814 students were hauled out of the building and jailed.

After the demonstrations, university and state college students suddenly found themselves accused of being merely demonstrators who wasted the taxpayers' money. But Kerr said he had noticed signs of public discontent even before the Free Speech Movement. While touring the state in 1964 on behalf of a university and college construction bond issue, he became aware that the university was dropping in public regard. "I have made a lot of speeches over the years," he said. "Particularly toward the end, I became aware of three shifts in attitudes."

One was a growing disapproval of dissent on campus, and a hostile attitude toward faculty members whom the public blamed for encouraging student dissent. Another went to the very heart of the university's role as a scientific innovator. "Back when I started out as chancellor, you could sell what we did for science; we were saving the world for democracy," Kerr said. But in the sixties he became "aware of a kind of concern that science was changing people's lives in a way they did not like." Scientific investigation into genetics was an example. "When people hear about work on the genetic code, it gives them a kind of gut reaction—they don't like it. There was a feeling the university was a source of change, and they were fed up with change, and they didn't like the changes that were coming." He also found a vague, "almost inarticulate" resentment against what he called "the meritocracy," those who had risen to positions of influence and authority because of their education and ability. There was a feeling, Kerr said, of "meritocracy versus the people," a persistent resentment on the part of the people expressed in the question: "Who are these experts?" To them, "the university is elitist—some people are being raised up above others.

"These three things I saw coming along," he said. "Reagan was against change. He rode these things. How much he believed, I don't know."

Just after the election, Kerr had the first indication that he would be replaced—and the first sign, in his view, that Reagan was taking a personal hand in his removal. One of the chancellors "told me and told other people that he had been approached [about the university presidency] and asked if he would take it. He said he wasn't a candidate, but would take it." Kerr said the approach was made by some of Reagan's advisers. There is no doubt that there was a conversation between at least one Reagan adviser and a chancellor. Taft Schreiber, one of Reagan's informal advisers, confirmed he had talked to an unnamed chancellor and had asked casually: "Have you ever thought about the presidency?" But he denied he was acting as an emissary from the governor. He said he spoke to the man only as a friend and had no authority to offer the job. Schreiber correctly pointed out that only the regents can name a president.

In late November there was another event that helped convince Kerr that his future had already been decided. Regents' chairman Theodore Meyer "advised me to look for another position." The conversation took place in Kerr's office. "I asked him how he saw my future," Kerr said. "He indicated that it was quite doubtful." Meyer told the president that if an opportunity came along, he should take it.

Then in late December another regent urged him to quit. The regent, a Republican once active in state politics, told Kerr that "[my] days were numbered, that it would be better if I resigned than be fired. He said that since I had served with Brown, it would be better if I resigned when Brown were governor and not embarrass the new governor. He did not say he was speaking on behalf of Reagan, but he was quite concerned that Reagan not be embarrassed and the new governor have a clean slate." Kerr said the regent concluded the conversation by saying: "I don't expect you will make a fight of it because I know how devoted you are to the university." Later that day Kerr approached the regent and resumed the conversation. He asked what purpose his resignation would serve the university. The regent replied that his fellow members of the board "would be friends again." And the regent added: "We wouldn't have any trouble in Sacramento." Kerr replied: "We will have trouble regardless of who is president." Kerr also told him that the university might have difficulty finding a replacement. "We don't expect any trouble in getting your replacement," the regent said.

Governor Brown recalled hearing at about this time that "somebody met with him [Kerr] and said 'You'd better resign.' I called him up," Brown said. "I told him: 'Don't let him fire you. Don't let him bluff you.' " Brown, like Kerr, believed the push to fire Kerr was coming directly from Reagan.

On January 3, 1967, Reagan's finance director, Gordon Smith, informed university and state college officials that the new administration was proposing to cut higher education budgets by 10 percent and to ask for tuition. "It was the worst setback for higher education in the state since the Depression," said a university official. Kerr opposed the cuts and was thrust in the middle of the fight. It was a confusing time, one that cast considerable doubt on the credibility of the Reagan administration. University and state college officials leaked to the press details of what Smith had told them, and protests were staged on college campuses. Reagan insisted that he had not decided on any budget cuts, that Smith had just talked about tentative plans. "A lot of tentative things have been proposed in an effort to balance the budget and get the state out of the mess Governor Brown left it in, but there has been no final decision on anything including tuition," said Reagan's aide, Nofziger. Reagan's language was more colorful. "It is like Chicken Little running around saying the sky is falling in," he said of those who were protesting his financial plans. "They have invented a boogeyman." He reiterated that no final decision had been made. But the concern of the university and colleges was well founded. Within weeks, Reagan presented a budget that imposed 10 percent cuts and asked for tuition.

The uproar that resulted surprised the young administration, and Reagan blamed Kerr for much of his trouble. On January 12, Kerr went to Sacramento to confer with the governor and a group of regents, and left more convinced than ever that Reagan and some of the regents were planning to oust him. For after the meeting regents Theodore Meyer, H. R. Haldeman and Philip Boyd returned to the governor's office for another discussion from which Kerr was excluded.

That had happened on a Thursday, and Kerr had an appointment with Reagan and Lieutenant Governor Robert Finch the following Monday. He was concerned that he had been left out of the meeting and asked Meyer "if there was anything I should know before I talked to the governor." Meyer replied: "The governor will tell you." The president renewed his plea to Meyer for an inkling of what was on Reagan's mind. "I told him I did not want him to break his confidence, but it would help to say whether the regents acted favorably or unfavorably on what he [Reagan] had to say. I may have to make some fast decisions." Meyer replied: "I can't tell you that either."

By now Kerr was convinced that his firing was just a matter of time. But he sought a reprieve. He sent an emissary, the university's vice-president, Harry Wellman, to regents Meyer and Boyd to offer a compromise. He would resign effective June, 1968, giving the regents more time to find a replacement. This would have allowed Kerr to remain president through the university's centennial year, something he wanted to do very much. More important, it would have avoided a dangerous precedent, appointment of a new president with the election of a new governor. But Wellman returned and reported that it looked "like the situation was without solution."

On Monday, Kerr prepared for his appointment with the governor. But just before he left his office, the university's lobbyist in the capitol phoned him and reported that Reagan and Finch had canceled the meeting. Kerr went to Sacramento anyway, for this was the evening of the university's annual reception for legislators. Before the reception he tried to see Executive Secretary Battaglia in hope that his position could be clarified, but he was refused an appointment.

At the reception Kerr found himself in the position of a doomed man, appealing to judge after judge and being coldly ignored. Assemblyman William Bagley warned him there was a move afoot to fire him. Bagley had heard of it from a university official the day before. The assemblyman urged Kerr to make a public statement that he wanted to get along with the governor. "I said I was sure we could, that things could be worked out," Kerr said. He felt there were two immediate sources of contention between him and Reagan. One was an order Vice-President Wellman had relayed on Kerr's behalf to the chancellors suspending the enrollment of new students until the budget was clarified. The order was sent by confidential telegram, but someone at the University of California at Riverside gave it to the press, and it became public. Reagan attacked Kerr for sending the wire, although Kerr remembered that Chancellor Glenn S. Dumke of the state colleges had publicly suspended enrollments and "nothing was said about Dumke." The other source of irritation was a meeting between the regents and Finance Director Smith on January 12, which turned out to be an angry confrontation between Smith and the university. Kerr was in the Far East when the meeting was called, and he had advised Wellman and Meyer against holding it because he didn't want to challenge the governor. Nevertheless, "Reagan and Smith had the idea I called it," said Kerr.

After discussing the idea of a public statement, Bagley and Kerr met with Meyer outside the room in the Sutter Club where the reception was being held. The assemblyman repeated his suggestion. Kerr recalled saying: " 'Well, Ted, I'm prepared to. What about you?' He just put his head down and shook it." Kerr then asked him to help clear up the misunderstanding about the special regents meeting and the enrollment. But Meyer refused.

At the reception, legislators were happily drinking and eating from the Sutter Club's ample table. Kerr, however, was worried. "I was in some state of confusion because it looked like Reagan and the regents had agreed to act," he said. Almost desperately he began looking for Reagan's assistants in the crowded room. First he saw Nofziger. "I told him there had been no effort on my part to have any conflict with the new administration," Kerr said. "He just listened." Then Kerr talked to Battaglia and two other Reagan assistants, Dirk Eldredge and Jack Lindsay. "I went into it with a good deal more detail. I said again we did not want any trouble. They listened. They did not say a word. They asked no questions.

"So I went home."

During the week, two news stories appeared that said the Reagan administration had decided to postpone pressing for Kerr's firing until February. These confirmed in Kerr's mind what he already believed was about to happen.

On Thursday and Friday the regents held their regular meeting at the statewide university administration building, across the street from the Berkeley campus. Reagan, the president of the board, was attending his first meeting so he allowed Meyer, the chairman, to preside. Kerr was also at the table. He was a member of the board and acted as an executive officer who presents proposals to board members for a decision. Before the Friday session began, Kerr tried once again to clarify his status. He went into another room with Chairman Meyer and Mrs. Dorothy Chandler, the vice-chairman. His intention was not to seek a vote of confidence, for he believed Reagan and a majority of regents had already decided to fire him. Instead he brought up the news stories and said that if a decision had been made to let him go, action should be taken now instead of waiting another month. He said it would be impossible to represent the university in budget negotiations with Reagan as a lame-duck president. Meyer and Mrs. Chandler, in turn, asked him to resign. He refused. In asking for the board to take action immediately, Kerr said later: "If I was asking for anything, it was quick execution." This was a crucial point in the dispute between Reagan and Kerr. The governor insisted that Kerr, in talking to Meyer and Mrs. Chandler, precipitated the vote on his job and was responsible for his own firing. Thus Reagan exonerated himself from any blame

for Kerr's dismissal. In fact, when he arrived at the Los
Angeles airport after the meeting and reporters asked him
about the firing, the governor appeared surprised at their
questions.

After their conversation, Kerr, Meyer and Mrs. Chandler
rejoined the other regents. Late in the morning session, Kerr
turned to Chairman Meyer and asked if Chancellor Franklin
Murphy of the University of California at Los Angeles could
make a brief presentation. Meyer refused, saying: "I've
promised some of the regents we would have a chance to
talk about you at twelve-thirty." At 12:30, Meyer asked Kerr
to leave the room. Looking back on it, Kerr believes this is
more evidence than Reagan was part of a plot to fire him,
for the governor planned to leave the meeting early in the
afternoon, before adjournment. Kerr is convinced that Meyer
set the 12:30 time to accommodate Reagan.

Once Kerr left the room, the regents began a long discussion of him. Speaker Unruh, who was there, remembered he
became so disgusted by two hours of talk that he finally said
to the regents: "You have vacillated for two years. I don't
see how you can vacillate any more." Although opposed to
Kerr's firing, he was tempted to move to dismiss the president
to end the lengthy discussion. But finally Alan Grant, president of the state board of agriculture, made the necessary
motion. Someone pointed out that it would be injudicious
for Grant, a Reagan appointee attending his first meeting, to
strike the death blow. The motion was made by Laurence
Kennedy, Jr., one of Brown's appointees. The vote was
fourteen to eight against Kerr.

Meyer and Mrs. Chandler left the room and talked once
more to Kerr. They again gave him the option of resigning.
"I've fought a lot of tough battles for you," Kerr replied.
"This is one you'll have to fight for yourself. On this matter,

about Kerr's dismissal. The day of the firing, he indicated to newsmen that "certain regents"—not Kerr—initiated the vote. "I was informed that certain regents wanted to have this matter discussed," he said. "I mentioned it to Dr. Kerr and he and I agreed that he should be absent from the room during the discussion." Meyer was asked if Reagan had conveyed to him a wish to be rid of Kerr prior to the afternoon meeting. He replied: "Well, the governor had discussed the subject with me and others. I think he should be the one to say what he said to me and to anyone else. I'd regard that as confidential."

On Monday, Meyer issued another statement. "A few minutes after the convening of last Friday's regents meeting, Mrs. Dorothy Chandler, board vice-chairman, and I met with Dr. Kerr at his request. He told us that he could not carry on effectively under existing conditions and that if the question of his continuance in office was likely to come up at any board meeting in the near future, he thought the regents should face up to it and decide it now one way or another." With these words, Meyer contradicted what he had said on Friday and supported Reagan's contention that Kerr had touched off the action by seeking a vote of confidence.

With Kerr gone, relations between Reagan and the educators were more quiet. After fighting through a legislative session, the university and the state colleges received more money than Reagan originally granted them, enough to keep them operating—at least temporarily—at about the same level as the year before. When Kerr was fired and the fight over the budget cuts was raging, Roger Heyns, the chancellor at Berkeley, said faculty recruiting at his campus had been hurt. "We have already had offers declined where political uncertainty of the state was cited as a reason," he said. For the university as a whole, however, recruiting went better than expected. "In the end it seemed to be that the chancellors felt this made life a little more difficult but it wasn't absolutely catastrophic," said Dr. Angus Taylor, vice-president in charge of academic affairs. "They were able to recruit good people, but they had to work a hell of a lot harder." Another year of economy would hurt faculty recruiting, he said.

For the state colleges, where salaries are lower than at the university, the budget cuts worked a major hardship. The Los Angeles *Times* surveyed the colleges at the beginning of the fall semester in 1967 and found a shortage of qualified faculty members. Classes were overcrowded as a result, and students sometimes found it impossible to gain admission to classes they needed for their major. At one college, class size was increased from forty to fifty or fifty-five, but there was still no space available for many students in English, history or other basic courses.

Kerr believes that Reagan has had a major and permanent impact on California's public higher education. He contends that advanced planning at the university has stopped; the university administration is now afraid to fight Reagan on budgetary matters and the conservatives are now firmly in the control of the board of regents.

At the university headquarters, officials expressed the quiet hope that Reagan's war with higher education had ended and that there would be a peaceful era under the new president, Charles J. Hitch. He was comptroller and assistant secretary of defense under Robert McNamara before coming to the university as a vice-president in charge of financial planning. He was, according to Kerr, not the regents' first choice. "They were turned down by seven people," Kerr said. "The presidency has deteriorated. It was once looked up to like the presidency of Harvard, as one of the two top presidencies in the country."

But now the future of the university and the state colleges was out of the hands of the men who administered them. It would be up to Reagan and would be molded by his view of public higher education. Through his first year in office, he continued the basically anti-intellectual approach he espoused in his campaign, never relenting in his hostility toward the academic community. In the later fall and winter of 1967, disturbances broke out on several state college campuses, caused by white students protesting the Vietnam war and black students who accused college officials of discrimination. In December an emergency meeting of the state college trustees was called after a campus disturbance, and Reagan canceled a political speech in Ohio to fly back to attend. At the meeting he showed he was still riding the popular resentment against public higher education. "This meeting reflects the concern of millions of Californians over higher education," he said—talking more to the millions outside the room than to the trustees seated around the U-shaped table. In answering reporters' questions after the meeting, he said that at least part of the trouble was due to professors who indoctrinate their students with "political ideologies."

"I'm in favor of education," he had said shortly after Kerr's firing. He added that education budget cuts did "not represent any anti-intellectual approach on my part or any criticism of the gain or the goals or the aspirations of the university or colleges." But at the end of his first year in office, he went on television again to tell about his program for the coming year. "This administration will do whatever is possible to maintain order on our campuses so that the vast majority of students who attend to learn and to study can have that right," he said. "Currently, the taxpayer foots a bill that averages out $2,900 a year per student at the university level. And he pays it whether or not he is able to afford to send his own children to college, whether or not he is educating them in a private school or whether or not he has children at all."

His words made it clear that his education policy would continue to consist of tight budgets and a hard line toward dissent on campuses. "One of California's greatest resources is our system of state-supported higher education. As governor, I am determined to maintain and protect that resource for those currently attending one of the many campuses, for those who will attend in the future and for those who foot the bill—you and I."

⊠ **CHAPTER FIFTEEN**

THE FUTURE

IN JANUARY, 1968, one year after Reagan had been sworn into office, his problems in the state government were still unsolved, but national politics occupied an increasing share of his attention. In Los Angeles, Bill Roberts and Stu Spencer were working on another Reagan campaign. In six months he would run in the California Presidential primary as a favorite son, and while he expected no major opposition, his advisers recalled how Governor Brown had been embarrassed in the 1960 primary by the strong showing of a minor challenger. In Oregon, Robert H. Hazen, the past president of the Portland chamber of commerce, accepted the state chairmanship of a group organizing to draft Reagan for their state's primary. Reagan continued to insist he was not seeking the Presidential nomination, but polls reported he had substantial support among the voters and Republican party workers. In a series of speeches in other states, he had raised the impressive amount of $1.5 million for the Republican party—and put party officials throughout the country in his debt.

Delighted with the past year, Holmes Tuttle, Henry Salvatori and some of the other original Reagan backers were making plans for a dinner and ball in Sacramento to celebrate the completion of the governor's first twelve months. The price was $1,000 a couple and the proceeds would be used to elect more Republican state senators and assemblymen in California and give Reagan the legislative majority he wanted. But such ambitious political activity didn't hide the fact that Reagan was facing the second budget crisis of his short administration. He had hoped his $1 billion tax increase would permit him to coast through the Presidential election year without state financial problems. But as Unruh had anticipated, Reagan would be forced to spend much of his tax surplus if he wanted to keep a promise of local property tax reductions.

To the nation, however, these were dull technicalities. Reagan was being pulled toward the Presidential race by forces over which he had no control. He was the heir to the Goldwater tradition, questioning the entire direction of American political life since the New Deal. The more liberal Republicans were also interested in him, for he was a winner in a state with a heavy Democratic majority. Some of his more old-fashioned backers felt he should first succeed as governor before moving up to the Presidency. "If he can run California for four years he would be a sound candidate in 1972," one man said. He did not understand that Reagan's importance was not as an administrator but as an evangelist warning of the destruction of the American dream. He and his team were most effective when there was an election to be won or a message to be delivered.

His popularity remained high despite a number of news stories which reported that two members of his staff had been dismissed after they were accused of homosexuality. Of all the charges made in politics, few are more devastating than that of homosexual activities. No evidence was made public to substantiate the charges and there were no arrests on the public record to back up the gossip that circulated so widely in political circles. Nevertheless, in late September, *Newsweek* reported "a top GOP Presidential prospect has a potentially sordid scandal on his hands. Private investigators he hired found evidence that two of his aides had committed homosexual acts. The men are no longer working for the GOP leader but the whole story may surface any day." Drew Pearson, the columnist, was more specific. He wrote: "The most interesting speculation among political leaders in this key state of California is whether the magic charm of Governor Ronald Reagan can survive the discovery that a homosexual ring has been operating in his office."

The political managers and reporters who watch potential candidates for the Presidency awaited Reagan's reaction to see if he would make an error that would eliminate him from Presidential contention. Reagan's response came at his weekly news conference on October 31 when, pressed by reporters, he made an emotional denial of Pearson's column. The first question was:

"Governor, is there any truth to a published report that a homosexual ring has been uncovered among your administration?"

Reagan: "No, there is no truth to the report, and I know where the report comes from. I was informed last night, while most Californians won't see it, because I think that's the best clue to the veracity of the report—is the fact that as far as we know most of the major papers are refusing to run the Drew Pearson column in which it appears. Drew Pearson has been sort of riding on my back for a number of years, long before I ever got into this business, back when I was just making speeches along the banquet trail. . . . I myself wonder how respectable newspapers can continue to carry this column of a man who has done what he's done, and this is about the lowest, this is just stooping to destroy human beings, innocent people, and there is just no sense in getting into that kind of contest with him."

Reagan slapped the rostrum in anger when a reporter suggested that he extracted an agreement from California newspapers not to print the Pearson column. Pearson had reported that the governor's office had conducted an investigation into the staff members in question. When asked about it, Reagan said: "I just don't know what you are talking about, really."

He was asked if Nofziger had repeated the story at any time.

Reagan: "Yes, he's here and you can ask him directly. I am prepared to say that nothing like that ever happened. I've also—and we heard these rumors even before we got off the ship. I've even heard rumors also like that behind closed doors I gave statements to the press, and this is just not absolutely true. Want to confirm it, Lyn?"

Nofziger: "Confirmed."

But the following day, political writer Jack S. McDowell said in the San Francisco *Examiner:* "The resignations of certain officials serving in Governor Reagan's administration were demanded and were received. Their departure from state service came after a private investigation was made into some of their activities, personal and political. The investigation was ordered without Reagan's knowledge. Later, when this investigation was completed, Reagan was made aware of it. He immediately demanded the resignations of the officials involved."

A few days later, a story by Tom Wicker in the *New York Times* raised a question about Reagan's denial that communications director Nofziger had, in fact, told a few news-

men that the two aides had been fired for suspected homosexuality. He wrote:

"Although Governor Ronald Reagan of California publicly
has denied that Lyn Nofziger, his press secretary, told reporters that two Reagan staff members had been dismissed
as homosexuals, the *New York Times* learned that Nofziger
did make such a statement on several occasions. Nofziger gave
that explanation of the firings to at least three reporters
aboard the *S.S. Independence,* as it sailed to the Virgin Islands
last month with the 1967 governors' conference aboard."

Wicker also said that "before that, Nofziger made the same
allegation to three West Coast reporters. . . ."

On November 8 the Washington *Star* said in an editorial
that "the fact is that Nofziger, during the governors' cruise
aboard the *S.S. Independence,* did tell a handful of newsmen
—the *Star*'s Paul Hope among them—that two of Reagan's
aides had been fired for homosexual activities. The black
mark on Reagan's record is not that he hired such men, or
that he was slow in firing them. Where he stumbled was in
his histrionic denial and in calling Drew Pearson a liar when
he must have known Pearson's article was factually correct.
The motivation of this extraordinary performance is not
easily discerned."

On November 14 Reagan was again questioned about this
affair at his news conference and he seemed to moderate his
denial. This time he concentrated on one aspect of the Pearson column, the statement that he had waited six months
before asking for the assistants' dismissal. "Gentlemen," he
replied, "I told you last week the story that I had known for
six months of such a ring in my administration and had
refused to do anything about it was totally false and I reiterate
it was totally false." Reagan's advisers also insisted privately
that Reagan acted promptly.

Disregarding the six months' delay, a reporter asked whether the story was substantially true.

Reagan: "Look, let me ask you something. I just can't believe you fellows want to continue to pursue this thing. Now I told you a few days ago that I had made my last statement on the subject. I have never had and do not have any evidence that would warrant an accusation, no accusation or charge has been made. Now, if there is a credibility gap, and I'm responsible, it is because I refuse to participate in trying to destroy human beings with no factual evidence, and I'm not going to do that, and if that means there is a credibility gap, so be it. There is a credibility gap."

Question: "Mr. Nofziger has been accused by six newsmen of not owning up to telling them confidentially that people left the administration because of immoral behavior."

Reagan: "Yes, I don't know that that is true, and I told you this subject, as far as I'm concerned, is closed. Now do we want to have a press conference or do we want to just stand here with me refusing to talk?"

Question: "Well, the question bandied about is that someone is lying. Is it Mr. Nofziger?"

Reagan: "No, I don't think that there is any lying been going on at all. I've told you that if there is a credibility gap, what the basis for it is and that basis still remains, and the credibility gap will have to remain if that is the way you choose to interpret it."

Publicly and privately, the governor was subjected to some of the strongest criticism of his political career. But, aside from the gossip among politicians and newsmen who knew about the affair, there was no evidence that Reagan's standing had fallen. In fact, two months after the furor, the Gallup poll reported that Reagan was a solid second choice of the Republican party county chairmen for the Presidential nomination.

The incident recalled the case of Walter Jenkins, President Johnson's close personal assistant, who had been arrested with another man for disorderly conduct in the basement of the Washington Y.M.C.A., a meeting place for homosexuals. Jenkins' arrest, a month before the 1964 election, was a matter of public record, and the Johnson Administration had to admit it. But Johnson's popularity did not drop. Theodore H. White, in *The Making of the President, 1964,* reported that soon after Jenkins' arrest was made public, the President ordered Oliver Quayle, who handled his public-opinion polls, to do a hasty survey of voter reaction. Quayle replied that the Jenkins case caused no significant shift in public opinion.

To reporters, Reagan's treatment of the homosexual charges was another case of conflicting statements about important government matters. There had been previous conflicts on Kerr's firing, higher education budget cuts, tuition and major personnel changes. There were two stories about the firing of a public-works director—Reagan's and the director's. John Errecca, a popular Democrat, had been held over from the Brown administration, but he was suddenly dismissed in September, which angered some legislators and segments of private industry. An administration spokesman maintained that Errecca had never been reappointed by the governor, but had just been given temporary charge of the department until a replacement was found. But Errecca replied that Reagan told him he had been reappointed—a statement that appeared to be confirmed by a press release issued at that time: "Governor Ronald Reagan today announced the reappointment of John Errecca, as director of public works." Errecca said: "Whoever says I wasn't reappointed is lying." On another occasion, a young businessman who was working as an aide in the Reagan administration called a newsman into his office and told why he was quitting his job—to return to a multimillion-dollar business and to take charge of a volunteer political organization that would be valuable to Reagan during the 1968 election year. That was also Reagan's story. Days later, however, other sources in the administration reported that the man was leaving because his superiors wanted him shifted out of the governor's office and he rebelled. In another instance, the public was assured Reagan had nothing to do with the selection of Kerr's successor. But there was some doubt about this after a disclosure that Reagan had conferred privately with the new University of California president, Charles J. Hitch, before he was given the job.

Reagan's critics kept alive the issue of a "credibility gap," the fashionable phrase used to describe the difference between a government statement and the facts. Reagan was self-righteous about such a failing when talking about other politicians. Of President Johnson, he said: "I think there has been a tendency throughout the country not to keep the people fully informed, and we are not practicing that and are not going to practice it in California." But in the state government, Reagan himself sometimes fell short of the rough-hewn frankness practiced by some of the best men in politics, a quality that Lincoln Steffens described when he wrote about Richard Croker, the New York political boss of the turn of the century: "Richard Croker never said anything to me that wasn't true unless it was a statement for publication, and then, if it was a lie, he had a way of letting you know. He was true to the professional ethic." Reagan prefers to tell the people his story through the special reports on television or through news conferences that are so well attended that reporters find it difficult to explore a single subject during the half hour or so set aside for the meeting. He is angry when a reporter probes beneath the surface, and is more like a businessman who believes that the changes he makes in his company are of interest only to himself and his stockholders. He considers the press an adversary.

Reporters are often fascinated by his image. Too many stories are written about his glamour, his style and his personal habits, and not enough about what he does on the job. This concentration on Reagan as a phenomenon is so intense that it overshadows his views on issues. His opinions on foreign policy, for example, are almost as controversial as anything Goldwater said during the 1964 Presidential campaign. Reagan questions some of the basic assumptions of United States foreign policy. He feels that there is not much chance at present for an accommodation between the Soviet Union and the United States. He talks of Soviet Russia and the nations behind the Iron Curtain in the language of John Foster Dulles of a decade ago. "A totalitarian force in the world has made plain its goal is world domination," he said. "This had been reiterated by Nikita Khrushchev and by the present rulers of Russia. Each one has stated he will not retreat one inch from the Marxian concept of a one-world socialistic state." Reagan still speaks of the eastern European nations as "captive nations," ignoring signs of independence behind the Iron Curtain. "Each year," he said, "we observe a Captive Nations' Day. At one time, pronouncements on that day here in our own land anticipated the future freedom of those now held captive and enslaved. But more and more we have diluted that theme until now we use the day to speak of peace with no mention of freedom. Is it possible that while we are sorry for the captives, we do not want to offend the captors?"

Reagan also wants some sort of change in the present structure of the United Nations to prevent the United States from being overruled by a group of smaller nations in the General Assembly. He said the United States cannot "safely rest the case of freedom with the United Nations as it is presently constituted. Not until reconstruction of this organization puts realistic power in the hands of those nations which must, through size and strength, be ultimately responsible for world order, can we submit questions affecting our national interest to the U.N. and be confident of a fair hearing."

On Vietnam, he is a hawk. In response to a question in September, 1967, he said that he favored a sharp escalation of the war to "win as quickly as possible" and that the military should recommend how to win it. But later he carefully added: "The military can only advise. It is for the government and the people, and only they, to decide what is to be done with such advice, if anything is to be done at all." Reagan finally came up with an answer that freed him from the necessity of going into detail. "I believe we've turned the corner, and the situation is better than we have been told." This combined the Johnson view—we are winning—with the Republican view—the President is lying. And, if the nation is winning the war, why talk about it?

It was a skillful answer for a muddled political issue. The black-and-white picture of 1964—Johnson the peaceful man against Goldwater the hawk—had changed, and Reagan was aware of it. He found that out in 1966 when the audiences laughed hardest at his story about a man whose friends warned him that if he voted for Goldwater in 1964, "we'd be at war in a year. He did—and we are."

Reagan's message of old-fashioned conservatism was more relevant to domestic issues, and it was here he hopefully predicted the battle would be fought. Reagan truly reflected the new currents in American political life, the political ascendency of the white suburbs, the growing willingness to solve the problems of the urban slums with force rather than with government spending. On social issues he would invariably side with the middle class in a way that inflamed feelings against the poor. Early in December he spoke about one of the nation's most complex social problems—providing the poor with the same quality of medical care as the middle class or the wealthy. In 1964 Congress offered free health care to those whose incomes were too high to make them eligible for welfare, but were too low to afford private medical care. This program—passed at the same time as the better-known Medicare–Social Security plan—was offered to any state that would share the costs. Under Governor Brown, California accepted the obligation and joined the Federal Government in providing the benefits. By 1967 the state was paying the drug and doctor bills for 1,575,389 people, and Reagan said that spending exceeded appropriations. It was up to the governor to act.

Reagan's solution was to suggest reductions of medical care. These were ruled illegal by the courts, and the Democrats refused to change the law to allow him to act. Reagan again took his problems to the people on a television broadcast of less than two minutes. The main emphasis of his talk was that the program itself was wrong. He held up a small identification card issued to recipients, and, in words directed toward his middle-class constituency, said it was really a free credit card for "medical *carte blanche.* You are actually being taxed to provide better medical care for these card holders than you can afford for yourself or your family." This was the Reagan of the Goldwater days, warning against socialized medicine, and Speaker Unruh charged the governor didn't "really want this program at all."

Reagan was governor at a time when the government was being called on to provide more services than ever before. But he thought that there was a limit to what government should do, and he was annoyed—and sometimes angry—when demands for services continued. Groups of citizens, protesting his mental health budget cuts, asked that he make a surprise visit to a few rear wards of any state mental hospital. Reagan refused and replied that such requests were "a kind of attempted blackmail." He said: "Now, if these cases [of inadequate staff] were true, and perhaps in some instances they are, I don't think there is an institution of this kind in the United States that you cannot go into and find at some point in a ward a shortage or some doubling up." One psychiatrist said that Reagan must have been under "great strain" to make the blackmail charge. Reagan replied: "Well, you know a head shrinker. He's probably sitting there right now looking at the pupils of my eyes on television. He can see me on a couch now. Well, I want to tell you, if I get on that couch it will be to take a nap."

These were the words of a man out of tune with the complexities of modern urban life. Yet Reagan was convinced of the correctness of his simple conservative approach to problems. Newsmen from the East study his giant budget and tax increase and conclude that the ultraconservative Reagan of Goldwater days is now a moderate, not realizing that he has simply failed to put his budget cuts into effect.

His attempts to cut back the size of the California government show that he would be the most conservative President since Herbert Hoover—if the dreams of his fervent admirers come true. For he questions all of the domestic political decisions that have been made since 1933 and revives arguments that have been settled in the past. When the Republicans returned to power under Eisenhower in 1952, they accepted the New Deal programs, revising them in some cases, but never in the belief that the programs were wrong. It had become a maxim of political life that the Depression had taught the nation a lesson that government must sometimes intervene to solve social and economic problems. The dominance of urban life in recent years had reinforced that lesson. Republican as well as Democratic governors had tried to use their governments to find ways of improving transit facilities, supplying medical aid to the poor, curing mental illness, cleaning up the slums, improving welfare without persecuting those receiving it.

But in the 1960s there are signs that the people's desire for the progressive drive that started in the Depression has ended and that the idea of a problem-solving government is out of style. Reagan thought that government was too ambitious even under Eisenhower, and both Democrats and Republicans agreed. He shattered the Democratic registration majority in California, and in this spectacular accomplishment lies a lesson for the rest of the nation. After Reagan's victory in 1966, one of the Democratic party's brightest young strategists looked over the wreckage one winter day and theorized about what had happened. As vice-chairman Robert L. Coate saw it, the traditional Democrats—those who believed in social progress—were now a minority party, outnumbered by people who were mostly worried about conserving the economic gains they had made under the Democratic administration. Ever since Franklin D. Roosevelt and the Depression, the Democratic party had favored social and economic reform for the workingman. In the prosperity of post-World War II, the white workingman had achieved his goal, although the black man had not. True to its ideals, the Democratic party pressed ahead to extend social and economic justice to the Negro. The white majority rebelled at this, more worried that Negroes would move into their neighborhoods and take their jobs. "Whether we like it or not," said Governor Brown after his defeat, "the people want a separation of the races."

Reagan was able to take advantage of the emotions of the white majority and to put together a new alliance of Democrats and Republicans, a patchwork marriage nurtured by violence in Negro districts; by student demonstrations; by newspaper stories of violent crime in the streets; by parents' fears that their children were abandoning traditional moral codes in favor of new standards which permitted promiscuity and use of drugs; and by rising taxes, especially the property tax that hit hardest at newly prosperous residents of the white suburbs.

Lyndon Johnson and the other sons of the New Deal had no easy answers for these worries. The American dream had changed since their youth, become more inward-looking. Law and order, morality and bigotry were now more important than clearing slums or putting young men to work. In the minds of the new middle-class majority, the government should now become a protector of their material wealth, rather than a creative mechanism designed to extend equal opportunity to all.

Besides the issue of war and peace, the greatest dilemmas the nation faced in the 1960s were the related problems of ending the decay of the cities and assuring economic and racial equality to all. But the new middle-class majority was running to escape these problems, hurrying into the suburbs and then carefully guaranteeing their isolation by building unbreakable barriers of discrimination. These suburbanites would consider themselves betrayed by politicians who would raise their taxes to help pay for those locked away in the city slums. Reagan understands the hearts and minds of this majority. He, too, does not want to tax the suburbs to pay for the sins of the city.

At a conference on welfare fraud, Reagan discussed the main programs for the poor and then wondered why nobody helped "the forgotten American, the man in the suburbs working sixty hours a week to support his family and being taxed heavily for the benefit of someone else." The Forgotten Man was Franklin Roosevelt's constituent in 1932. The Forgotten Man was a revolutionary, in a way. He wanted the economic system changed. Reagan's Forgotten American is a counterrevolutionary. He wants no more change. In fact, he favors retrenchment. In a time of complexity, he looks for simple answers, and in Ronald Reagan he finds a spokesman and a leader.

Index

ABOUT THE AUTHOR

BILL BOYARSKY has covered California politics for a national wire service since 1960 and he has known and traveled with Governor Reagan since the fall of 1965, following his campaign for governor from the start. There is probably no reporter in the country who has had a better opportunity to observe Reagan first-hand. Mr. Boyarsky lives in Sacramento with his wife, Nancy, and their two daughters.